Changing Employee Behavior

Springer Nature More Media App

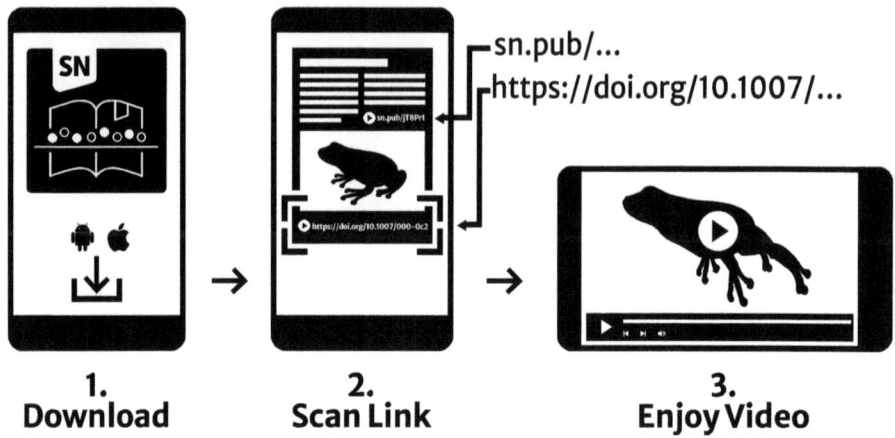

1. Download
2. Scan Link
3. Enjoy Video

Support: customerservice@springernature.com

Nik Kinley • Shlomo Ben-Hur

Changing Employee Behavior

How to Drive Performance by Bringing out the Best in People

2nd ed. 2023

Nik Kinley
Woking, Surrey, UK

Shlomo Ben-Hur
IMD Business School
Lausanne, Vaud, Switzerland

This work contains media enhancements, which are displayed with a "play" icon. Material in the print book can be viewed on a mobile device by downloading the Springer Nature "More Media" app available in the major app stores. The media enhancements in the online version of the work can be accessed directly by authorized users.

ISBN 978-3-031-29339-9   ISBN 978-3-031-29340-5 (eBook)
https://doi.org/10.1007/978-3-031-29340-5

© The Editor(s) (if applicable) and The Author(s), under exclusive licence to Springer Nature Switzerland AG 2015, 2023

This work is subject to copyright. All rights are solely and exclusively licensed by the Publisher, whether the whole or part of the material is concerned, specifically the rights of translation, reprinting, reuse of illustrations, recitation, broadcasting, reproduction on microfilms or in any other physical way, and transmission or information storage and retrieval, electronic adaptation, computer software, or by similar or dissimilar methodology now known or hereafter developed.

The use of general descriptive names, registered names, trademarks, service marks, etc. in this publication does not imply, even in the absence of a specific statement, that such names are exempt from the relevant protective laws and regulations and therefore free for general use.

The publisher, the authors, and the editors are safe to assume that the advice and information in this book are believed to be true and accurate at the date of publication. Neither the publisher nor the authors or the editors give a warranty, expressed or implied, with respect to the material contained herein or for any errors or omissions that may have been made. The publisher remains neutral with regard to jurisdictional claims in published maps and institutional affiliations.

This Palgrave Macmillan imprint is published by the registered company Springer Nature Switzerland AG.
The registered company address is: Gewerbestrasse 11, 6330 Cham, Switzerland

*This is for Connie and Lukas. Again. Because some things do not change. N.K.
To my beloved Jean and Burt. For being the best in-laws I could have ever wished on myself. S.B-H.*

Preface

Back in 2015, when we wrote the first edition of this book, our premise was simple. We argued that the key factor that determines whether a change in behavior is sustained or not is the context in which it occurs. So, if the environment in which you live or work supports a new behavior you are trying to adopt, then you have a good chance of being successful and sustaining that new behavior. But if your context does not support the new behavior, then you're not likely to sustain it for long. And we then went on to show that as the most important part of most employee's working context, managers are uniquely placed to help people change behavior.

We had evidence to support this, too—a range of academic studies all showing the importance of context to behavior change. Never in our wildest imagination, though, did we dream that our premise would be demonstrated in quite the way it came to be in 2020.

Flashback to March 2020. We remember watching news reports of the lockdown in Wuhan coming into effect, and confidently declaring that this could never happen to us in the west. We could not have been more wrong. The COVID pandemic was an unprecedented sudden and dramatic change in the context of millions of people's lives across the world. It was a shock for almost all of us; a hard time for most; and a tragedy for many. And it was also an incredible demonstration of the sheer power of context to change behavior.

The vast majority of people (one study reports the figure being as high as 97%) say that they changed at least one significant behavior during the pandemic. The most common changes—over and above just being at home more or having to work remotely—were handwashing frequency, mask wearing, and avoiding crowded areas. And while many of these behavior changes were mandated by governments, some of them appear to have been sustained even after the pandemic officially ended.

The World Economic Forum recently reported that changes in personal hygiene measures, such as handwashing and using sanitizer, have continued post-pandemic, and that more people are wearing masks in public places than before COVID. A heightened awareness of physical space and surface cleanliness has also been found in many people compared to pre-pandemic. Personal safety has thus become a more conscious and common concern, and many reports suggest that awareness of and attitudes to mental health issues in the workplace have improved. There have also been sustained changes in digital adoption for day-to-day needs, remote working is more common than pre-pandemic, and as a result, the use of public transport has decreased. Before the pandemic, less than 30 percent of firms reported that a majority of employees worked from home at least one day a week; now, that figure is almost 70 percent.

Imagine, for a second, if back in 2019 your boss had called you into her office one day and told you that she wanted you to make some changes in your team. For starters, she wanted people to wash their hands for longer and more frequently, wear masks in public, and avoid crowded areas. And not just for a week, but for a whole year. How successful do you think you would have been? It is hard to imagine any other circumstance other than the pandemic in which so many people could have been persuaded to so suddenly change their behaviors in so many ways.

Yet, provided with clear motivation (avoiding illness), and given the means to act (repeated information and instructions, and free masks), many, if not most people in a lot of countries really *did* change their behavior. And even more impressively, a sizeable proportion of them appear to have then sustained these changes even after the initial event passed. It was not the test of our premise that we or anyone else would have wanted; but it was conclusive, nonetheless: when it comes to changing people's behavior, context really is king.

Given all of this, a second edition of this book seemed required, not because of any changes to our model, but because of the many questions that we have received related to the pandemic, and the changes the ongoing situation is still requiring businesses, leaders, and employees to make. In what follows, then, you will find the original book we wrote in 2015, with brand-new additions that develop the ideas in the original book and extend how they can be applied to day-to-day leadership challenges.

There is a new chapter describing the research on behavior change that has emerged since the first edition of the book, and the implications of these findings for how we think about and approach change.

There is a new chapter describing how our own research and work in the field has moved on, and in particular how we have extended the approach taken in this book to both culture change (changing the mindset and behavior of large groups of people) and how leaders can drive performance through creating the optimal working environment for their people.

Throughout the book, and most notably at the end of each of the original chapters, you will find links to brief videos in which we expand on some of the ideas described, and share with you some of our experiences of implementing these ideas within organizations.

Finally, there is a new chapter in which we share and answer some of the most common questions we are asked about behavior change. And.

One final thing. When we first wrote this book, we chose the title – *Changing Employee Behavior* – because we thought it was straightforward and descriptive. And it is. Yet some readers commented to us that they thought it sounded a little mechanistic or even manipulative: how to get people to do things you want them to. This was never our intention. Leaders do sometimes just need people to behave in a certain way, or to do more of one thing and less of another. But they should do so not for their own benefit, but to drive results, support organizational transformations, and bring out the best in people.

If the COVID pandemic and subsequent new normal has taught us anything, it is that context is most powerful when it supports people to look after themselves and help them to be the best they can be in any particular situation. In this vein, many leaders report that beyond immediate business continuity challenges, their main focus in the early months of the pandemic was simply caring for their people: making sure that their people were okay, and that the working environment still enabled them to connect with others and be effective. This, for us, is the true focus of this book: How to help people be safe, happy, *and* effective employees. Because if we can do that, we won't just create more efficient and productive workplaces, we might just make the everyday lives of our people a little better, too.

Woking, UK Nik Kinley
Lausanne, Switzerland Shlomo Ben-Hur
January 2023

Acknowledgments

Many people have been involved in writing this book. There are some without whom it would never have happened. There are others who have helped us develop our thinking and form our ideas, both recently and over the years. And then there are those who have helped us hone the text. It is a long list and we are grateful to them all.

Unfortunately, there is not enough space to name everyone, but there are some people we absolutely must mention – people who have directly contributed time and effort to help us write this. Top of this list has to be our brilliant researcher, Noemi Dreksler. Without her, this book genuinely would not have been written. There just would not have been enough hours in the day. A huge thank-you also has to goes to Lindsay McTeague, our fabulous copy-editor at IMD, and the fantastic Josephine Taylor and Aimee Dibbens at Palgrave Macmillan.

Then, in alphabetical order: Alan Arnett, Bertolt Stein, Brenda Steinberg, David Gray, David Royston-Lee, Derek Draper, Emma Wilson, Eyal Pavell, Francesca Elston, Francesca Giulia-Mereu, Gurprriet Singh, Harriet Brook, Ilaria Vilkelis, Jean-Stéphane Szijarto, Jurgen Hell, Lynn Verdina-Henchoz, Marjon Oosterhout, Nicola Graham, Palle Grzona, Rachel Robinson, Rob Morris, Ron Gorlick, Sarah Tyler, Sean Dineen, Simon Fincham, and Stuart Schofield.

Praise for *Changing Employee Behavior*

"This book begins with a real premise: changing employee behavior is hard. Then, with their terrific MAPS model, the authors offer insights, tools, techniques, examples, and assessments that will help any leader to change employee behavior. Rapid change has become the new normal, and this book is a tremendous asset for leaders who want to become architects of change in the twenty-first century. Congratulations to the authors for writing this masterpiece."
 —Nick van Dam, PhD, *Global Chief Learning Officer, McKinsey & Company*

"This book drives home the reality that, ultimately, our success as leaders is defined by our ability to change behavior. All too often our agendas are focused on tools, processes, and even vision without a deeper appreciation for the changes in behavior required to make them happen. Through their highly practical yet comprehensive MAPS framework, the authors show that there is a wealth of wisdom and science to guide us in this challenge. The result is an invaluable primer and compelling resource on change and behavior for managers, HR professionals, and leaders everywhere."
 —Jonathan Donner, *Vice President Global Learning and Capability Development at Unilever plc*

"This is not just another book about change management; it is about human beings and how and why they change, and is packed with great tools and insights for creating the right context to lead sustainable change in both business and day-to-day life."
 —Fausto Palumbo, *VP Head of Corporate Training & Learning, Nestlé*

"This easy to read book decodes how to change the behavior of employees, and yourself, and how to make that change stick. It elegantly combines theory with practice and is packed full of over 100 tools that managers can experiment with. The book's significance is that it shines a light on the fundamental importance of the environment in which behavior change happens. The authors have done an excellent job of ensuring managers pay much more attention to this aspect in future."
 —Kim Lafferty, *Vice President Global Leadership Development, GlaxoSmithKline*

"Business models and customer choices are changing. The hyper connected millennials demand that we rethink competencies and leadership models. The book tells us how to change behavior without swapping the existing employees for new ones."
 —Abhijit Bhaduri, *Chief Learning Officer, Wipro*

"This excellent book makes the authors' extensive expertise in making change happen available to a wider audience. Providing a unique perspective and an impressive insight in behavioral change, this resource will be of great help to leaders wanting to drive change in their organizations."

—Rune Bjerke, *Group CEO, DNB ASA*

"This engaging, practical, and evidence-based book definitively addresses the timeless question of how do you get people change their behavior. It is a must read for any leader who is serious about driving change in his or her organization."

—Bernie Jaworski, *Peter F. Drucker Chair in Management, Claremont Graduate University*

"Behavior is a key enabler for sustainable growth and continuous success. This book will help you to change the behavior of not only your employees but also YOU as a manager and the working environment that you create. It is full of tools that can be used immediately to drive business results through behavior changes."

—Takehiko Tsutsui, *Senior VP, Business Development and Corporate Strategy, Japan Tobacco Inc*

"Organizations are engaged in a transformation journey as they try to become higher performing, more flexible and agile in an increasingly global and complex world. As the path to this transformation involves people engagement and development the solutions inevitably involve deep and sustainable behavioral change. This book is a must read for any manager wanting to understand the 'how' of achieving change as well as the 'what' and it paves the way for an essential management revolution."

—Yannick Bonnaire, *Corporate VP for Leadership and Managerial Development, Safran*

"An extremely valuable book about the massive challenges all leaders face in their efforts to drive sustainable improvements to individual performance. Filled with practical tools to help ensure higher return on our continuous and enormous investments in human capital and based on a profound and deep understanding of human nature and its complexities."

—Karsten Breum, *Chief HR Officer Panalpina World Transport Ltd*

"In an ocean of books on leadership and development, this one has an edge as it is profound, yet also practical and accessible. Intellectually rigorous, it addresses a fundamental issue: how to help people change their behavior. It has a conversational style and it presents its arguments in a simple, easy to understand way. The MAPS model is innovative and thoroughly researched, and the moment I finished the book I got an urge to apply the model immediately!"

—Sertac Yeltekin, *Senior Vice President, Corporate Learning, Unicredit SpA*

"This book draws together some incredible insights and new thinking about the power of context that can help ensure learning and development efforts yield real change. The focus on behavioral change being deeply informed by context has been a missing chapter in the litany of books on learning, development, and coaching. The attention to application and practical tools for managers is a critical piece of the puzzle in helping organizations deliver on their investments in development. Too many learning and development efforts yield little to no value to organizations, and the keys, identified in this book, lie in the hands of leaders and the contexts that they create. It provides a great guide to utilizing development as a transformative tool for organizations."

—Todd M. Warner, *Vice President, Learning, Group Human Resources, BHP Biliton*

Contents

1	How to Help Change Happen	1
2	Four Ways to Think about Change	17
3	Intrinsic Motivation: The Science of Commitment	35
4	Extrinsic Motivation: Using Reward and Punishment	59
5	Ability	85
6	Psychological Capital: Believing You Can Succeed	97
7	Psychological Capital: Willpower and Resilience	117
8	How to Build, Break, and Change Habits	135
9	Gamification	159
10	Nudging	179
11	Becoming an Architect of Change	201
12	What We've Learnt	209

| 13 | What We Do Differently | 219 |
| 14 | Frequently Asked Questions | 231 |

Appendix A	245
Appendix B	249
Appendix C	255
Index	257

About the Authors

Nik Kinley is a London-based director for the global leadership consultancy YSC. His prior roles include global head of assessment and coaching for the BP Group, and global head of learning at Barclays GRBF. He has specialized in the field of behavior change for over 30 years and in this time has worked with CEOs, factory-floor workers, life-sentence prisoners, government officials, and children.

He began his career in commercial roles, spent the next decade working with prisoners as a forensic psychotherapist, then returned to work with businesses around twenty years ago. As a consultant, he has worked with over half of the top 20 FTSE companies, helping firms create the leadership strategies they need to succeed. As a coach, he has worked with boards, CEOs and executive teams across industries and regions, in organizations big and small. He has written books on leadership and talent management, has published award-winning papers in academic journals, and is a regular speaker at conferences.

Shlomo Ben-Hur is an organizational psychologist and a professor of leadership and organizational behavior at the IMD business school in Lausanne, Switzerland. His areas of focus are the psychological and cultural aspects of leadership and the strategic and operational elements of corporate learning and talent management. In addition to teaching leadership on two of IMD's top programs for senior executives, Shlomo creates programs for and consults with a wide variety of organizations across the globe.

Prior to joining IMD, Shlomo spent more than 20 years in the corporate world holding senior executive positions including vice president of leadership development and learning for the BP Group in London and chief learning officer of DaimlerChrysler Services AG in Berlin. Shlomo earned his doctoral degree in psychology from the Humboldt University of Berlin, Germany.

List of Figures

Fig. 1.1	What managers think	4
Fig. 1.2	The basic two-step method of behavior change	5
Fig. 1.3	A typical coaching model for changing behavior	6
Fig. 1.4	The MAPS model for behavior change	10
Fig. 1.5	MAPS in coaching	12
Fig. 2.1	Four approaches to behavior change	18
Fig. 2.2	Basic cognitive model of behavior	23
Fig. 3.1	Three ingredients for intrinsic motivation	38
Fig. 3.2	Techniques to build intrinsic motivation	48
Fig. 3.3	Likely key intrinsic motivators for each profile	52
Fig. 3.4	Intrinsic motivators for promotion- and prevention-focused people	54
Fig. 3.5	The Effect of motivation on judgement (▶ https://doi.org/10.1007/000-ak1)	55
Fig. 4.1	Positive extrinsic motivator	60
Fig. 4.2	Negative extrinsic motivators	61
Fig. 4.3	Four rules for when to extrinsically motivate	67
Fig. 4.4	Three rules for who to extrinsically motivate	70
Fig. 4.5	Four rules for what to extrinsically motivate people with	73
Fig. 6.1	Psychological capital	98
Fig. 6.2	The benefits of psychological capital	100
Fig. 7.1	The inner steel to see things through	118
Fig. 8.1	Transferring cues through classical conditioning	139
Fig. 8.2	The role of reinforcer	140
Fig. 8.3	How to build a habit	142
Fig. 8.4	Six techniques for promoting repetition	146
Fig. 8.5	The role of underlying needs in habits	153
Fig. 8.6	Examples of substitute behaviors	154
Fig. 9.1	Gamification player types	166

Fig. 9.2	Five gamification methods	167
Fig. 9.3	A simple progress bar	168
Fig. 10.1	Five types of nudges	183
Fig. 11.1	Using MAPS	202
Fig. 11.2	Plotting MAPS	203
Fig. 11.3	Simple action plan with MAPS	205
Fig. 11.4	Comprehensive MAPS action plan	206
Fig. AB.1	Motivation	250
Fig. AB.2	Ability	251
Fig. AB.3	Psychological capital	252
Fig. AB.4	Supporting environment	253

List of Video Figures

Video Fig. 1.1	Scaffolding (▶ https://doi.org/10.1007/000-ajz)	13
Video Fig. 2.1	Taking a more active role (▶ https://doi.org/10.1007/000-ak0)	32
Video Fig. 4.1	Could delayed feedback be best? (▶ https://doi.org/10.1007/000-ak2)	79
Video Fig. 5.1	The importance of hard knowledge (▶ https://doi.org/10.1007/000-ak3)	95
Video Fig. 6.1	The downside of optimism (▶ https://doi.org/10.1007/000-ak4)	112
Video Fig. 7.1	Is willpower really limited? (▶ https://doi.org/10.1007/000-ak5)	130
Video Fig. 9.1	Superfluous neuroscience (▶ https://doi.org/10.1007/000-ak6)	176
Video Fig. 10.1	A quick thought on social norms (▶ https://doi.org/10.1007/000-ak7)	196
Video Fig. 13.1	A MAPS approach to culture change (▶ https://doi.org/10.1007/000-aka)	223
Video Fig. 13.2	One key difference in a MAPS approach to culture change (▶ https://doi.org/10.1007/000-ak9)	224
Video Fig. 13.3	The research into leader-employee relationships (▶ https://doi.org/10.1007/000-ak8)	227
Video Fig. 13.4	Being a high performer vs. being a high-performing leader (▶ https://doi.org/10.1007/000-akb)	228
Video Fig. 14.1	How to help people improve creative thinking and innovation (▶ https://doi.org/10.1007/000-akc)	239

1

How to Help Change Happen

Almost always, it is about improving performance

Often, behavior change is about helping and supporting people to develop themselves. Other times, it is driven more by a manager, who may need people to do certain things or behave in certain ways. Almost always, it is about improving performance.

It can involve training people in essential skills, improving their ability to work with colleagues, or even trying to stop them from doing something. We may call it coaching, feedback, training, learning, or development, but whatever word we use, what we are doing is trying to change how people behave. We are endeavoring to get them to do something better or different.

The challenge is that changing people's behavior can be one of the most difficult and complex management tasks. Think about yourself. When was the last time you tried to change your behavior? Deliberately and actively. Not just thought about it, but seriously tried. What was it that you were attempting to change? Perhaps it was something big, like trying to improve a relationship, or something seemingly simpler like reading more books. How did you go about it? And now, be honest: how successful were you? Really. Because if you succeeded, you are probably in a minority.

Take a look at the global annual ritual of new year's resolutions. Resolving to change some aspect of your behavior or circumstances at the turn of the

---

Supplementary Information The online version contains supplementary material available at https://doi.org/10.1007/978-3-031-29340-5_1. The videos can be accessed individually by clicking the DOI link in the accompanying figure caption or by scanning this link with the SN More Media App.

year is common to many cultures. And somewhere between 50% and 60% of people in these cultures say they make just such a resolution. There is a lot of variability in what people resolve to do, but some of the most common goals are getting fit, stopping smoking, and improving personal finances.(Pichyl 2013). If you ask people a few weeks into the new year how they are doing with these resolutions, the vast majority—around 80%—say they are doing well. Even after a month, about 65% of people still say they are on track (Peak Performance Episode 56 – The Real Truth About New Year's Resolutions 2013). Ask them two years later, though, and fewer than one in five people say they succeeded in changing, and even this figure is probably optimistic.

Perhaps this is why bookstores are heaving with shelves of self-improvement books. They are a weighty testament to the fact that people hope and believe that they *can* change. Yet they are also proof that people feel they need some help. For all their initial motivation and confidence, translating good intentions into sustained behavior change is far from easy.

If you think changing your own behavior is difficult, how tough must it be to change other people's behavior? It may not be easy, but it can be done. You just need to know how. You just need to know what to do and which techniques to use. Unfortunately, most managers are working with only a limited set of tools and techniques. They have been taught a model of how to give feedback and coach their staff, and they have resources such as training programs at their disposal. Yet as good and useful as these may be, too often they are just not enough.

only 19 percent believe that the coaching going on in their business is effective

Take training programs and development workshops. Even the most wildly optimistic estimates of how much learning from these events is transferred into real behaviors back in the workplace do not go much beyond 34% (Saks and Belcourt 2006). Then there is coaching. An increasing number of organizations use coaching by line managers as a tool for developing people and changing behavior. It has become a standard part of the managerial toolkit, and an amazing 99% of HR professionals believe that it can be of benefit (Jarvis 2004a). Yet only 19% believe that the coaching going on in their business is effective, and less than 3% of firms even check whether it works (Jarvis 2004b).

These statistics are really sobering when we remember just how much is spent on this activity. The training market alone was estimated to be worth over $135 billion in 2013 (O'Leonard 2013). Even if we take the most optimistic success rates of 34%, that still means $88 billion invested with not much to show for it—every year. And that does not include the coaching and broader development market.

We want to be clear here: we are fans of feedback, training, and coaching. They are essential tools and, done well, they can be highly effective. But most of the time they do *not* appear to be particularly effective. And this begs the question, why?

What Managers Think

As research for this book, we conducted a global survey with over 500 business leaders and managers. When we asked them what main behaviors they needed to address or improve in others, the top five responses were:

1. Drive and work motivation
2. Management and supervisory skills
3. Collaboration and teamwork
4. Interpersonal skills
5. Attitude

Nothing surprising there, nor is there anything unusual in the list of main methods that people report using to change these behaviors. They are the usual suspects of giving feedback, coaching, and training. However, when we asked these leaders and managers how often their attempts to change people's behavior worked, the response—on average—was around 50% of the time. Half the time it seems to work; the other half it does not. In our experience that is an optimistic figure, but even if we take it at face value, it does not look good. Frankly, if you told your boss that in any other aspect of your role you were only successful half the time, they would want to know why and what was going wrong.

So we asked managers this. About three-quarters said they felt confident about helping people to identify and understand which behaviors they needed to change to be more effective. And almost the same number said they felt confident about giving people feedback. Yet only 28% of managers said they felt confident about being able to motivate people so that they wanted to change, and only 31% said they felt confident about which techniques to use to then help people actually change. Most worryingly of all, less than 10% said they felt confident about making sure behaviors stayed changed over time (see Fig. 1.1). The issue for managers, then, is not *what* people need to change, but *how* to do it.

Fig. 1.1 What managers think

We know behavior change is hard and complex, but it ought to feel easier than this. We should have better success rates than we do and, at the very least, managers ought to feel well equipped for the task. So, something is missing. And this book is designed to fill the gap.

What Is Missing

The basic approach to changing behavior that the majority of people use most of the time involves two simple steps. They identify what needs to change and then they try to resolve the issue, usually by providing information—in the form of advice, feedback, or even training—about what new behaviors are needed. "Don't do this, do that." "This is the issue, and this is what you need to do about it." Or, "What do you want to achieve? Now let's think together about how you can do it." They identify, and they resolve (see Fig. 1.2).

This two-step problem-solving method is common to all aspects of life. It is simple, basic, and fundamental. Parents do it. Friends do it. Managers do it. Over the past 20 years, managers have become increasingly sophisticated about *how* they do it, too. Since the early 1990s, training managers how to coach people has become commonplace, and these days coaching is a standard piece of the managerial toolkit.

To help managers coach their people, a large number of different coaching models and approaches have emerged. Probably the most famous of such a model is the GROW model (Whitmore 1992) The G stands for "goal" and is all about helping people identify what they want to achieve. The R stands for "reality" and is about helping people understand where they are now and how far they are away from their goal. The O is all about identifying both the "obstacles" and "options" facing people. Finally, the W refers to planning a "way forward." As models go, GROW is pretty good, too. It is clear, practical, and results focused.

What GROW and all the other coaching models do is to offer a more structured and sophisticated way of approaching the basic two-step method for changing behavior (see Fig. 1.3). They enable us to question the issues involved and make sure we really understand them. They help us set better goals and develop effective action plans. And they remind us to track people's progress.

Fig. 1.2 The basic two-step method of behavior change

Fig. 1.3 A typical coaching model for changing behavior

Yet despite the seemingly endless range of coaching models available almost all of them share two basic faults. First, they have more to say about the process managers have to follow and the steps they have to take than about the techniques they can use. For example, they may suggest that you "first discuss this, then that," but tend to be less clear on *how* to discuss it. Or they may suggest that you write a plan for changing a behavior, but say less about what kinds of activities can be included in the plan. And when they do suggest techniques, they tend to describe only a very limited range. So they set a clear path for people to follow, but tend not to provide all the tools to get there. Part of the aim of this book is to set this right and to provide a much broader set of tools and techniques for managers to use.

Our second concern with so many coaching models is that their main focus is still on the two basic steps. It may be a more sophisticated version, but the focus is still on identifying *what* people need to change and *what* they need to do. This may sound reasonable and essential, and it is. Managers undoubtedly need to help people do these things. In fact, behavior change cannot work unless managers *do* help people to do them. But these two steps ignore everything else that is going on around the change and which can have a huge impact on it: the environment and conditions in which change happens.

The Power of Context

One of the clearest examples of the importance of context in behavior change comes from an unusual place: studies of whether criminals reoffend after they have been released from prison. Reoffending rates vary depending on the type of prisoner and the type of offense they committed. Overall, though, evidence from the UK, Europe, the US, and Australia suggests that between 40 and 60% of prisoners released from prison reoffend within 12 months (Sapouna et al. 2011).

Looking at the difference between those who reoffend and those who manage not to, two major factors stand out. First, treatment or attending some kind of change program seems to help, although exactly how much depends on the quality of the program. Second, the context and life circumstances that individuals return to after participating in a change program or being in prison are critical. The amount and quality of family support, whether or not they can find a job, and the types of friends they have can all affect how likely they are to reoffend. In fact, these factors can be even more influential in determining whether people reoffend than the quality of any change or treatment program they attend. No matter how well intentioned, well treated, and rehabilitated a criminal may be, if they have little family support, poor personal relationships, friends who are criminals, no job, and housing problems, it is much harder to stay on the right side of the law.

The key lesson here is that if you want to change someone's behavior, their context—the environment and situations in which they operate—has to act like a life-support machine for the new, desired behavior. If it does not, then the chances are that the new behavior will not hold and old ones will reemerge. This is why one of the most consistent findings from research into the effectiveness of development activities such as coaching and training is that contextual factors (what happens outside the coaching or training room) are *more* important in ensuring behavior change happens than the quality of the training, development workshop, or coaching (Rouiller and Goldstein 1993; Tracey et al. 1995).

In fact, research from almost every type of behavior change intervention you can imagine shows the same thing. Take what is perhaps one of the most extreme examples: brainwashing. In the Korean War of the early 1950s, some American soldiers emerged from prisoner-of-war camps as seemingly devout and passionate Communists (Hunter 1956). Subsequent investigations by the CIA showed that they had been through extraordinary ordeals, which included interrogation, torture, isolation, restriction of food and water, and the use of drugs (Dulles 1956). Their sense of free will and free thought had very literally, deliberately, and systematically been broken down. And yet, even so, the vast majority of these individuals did not stay brainwashed for long once they had rejoined their colleagues and returned to their normal environment.

Then there are the victims of depression. Studies have repeatedly found that although therapies can be effective at treating depression, someone's life context is a significant determinant of whether their depression returns. Simply put, those who fall back into depression tend to have experienced more negative life events and less family support than those who manage to avoid further bouts of depression (Holahan et al. 2004). It is the same for people treated for alcoholism and drug addiction: the environment they return to after treatment has a big influence on whether or not they relapse (Wallace 1989).

Context Is Internal, Too

We usually think of context as what lies outside people—their circumstances and the environment they live in. Yet there is another type of context, which researchers have shown to be just as important. That is what is going on *inside* people, what they bring to any attempt to change their behavior. One obvious such factor is their current level of capability—what they are able to do. Yet there are other, less obvious, factors at play here as well. Things like how much confidence or self-belief people have that they *can* change, and how committed they feel to the change. Then there is the degree of willpower individuals have, and their level of perseverance and resilience. These are as much part of the context for change as external factors, and all have been shown by researchers to be critical in determining whether or not behavior change succeeds.

For example, people with higher levels of motivation to change are more likely to persevere and sustain the change over time (Ryan and Connell 1989; Ryan et al. 2008). People with higher levels of self-confidence are more likely to achieve behavioral changes such as losing weight, stopping smoking, and quitting drugs (Bandura 1982; Strecher et al. 1986). And people with higher levels of resilience are more likely to succeed in their goals and find ways around potential obstacles and challenges (Youssef and Luthans 2007).

Both inner and outer context matter, then, and they often matter more than anything else. Yet you would never guess so from looking at most behavior change and development interventions, because in most of them contextual factors simply do not receive the attention they deserve.

The exception here is people's level of current ability, which *is* usually considered. And, to be fair, things like motivation to change and confidence *are* sometimes explored. Incentives may even be offered. But the central focus in the vast majority of cases is on the information to be taught, the skill to be learned, and the behavior to be changed.

As a result, many coaching, training, and development interventions are fundamentally limited. It is as if we have been focusing on only half an equation and hoping to get the right answer. It is why less than 10% of managers have any confidence that the behavior changes that people try to make will stick over time. And it is why this success rate will stay low until managers have the necessary tools and techniques to understand and do something about these contextual factors.

It is not all bad news, though. Because *you*—as a manager—are ideally placed to influence this context for change. After all, you are a large and vital part of it.

What You Need to Do

Part of your role as a manager in supporting people to change behavior is to help them through the two basic steps of identifying the issue and resolving how they ought to behave going forward. You need to help them set goals and create action plans. And to do this, you have coaching models a-plenty to help you. But these steps, although important, are not enough on their own. There is a second, critical part to your role.

You need to shape, adapt, and fine-tune the context in which people are trying to change, in order to help the change happen and to give it a decent chance of succeeding and being sustained. You need to make sure that people's inner and external contexts can act as a kind of life-support system for the change.

Context, of course, includes a lot of different elements, many of which are simply beyond managers' sphere of influence. So what are the things you *can* do? What are the aspects of someone's context that you, as a manager, can easily influence and that will make a real difference to any attempts to change behavior?

Four factors stand out above the rest. For each one, the scientific evidence is clear that it can significantly affect people's chances of success at changing behavior. And for each, there are proven and easy-to-apply techniques that managers can use to boost it. We have combined and developed these four factors into the *MAPS model for change*. It describes the contextual factors that are most critical in supporting people to change their behavior. And in doing so, it shows you the levers you can pull to support change. The four factors, shown in Fig. 1.4, are:

- **M**otivation—do they want to change?
- **A**bility—do they know what to do and do they have the skills required to change?

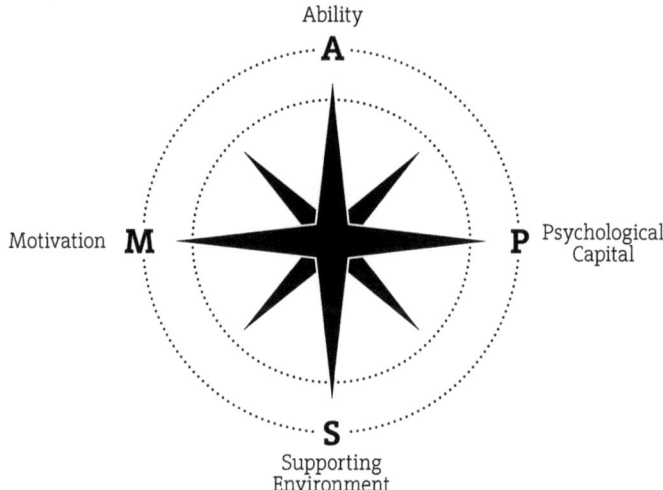

Fig. 1.4 The MAPS model for behavior change

- **P**sychological capital—do they have the inner resources, such as self-belief, willpower, and resilience, they need to sustain change?
- **S**upporting environment—do key elements in their working environment, such as incentives, situational cues, and social norms, support them changing?

To maximize the chances that any attempt to change behavior will succeed and be sustained, as many of these factors as possible have to be right. In the following chapters, we are going to outline the research into why each of the four is so important and describe a range of simple techniques you can use to affect them.

The importance of the first factor—motivation—is simple. If people do not want to change, then the chances are they will not. The subject has been much talked about in recent years, with a spate of popular books and some highly viewed TED talks. Much of this, however, has been about how to motivate people to perform better, and although motivating people to change is similar, there are some key and significant differences. Later, we will explain what these are and what you can do about them.

The second element—ability—is a basic consideration in all behavior change. People need to know what they have to do, and they need to be able to do it. This is the factor more than any other that coaching and other change models have succeeded in helping us get better at—through goal setting and action planning. But we will briefly revisit the research and reveal some perhaps surprising ways of looking at whether people have the ability to change.

The third element—psychological capital—may be a new phrase to you, but psychologists have been studying it for many years. Through this research, they have identified a cluster of four inner resources that significantly impact whether people can sustain behavior change: self-belief, optimism, willpower, and resilience. Not all of these are easy for managers to affect (it can be tough to change someone's level of optimism, for example), but there are some simple things you *can* do, and we will show you what they are.

Finally, there is the supporting environment. These are things outside individuals that *you* can change to help them change. Like motivation, it is a subject that has received growing attention in recent years, in particular through the focus on habits and how to form them. This research has shown how physical changes to people's environments can help trigger and reinforce new, desired behaviors and transform them into automatic habits – things we do without really thinking about it. So we will look at how you can create these kinds of triggers as well as how you can use incentives to encourage certain behaviors and discourage others. We will also explore the power of social support and norms, the impact of the environment on how people choose to behave, and even how you can use economics to help change happen.

In this book, we will use the MAPS model to show how you can create a context or environment that gives change a better chance of succeeding. One question we are often asked is how the MAPS model fits in with the two-step behavior change model or a typical coaching model. We suggest that you need to think about the MAPS contextual factors after you have set clear behavior change goals, but before you create an action plan (see Fig. 1.5). The reason for this is that you should be clear what behaviors you are changing and what goals you have before you can understand what impact the MAPS contextual factors will have on these things. Yet you should do this before you make a plan because, in effect, we believe you have to create *two* plans: one for the person, describing what they need to do to change their behavior, and another for *you*, outlining what you need to do to create a context or environment in which the change can happen and be sustained.

What Is in this Book

This book is a practical one. It is about tools and techniques that you can incorporate into your day-to-day activities without adding endless amounts of time or extra activity.

We are going to begin, though, with some theory; because in order to understand how to shape the context for change, you need to understand

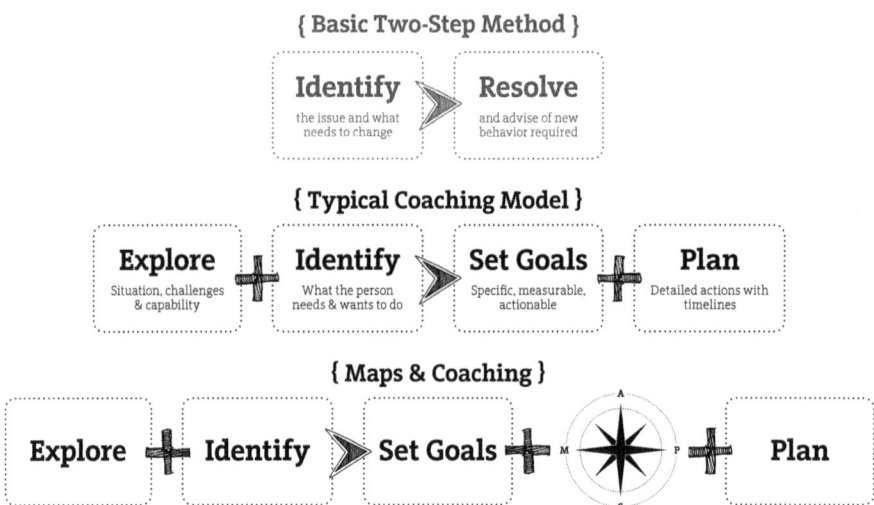

Fig. 1.5 MAPS in coaching

what is involved in change. So in Chap. 2, we briefly present four key approaches to understanding the challenges involved in behavior change. These approaches have been developed by the world's greatest experts in human behavior over the last 100 years. They are significant because each provides us with a different way of identifying the most important contextual factors for individuals engaged in change, and because all of the techniques used in this book stem from one of the four.

In Chaps. 3 and 4 we turn to the factor of motivation. We look at how to motivate people to want to change, as well as covering the thorny question of whether and how to use rewards and even punishment. Two chapters solely about motivation may sound a lot, but it really is *that* important. After all, if someone does not want to change a behavior, then they invariably will not do so.

In Chap. 5 we briefly examine ability. We say briefly because of the four factors in our model, this is the one you will already be most familiar with. We will, however, look at how you can make sure that people do know how to change, as well as providing a couple of easy techniques you can use to ensure they understand the challenges involved.

In Chaps. 6 and 7, we explore psychological capital and what you can do to strengthen people's sense of self-belief, optimism, willpower, and resilience. Along the way, we look at how groups as varied as athletes, teachers, and even the US Army have used these concepts to drive behavior change.

In Chaps. 8, 9, and 10 we delve into three very different approaches to creating a supportive environment. We begin by exploring the science of habits, before moving on to two new, but scientifically grounded, approaches to changing people's behavior: gamification and nudging.

Finally, as there are a *lot* of tools and techniques in this book, in Chap. 11 we show you where you need to start. We show how you can identify which areas of the MAPS model you most need to focus on, and how you can choose which techniques to use.

* * *

The psychotherapist Gianfranco Cecchin once said that the secret to being a good therapist is to create a context so that no matter what you do, you will be successful. This was, of course, an ideal rather than a practical reality, but he had a point.

The problem solving, information giving, and skills teaching involved in so much current training, coaching, and development is undoubtedly essential. But if they are to stand a chance of working, the context people work within *has* to support change. Contextual factors *need* to be addressed.

What we will do in this book is to show you how to create this context or life-support system in which behavior change can be successful. We will give you the tools you need to make sure that the training, coaching, and development you give genuinely work and lead to lasting change. We will show you how to help change happen.

For brief reflections on the content of this chapter, new to the second edition, see Video Fig. 1.1.

Video Fig. 1.1 Scaffolding (▶ https://doi.org/10.1007/000-ajz)

References

Pichyl, T.A. (2013). New year's resolutions: ringing in the new with the old. *Psychology Today*. Retrieved August, 12, 2014, from http://goo.gl/jMZf2U.

Peak Performance Episode 56 – The Real Truth About New Year's Resolutions. (2013). Retrieved August, 12, 2014 from http://goo.gl/Sqt2gT.

Saks, Alan M. and Belcourt, M. (2006). An investigation\ of training activities and transfer of training in organisations. *Human Resource Management*, 45 (4), 629–48.

Jarvis, J. (2004a). *Coaching and Buying Coaching Services*. London: Chartered Institute of Personnel and Development.

Jarvis, J. (2004b). *Coaching and Buying Coaching Services*.

O'Leonard, K. (2013). *The Corporate Learning Factbook 2013*. New York: Bersin & Associates.

Whitmore, Sir John (1992). *Coaching for Performance: GROWing Human Potential and Purpose* (4th edition). Boston: Nicholas Brealey.

Payne, J. (2007). *Recidivism in Australia: Findings and Future Research* (No. 80). Canberra: Australian Institute of Criminology.

Sapouna, M., Bisset, C., and Conlong, A. (2011). What works to reduce reoffending: a summary of the evidence. *Justice Analytical Services Scottish Government*.

Rouiller, J.Z., and Goldstein, I.L. (1993). The relationship between organizational transfer climate and positive transfer of training. *Human Resource Development Quarterly*, 4(4), 377–90.

Tracey, J.B., Tannenbaum, S.I., and Kavanagh, M.J. (1995). Applying trained skills on the job: the importance of the work environment. *Journal of Applied Psychology*, 80(2), 239.

Hunter, E. (1956). *Brainwashing: The Story of Men Who Defied*. London: World Distributors.

Dulles, A.W. (1956). A report on Communist brainwashing. Central Intelligence Agency memorandum for J. Edgar Hoover, April 25, 1956. Retrieved August 12, 2014, from http://ncoic.com/brainwsh.htm.

Holahan, C.J., Moos, R.H., Holahan, C.K., Cronkite, R.C., and Randall, P.K. (2004). Unipolar depression, life context vulnerabilities, and drinking to cope. *Journal of Consulting and Clinical Psychology*, 72(2), 269.

Wallace, B.C. (1989). Psychological and environmental determinants of relapse in crack cocaine smokers. *Journal of Substance Abuse Treatment*, 6(2), 95–106.

Ryan, R.M., and Connell, J.P. (1989). Perceived locus of causality and internalization: examining reasons for acting in two domains. *Journal of Personality and Social Psychology*, 57(5), 749.

Ryan, R.M., Patrick, H., Deci, E.L., and Williams, G.C. (2008). Facilitating health behaviour change and its maintenance: interventions based on self-determination theory. *The European Health Psychologist*, 10(1), 2–5.

Bandura, A. (1982). Self-efficacy mechanism in human agency. *American Psychologist*, 37(2), 122.

Strecher, V.J., DeVellis, B.M., Becker, M.H., and Rosenstock, I.M. (1986). The role of self-efficacy in achieving health behavior change. *Health Education & Behavior*, 13(1), 73–92.

Youssef, C.M. and Luthans, F. (2007). Positive organizational behavior in the workplace the impact of hope, optimism, and resilience. *Journal of Management*, 33(5), 774–800.

2

Four Ways to Think about Change

"They just aren't sweating enough." That was how the CEO of a South American conglomerate in our global survey described the problem. He felt that his people were not as committed to the business as he expected and that he was the one driving all the stretch targets and innovation.

He was a big character and a showman—engaging, entertaining, and dominant. Quick to voice an opinion, he was direct and decisive. He set a clear agenda for the business. And he was good at it: the firm was doing well. Yet he sometimes felt as if he was single-handedly pushing the business forward. He did not feel that those around him had the same sense of urgency and sheer ambition as he did, and which he believed were essential for the business to progress.

His HR director had suggested bringing in consultants to conduct a cultural review of the business and design a change program. But he was cautious about consultants and did not want a big, complex culture-change solution. Anyway, he was not sure that the culture of the business was the problem. He believed it was the behavior of his team—the business and functional leaders who reported to him—that was wrong. It was *their* behavior that had to change first.

After months of increasing frustration, he sought help and turned to a coach he had worked with some years before. He introduced a new leadership framework, laying out what he saw as the behaviors required in his leaders. He began to emphasize the importance of innovation and hired trainers to run

Supplementary Information The online version contains supplementary material available at https://doi.org/10.1007/978-3-031-29340-5_2. The videos can be accessed individually by clicking the DOI link in the accompanying figure caption or by scanning this link with the SN More Media App.

workshops on how to make the business more ambitious and entrepreneurial. He brought in motivational speakers, ensured bonuses were aligned with results, and made sure that everyone in his top team received 360-degree feedback about their leadership style. Yet he still could not shake his basic feeling that people just weren't sweating enough. And this is when we became involved.

* * *

This is not a chapter about techniques, about how to *do* things. That comes later. This is a chapter about how to *view* things. It is about four fundamentally different ways of understanding what is involved in changing behavior. It is thus not about the MAPS model or any of its elements, but about background information that you need to have in order to be able to use the model.

It is important because, in order to understand how to shape the context for change, you first have to understand what is involved in change. It is also important because one of the objectives of this book is to broaden the range of techniques available to you to help people change behavior. And all of the techniques in this book come from one of the four approaches described in this chapter (see Fig. 2.1).

The approaches we will look at come from fields as far apart as psychotherapy and economics. All have something to say about how to create the context for change. No single one is correct or best. Instead, they are a bit like

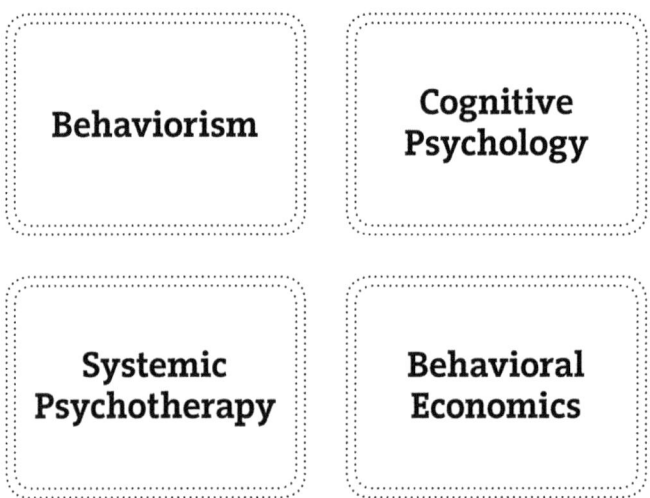

Fig. 2.1 Four approaches to behavior change

sunglasses, each providing a slightly different tint or perspective on how the world looks. And this is why having an understanding of them is so essential. By swapping from one to another, you can gain a fresh view and new ideas about how to make change happen and which techniques you need to use.

We begin with the emergence of the field of psychology, and the strand of it known as behaviorism. Its ideas about how to change behavior are among the most simple we will look at, but they are also some of the most fundamental and powerful.

Behaviorism

Douglas Merritte was just six years old when he died on May 10, 1925, of a neurological condition involving the buildup of fluid in the brain. He is probably not someone you have heard of, but before he died, he was the subject of one of the most famous and controversial series of experiments in the history of psychology.

The experiments were performed by an American psychologist called John Broadus Watson. When Douglas—referred to as Albert B., or Little Albert, during the experiments—was around nine months old, Watson introduced him to a series of objects, including a rat, a rabbit, a monkey, some masks, and even a burning newspaper. The boy initially showed no fear of any of the objects. But then Watson showed him the rat again, and this time he deliberately scared the boy by making a loud noise. Naturally, Douglas cried. Watson repeated the process again and again, presenting the rat and the noise together, until the boy cried at the mere sight of the rat, even when there was no scary noise. He had learned to associate the harmless rat with the noise and, as a result, was now conditioned to be scared of the rat on its own. And although he was not an uncaring man, Watson was pleased. It was the proof he needed and had been seeking for the past six years.

His objective was … to … transform the study of psychology

Six years earlier, on a cold December evening in Chicago, Watson had stepped on stage to deliver the presidential address at the 24th Annual Meeting of the American Psychological Association. He was a passionate and strongly opinioned man, and as he spoke that evening he would be more so than ever (Burnham 1994). His objective was both simple and substantial: to fundamentally transform the study of psychology.

As an academic discipline, psychology had only really existed since the 1880s. In the early years it had been dominated by a technique called *introspection*—essentially asking people to describe what and how they were thinking. For Watson and his followers, this simply was not scientific enough and so he used his address to argue that the only thing psychology should study was behavior, because while thoughts and feelings could not be measured reliably, behavior could.

Essentially Watson was arguing that we should stop worrying about concepts such as meaning, fulfillment, and how people feel, and focus instead on what people actually do. We can spot when someone is writing from this perspective because they use words like *stimulus* and *response*. They are interested in which stimuli, events, or conditions (like loud noises) produce which kind of responses in people (like fear or crying). And they believe that people primarily learn and develop either by associating certain stimuli with certain responses or through the consequences of their actions. For example, they believe that when we do something that produces a positive outcome, such as a reward, we are more likely to do it again, whereas if something produces a negative outcome, such as a punishment, we are less likely to do it again.

Thought and feeling are irrelevant. We do not need to know about them or try to affect them in order to change someone's behavior. We just need to know what behavior we want to produce, which stimuli will produce it, and then how best to present these stimuli.

This may sound like a very simplistic approach, and in fact this was one of the main criticisms initially leveled at it. As was the accusation that the research behind it had been conducted on animals and so was not applicable to more complex creatures like humans. But, when baby Douglas cried, Watson had his proof. It may have been a simplistic idea, but humans could indeed be *conditioned* to behave in certain ways just by using simple stimuli, without any requirement to understand internal thinking processes.

Watson and his followers won the debate that night in Chicago and the result was what we now call *behaviorism*. It was *the* main approach to psychology until the 1950s, and many of the ideas and methods it gave rise to are still used today. The study of habits may only recently have become popular, but it is heavily based on 100-year-old behaviorist research, as is almost everything you have ever read about the use of reward and punishment to change behavior.

To understand what it means to take a behaviorist perspective, let's return to our South American CEO and his insufficiently sweaty staff. From a purely behaviorist point of view, we first need to clarify what behavior we want to produce. If the CEO was literally trying to make people sweat more, we could simply turn up the heating, but let's assume it was something else. Perhaps it was the pace at which decisions were made, or perhaps the goals set by business leaders were not stretching enough.

Whatever it was, a pure behaviorist would not be interested in finding out more about what leaders think about these things or their underlying attitudes. They would merely focus on what stimuli, conditions, or incentives could be put in place to produce the required behaviors. If they did not know the best solution, they would try different things until, through trial and error, they found the most effective stimuli. In fact, in this case, one of the key behaviors the CEO found to be missing was punctuality—meetings always seemed to start and finish late. For him, this represented a lack of professionalism and discipline. So we worked with him to identify how he could stimulate these behaviors in his immediate team by rewarding those he saw doing it and punishing those who did not do it (for example, through praise and criticism). As solutions go, it was simple, but it was also powerful and helped promote the behaviors the CEO saw as essential.

There is no doubt that behaviorism can seem rather mechanical. Pull lever A to produce behavior B. And, indeed, it is referred to in some spheres as *behavioral engineering* or *behavior modification*. Because of its mechanical nature, and because of stories like that of Douglas Merritte, some people think that behaviorism seems unethical. But like any approach, if used in the right ways, it can be perfectly ethical.

Behaviorism may be the simplest approach to behavior change, but it is precisely this simplicity that gives it impact. As we will see in the chapters that follow, behaviorists developed a clear set of rules for how stimuli such as reward and punishment can best be used to produce certain behaviors. These days it may be rebranded as *organizational behavior management* or *applied behavior analysis*, but behaviorism is alive and kicking and is used in businesses to improve productivity, promote better safety behaviors, enhance customer service behavior, and more.

Seeing the power of the approach, Watson had the idea that behaviorism was all that psychology needed, that it could answer all the questions worth asking. But no single method can solve every issue, and the day inevitably dawned when psychologists realized that something was missing from behaviorism. It was time to bring what people think back into the equation.

Behaviorism Key Facts

The principal mechanism for change in behaviorism is using external stimuli and conditions—such as incentives—to introduce new behaviors, change existing ones, and create habits. The focus is thus firmly on the external context: the "S" (supporting environment) of our MAPS model. Yet, as we will go on to see, as behaviorism is interested in the effects of rewards and punishments, it also has a lot to say about the "M" of our model: motivation.

The key questions behaviorism leads us to ask are:

- Which specific behaviors do we want to change or promote?
- What are the stimuli, conditions, and incentives that would encourage or discourage this behavior?
- What is the best way to present these external stimuli, conditions, and incentives?

In later chapters, we try to answer the last question in particular. We look at the science of how best to reward and punish behaviors in order to help change happen. We also explore how to create habits and show how behaviorist techniques have recently been reborn in the form of *gamification*: the science of using incentive mechanisms that usually exist in games to change behaviors in the workplace.

Cognitive Psychology

Looking back, it seems a bit crazy that psychology—the study of the mind—for so many years reduced itself to studying only behavior. But the tide eventually turned. In the 1940s and 1950s researchers started investigating concepts like attention and memory, and slowly the field expanded to include all aspects of how people think. Today, cognitive psychology is the dominant approach in the field.

One early idea that researchers had was that people's attitudes toward a behavior—whether they saw it as positive or negative—should influence their engagement in that behavior. If you think shouting at someone is undesirable, you are less likely to do it than someone who thinks it is fine to shout. Unfortunately, early research showed that people's attitudes toward a particular behavior seemed to make surprisingly little difference to whether they engaged in it or not (Wicker 1969).

The breakthrough came when researchers realized there was more to what determined behavior than simple attitudes. Social norms—what you think other people do and see as normal—also appear to be important, as are confidence and the extent to which you feel you are able to control and achieve certain things. And finally, your intentions—what you set out to do—also

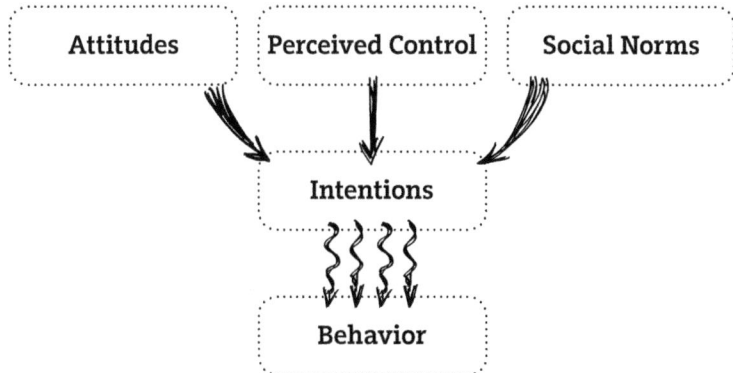

Fig. 2.2 Basic cognitive model of behavior

play a part in how you eventually behave. As a result of identifying these influences on behaviors, researchers came up with flow charts in which they tried to plot how all these influences come together to determine behavior (see Fig. 2.2).

This is just a simple model. Over the years, researchers' ideas about the thinking processes that lead to behavior became more complex. Indeed, one of the caricatures of cognitive psychology is that it has devolved into a series of ever more complex flow charts with arrows and lines heading off in all directions. Two elements are important for us here.

First, unlike behaviorism, cognitive psychology sees behavior as being the result of deliberate and conscious thinking processes. Although it recognizes that our thinking processes are not always effective, it does largely see us as rational, thinking beings. In more recent years, the approach has evolved to include some behaviorist ideas about automatic habits we may have that do not include much thinking at all. But the heart of it remains how what we think affects how we behave.

Second, there is the idea that by influencing or changing some of these thinking processes, we can help people change their behavior. Cognitive psychology has thus given rise to a whole new approach to therapy and coaching. In fact, most modern-day development programs about issues such as self-confidence, assertiveness, decisiveness, attitudes, and development planning are all based on this cognitive psychology focus on thinking processes. As such, cognitive psychology provides a rich set of tools and techniques that managers can use to help change people's behavior.

These methods generally try to do one of two things. When attempting to change or prevent undesirable behavior (such as a lack of confidence or the tendency to interrupt others), the focus tends to be on helping people recognize when their thinking is negative or unhelpful for them. Alternatively, when seeking to promote new behaviors, the focus is first on motivating people by helping them to think about the benefits of the behaviors, and then on helping them to plan when and how to behave in the new, desired way. To see more, let's return to our South American CEO.

Using a behaviorist approach, we had first worked with the CEO to improve what he perceived as professionalism and self-discipline by promoting punctuality. Then, using a cognitive lens, we also looked at individuals' thinking processes. We worked with the CEO and his immediate team to explore people's ideas about and attitudes to work ethic and leadership. We identified a set of desired, "sweaty" leadership behaviors that everyone could agree on. We looked at the advantages and disadvantages of these behaviors, and the potential benefits for the business. And we created structured development plans for how leaders could build these behaviors. All the time, we were focused on what and how people were thinking, and we sought to change this in order to drive changes in their behavior.

The popularity of the cognitive approach owes much to its easy application. Although at first glance all the flow charts can make it seem very theoretical, it is in fact deeply pragmatic and full of practical tools and techniques. Indeed, as we consider specific techniques in the chapters that follow, the cognitive ones will probably be the most familiar to you. Yet, like behaviorism, it has its limitations.

Because it focused on the psychological factors that influence behavior, elements that lie outside the individual were often ignored, or at least not seen as central to the task of behavior change. Yet, in the 1980s, research began to show that many of these external factors, such as relationships and the environments that people live and work in, can be significant influences on how we behave. Indeed, some researchers went on to suggest that at least 80 percent of the factors influencing behavior come from these external elements (Fliegenschnee and Schelakovsky 1998). This brings us to our third key approach to behavior change: systemic psychotherapy.

Cognitive Psychology Key Facts

The principal mechanism for change in cognitive psychology lies in influencing how and what people think. The focus is thus firmly on people's inner context and in particular the "M" (motivation) and "P" (psychological capital) of the MAPS model.

The key questions the cognitive approach leads us to ask are:

- What are the individual's attitudes toward both change, in general, and the specific behavior involved?
- Does the individual think that they are able to change their behavior?
- What motivates the individual and how motivated to change are they?

In later chapters we look at issues such as motivating people to change, exploring people's attitudes to change, and building confidence to change. We also discuss how a technique called *mindfulness* can help focus people on what they are trying to achieve.

Systemic Psychotherapy

Imagine that a member of your family suffers from a mental illness, like depression or schizophrenia. What would it be like? How would you feel? Now imagine how you would feel if a doctor said that you were part of what was causing that illness: that what was causing your loved one's depression or schizophrenia was not something about them as an individual, but something about how the family—and thus you personally—behave. That is effectively what systemic psychotherapy did when it arrived on the scene, and not everyone liked it.

For many, the story of systemic psychotherapy begins with a man called Gregory Bateson. He was an anthropologist who spent the early part of his career studying indigenous peoples in New Guinea and Bali. He was interested in how tribal social systems work and became convinced that in order to truly understand someone, you also need to understand the social and cultural environments in which they live.

There was nothing particularly contentious about that, but Bateson went further. In the 1950s, after researching communication patterns in families, he suggested that some symptoms of mentally ill individuals could be caused by particular patterns of behavior in their families—such as how anger was expressed or the level of authoritarianism. And he suggested that by changing these family behavior patterns, the mental illness symptoms could be stopped. At the time, it was a radical claim. Mental illness was generally considered to be the result of a flaw in the individual. In Bateson's eyes, though, it was not an individual's thinking patterns or biochemistry that were faulty, but the behavior of their families—of the social systems they lived in.

Bateson's work put him at the heart of a movement called *cybernetics*: the study of how things (social, mechanical, and biological) process information and react to it. The word comes from the Greek *kybernetes*, which means steersman or the art of steering. Imagine a pilot on a ship reacting to winds, waves, and currents. The systemic approach is interested in the relationship between the pilot and the elements—how they affect the pilot's behavior and how the pilot tries to steer a way through as a result. Indeed, as we will see in later chapters, some of its key techniques center on *feedback loops*: how what you do affects the people around you, and how they in turn affect you. And this does not only apply to interactions between people; it also applies between individuals and the targets they are set, the support they receive, and the environment they work in.

It is easy to see how this approach could be applied to work situations. Consider a common issue managers face. You are asked to help with an employee who is seen to be disengaged, demotivated, and ineffective, and who has gradually been getting worse. You could investigate which rewards or punishments would most encourage the individual to behave in the desired way. Or you might consider working on their attitudes or motivation. But from a systemic approach, you would also be interested in what in their current situation has caused them to act this way, in what has allowed them to become a poor performer. It may be that they are not suited to the role, but it could also be that the structure, processes, or culture of their team—or how they perceive these things—is not helping. If so, you would either try to change elements of this system or try to change how the individual thinks and reacts to them.

The systemic approach is thus fundamentally different from behaviorism or cognitive psychology. While behaviorism focuses on individuals' behavior and cognitive psychology on thinking processes, systemic therapy emphasizes the relationships and interactions between individuals and their environment. It is interested in how systems work. Because of this, Bateson and his colleagues started working not only with the individuals who were ill but also with their families. For a systemic therapist, having parents, siblings, grandparents, aunts, uncles, and even family friends in the room all at once was not unusual.

The early form of the systemic approach was in many ways just as mechanical as behaviorism. Granted, it took a more complex view of the world, since it acknowledged that what people think and feel is important, yet it was still seeking to pull some fairly simple levers to make change happen, such as asking person A to act differently in order to help person B to change. It developed some standardized techniques for uncovering what was happening in social systems and some simple yet effective tools for changing them.

Over time, of course, it has evolved. Some of Bateson's successors continued his research into communication patterns within systems and went on to focus on the role of language. They looked at how the way we describe issues can influence what we think of those issues and what we believe needs to happen to change things. This may sound rather esoteric and theoretical, but as any good speech writer will tell you, the words we use matter. Moreover, the systemic approach has remained consistently grounded in practical problem solving.

Let's return to our South American example. We described earlier how we used a behaviorist lens to identify some specific key behaviors that the CEO wanted to see, and then developed prompts and rewards to encourage these behaviors. And we have described how, by using a cognitive approach, we looked at the team's ideas about and attitudes to work ethic and leadership. Then, using a systemic approach, we examined how system elements such as the business culture and the CEO's behavior influenced the degree to which people were willing to sweat. We also looked at how the CEO's team thought and felt about these things and reacted to them. For example, we found that the CEO had a tendency to be directive, in response to which his team became more passive, which in turn led the CEO—in frustration—to become even more directive. We thus brought the CEO and his team together to discuss it. We coached the CEO on how to be less dominant and invite his people to take the lead more, and we coached his team on how to be more forthright and present themselves as less passive. We eventually went further, too, considering the relationship between the team and the broader business culture, but the basic feedback loop between the CEO and his team was an important start and a critical element in the eventual solution.

A systemic approach allowed us to see the patterns that connect people and influence how they behave. Just as cognitive psychology built upon behaviorism, systemic psychotherapy has built on both of them to develop an entirely new way of viewing people's behavior and how to change it. This may seem like an endpoint: having looked first at the behavior of individuals, then at how they think, and next at how they interact with the people around them, there is nothing else to look at. But the past 20 years have seen the emergence of one final approach to behavior change. So far we have focused on approaches that emerged from psychology and psychotherapy—studies of people. But for our fourth and final approach, we are going to see what happened when psychology met something very different: economics.

Systemic Psychotherapy Key Facts

The principal mechanism for change in systemic psychotherapy is influencing the relationship between individuals and the groups and social systems they live in. The emphasis is not on changing the individual or the environment, but on changing the relationship and interaction between the two. In terms of our MAPS models, systemic psychotherapy is interested in all four factors (motivation, ability, psychological capital, and supporting environment), but it has a special interest in the "S."

The key questions the systemic approach leads us to ask are:

- What is it about the environment the individual works in that has allowed undesirable behaviors to continue, or that could prevent desired behaviors from emerging?
- What are the behavior feedback loops that encourage or discourage particular behaviors?
- How do the individual and the people they interact with talk about the desired behavior change? What words do they use and how does this affect their attitudes toward it?

Pretty much any technique can be seen as a systemic one. This is because the systemic approach is essentially a way to use techniques. It focuses us on the impact of techniques and the feedback loops we are creating as we use them. Systemic psychotherapy has generated some new and specific techniques, however. So in later chapters, we show you how these systemic techniques can help you create a positive context for change.

Behavioral Economics

There is no two ways about it: it sounds bad. An increasing number of countries—such as the US, the UK, Australia, and Singapore—have in recent years either created special departments or used specialist external contractors for the sole purpose of changing citizens' behavior, to influence and adjust what they do and how they act. If you live in one of these countries, you may well have been on the receiving end of what these behavior change departments do—whether you know it or not. And no matter how you put it, that does not sound good. The irony, though, is that the approach behind this work is aimed at creating freedom of choice.

We tend to associate economics with money and the behavior of financial markets. Yet economists are also interested in the behavior of people and, in particular, in the choices and decisions that people make. For a long time, traditional economic theory viewed people as rational in their decision-making, capable of weighing up the costs and benefits of various options objectively and then choosing the best way forward. But during the twentieth century, economists increasingly started questioning whether people really do make decisions so coldly and rationally. And when cognitive psychology appeared in the 1940s and 1950s, it started shedding new light on the realities of decision-making.

The breakthrough came between 1974 and 1981, when two psychologists, Amos Tversky and Daniel Kahneman, published three important articles about decision-making (Tversky and Kahneman 1974; Kahneman and Tversky 1979; Tversky and Kahneman 1981). Describing some of the mental shortcuts that people take when making decisions, Tversky and Kahneman showed that, far from being logical and rational, people are hugely susceptible to being illogical and irrational. For example, the two men described what they called the *availability heuristic*—the fact that people tend to judge something as more likely to occur if it is memorable or something that springs to the front of the mind. It is why when one of your authors had his house burgled, he felt as if he had a far greater chance of being burgled again, even though he knew that statistically he was no more likely to be burgled afterwards than before. And it is why you probably should not watch a movie about a plane crash just before you take a flight, even though it does not in any way affect your plane's chances of crashing.

Tversky and Kahneman's work stimulated a huge amount of debate and further research, culminating in the field that we today call behavioral economics. It is primarily interested in developing as realistic an understanding as possible of how people make judgments and decisions, and then applying this knowledge to help people make better judgments and decisions. Researchers have documented a wide range of different thinking biases and shortcuts, and, for behavioral economists, each of these is a lever that can be used to change people's behavior. The idea is simple: if you know that people tend to make decisions in certain ways, you can use this knowledge to try to influence and improve the choices they make.

Traditional economists, believing people to be profoundly rational, saw the key tools of behavior change to be providing people with better information about the decisions they face and creating incentives to behave in certain ways. They believed that with the right information and the right incentives, people would make the right choices. What behavioral economics has added to our toolkit is something called *choice architecture*—using our knowledge of how people make choices and decisions to increase the chance that people will behave in a certain way or make the best choice for themselves.

This may sound sinister, and indeed it could be. But work in this area has mostly been confined to doing things like improving people's diets, helping them avoid fines, and encouraging them to save money. For example, research has shown that people tend to go along with default options (Madrian and Shea 2001). This is what happens when you do nothing—when you do not actively make a choice. When you get a new mobile phone, for instance, it comes with all sorts of options, such as a choice of background screens and ring tones. Phone manufacturers make an initial choice of background picture and ringtone for you—a default option—and studies show that, rather than change them, most people tend to stick with these default options.

Armed with this understanding of how people think, an increasing number of countries now require organizations to offer pension schemes that people contribute to by default. If they do not want to contribute to it, they actively have to opt out of doing so. This may seem like manipulation, and there is a degree to which it is. But another way of looking at it is that most people need a pension, and all that is being done is to present people with the choice of whether to save for their retirement in a way that increases their chances of doing so.

Critics of this approach see it as governments interfering in individuals' lives and assuming that they know what is best for them. But, as with the pensions example, it is possible to be open about the behavior being targeted and ensure people still have freedom of choice, while also trying to steer or nudge them in a particular direction. As with any other change technique, it is the intent and the manner in which it is used that makes it ethical or not, not the technique itself.

So behavioral economics is all about nudging people to make certain decisions and behave in certain ways. It provides a set of powerful methods that have to date predominantly been used to improve the effectiveness of public policy. But it can also provide us with techniques to help behavior change in specific individuals, and to see how, let's return to our South American CEO one last time.

We have described how we applied a behavioral, a cognitive, and a systemic lens to the issues we found at the South American conglomerate, and how each of these approaches led to a different type of solution. Finally, using a behavioral economics approach, we identified a few key choices and decision points that the CEO's immediate team had, such as how stretching targets should be and whether to speak up and challenge. We then identified nudges we could use to help shift these behaviors. We explored how sharing targets more publicly could lead to more stretch targets being set. We found that overall levels of challenge could be increased by giving a specific person at each team meeting the job of challenging what was being discussed and decided. And we used social norms to nudge people toward these behaviors—by putting up signs with sayings like, "An unchallenged idea is a weak one."

Behavioral economics, then, combines elements of the other three approaches and adds a little something of its own. It takes the use of incentives from behaviorism, the focus on how we think from cognitive psychology, the emphasis on relationships and feedback loops from the systemic approach, and works them into something different. It is one of the most exciting and high-profile developments of the past decade and, as we will see, it has much to say of real practical value.

Behavioral Economics Key Facts

The principal mechanism for change ... is ... how people make choices and decisions

The principal mechanism for change in behavioral economics is using our understanding of *how* people make choices and decisions, to make changes to their external context that can influence and change the behaviors they choose and decide to engage in. Just like systemic psychotherapy, it is interested in all four factors of our MAPS model (motivation, ability, psychological capital, and supporting environment), but it has a special interest in the "S."

The key questions a behavioral economics approach leads us to ask are:

- What are the key choices and decisions that people have to make in relation to the behavior we are trying to promote or prevent?
- What *choice architecture* are people currently using? Or, in other words, what are the assumptions, biases, and incentives that currently influence their choices and behavior?
- Under what conditions could they be incentivized to adopt or stop the behavior?

In later chapters we look at nudging techniques in detail and at how managers can build choice architecture. We explore how best to use social norms and we show how managers can use techniques such as loss avoidance and nonfinancial incentives to help guide and shape behavior.

Turning Approaches into Action

In this chapter we have laid the foundations for what comes next. For many readers, it is likely that the promise of techniques is what drew you to the book. But for the techniques to be useful, an understanding of these four different approaches is essential. Each leads us to ask very different questions about people's behavior and to pull very different levers to achieve change. No single one of them is best or correct. They are interchangeable and overlapping—like differently tinted sunglasses, each of which can help us gain a new perspective. They are not the only approaches, either, and in time new and possibly better ones may emerge. But for now, for us, they are enough.

We are sometimes asked which is our favorite approach or the most useful. Our response is that we do not have a favorite. Whenever you are thinking about how to help someone change a behavior, we simply recommend starting with behaviorism and working your way through the other approaches. By trying the different lenses one by one, you ensure you consider the issues involved from all angles.

Although the four approaches are all different, they do have one thing in common: they tell us something about how we can create the context for change. Each in its own way tries to change something about the environment in which behaviors happen, in order to try to push, coax, encourage, incentivize, and nudge behavior to change.

Now that we have considered how to view change, let's return to the question of how to *do* it. We begin with the "M" of our MAPS model, and with one of the aspects that managers most frequently cite as challenging when it comes to changing behavior: how to build motivation to change.

For brief reflections on the content of this chapter, new to the second edition, see Video Fig. 2.1.

Video Fig. 2.1 Taking a more active role (▶ https://doi.org/10.1007/000-ak0)

References

Burnham, J.C. (1994). John B. Watson: Interviewee, professional figure, symbol. In J.T. Todd and E. K. Morris, E. (Eds.), *Modern Perspectives on John B. Watson and Classical Behaviorism* (pp. 65–73). Westport, CT: Greenwood Press.

Wicker, A.W. (1969). Attitudes versus actions: the relationship of verbal and overt behavioral responses to attitude objects. *Journal of Social Issues*, 25(4), 41–78.

Fliegenschnee, M. and Schelakovsky, A. (1998). *Umweltpsychologie und Umweltbildung: Eine Einführung aus humanökologischer Sicht*. Wien: Facultas Universitäts Verlag.

Tversky, A. and Kahneman, D. (1974). Judgment under uncertainty: heuristics and biases. *Science*, 185(4157), 1124–31.

Kahneman, D. and Tversky, A. (1979). Prospect theory: an analysis of decision under risk. *Econometrica: Journal of the Econometric Society*, 47(2), 263–91.

Tversky, A. and Kahneman, D. (1981). The framing of decisions and the psychology of choice. *Science*, 211(4481), 453–8.

Madrian, B.C. and Shea, D.F. (2001). The power of suggestion: inertia in 401(k) participation and savings behavior. *The Quarterly Journal of Economics*, 116(4), 1149–87.

3

Intrinsic Motivation: The Science of Commitment

So there is a plan. Someone—perhaps with your help or at your request—has identified an issue they need to address or a behavior they need to change. And with your help, they have worked out what they ought to do instead, the new behavior they now need to display. Goals have been set, development plans written, and dates for a review of progress agreed. Now what?

In the traditional two-step problem-solving approach, that would pretty much be it: job done. Of course, there would be some challenges along the way, but through further identify/resolve problem solving, solutions could be found. It would just be a matter of seeing the plan through.

Our core argument in this book, though, is that if you want behavior change to succeed, this cannot be the end of it. More needs to be done and, specifically, you need to consider the situation and environment in which the person is working, and act to adjust it. In the chapters that follow we are going to look at this environment in some detail, and we begin with something fundamental: motivation, and whether the person really wants to change.

Motivation matters. If someone does not want to change, they probably will not. Even if they know that they ought to change and say that they want to, if deep down they feel ambivalent about it, they probably will not sustain any change they manage to make. Simply put: motivation matters.

For most managers, this will not be news. This is partly because motivating people is a core part of what they do, and partly because how best to motivate

---

Supplementary Information The online version contains supplementary material available at https://doi.org/10.1007/978-3-031-29340-5_3. The videos can be accessed individually by clicking the DOI link in the accompanying figure caption or by scanning this link with the SN More Media App.

people has been a much-discussed topic in recent years. First, there has been the public concern about the size of boardroom bonuses in the wake of the banking crisis, and the resulting debates about whether these bonuses work and encourage the right sorts of behaviors. Then, there has been a flurry of popular books and TED talks on the subject, as writers and academics such as Dan Pink and Dan Ariely (and even a few non-Dans), have entered the debate about how to motivate people.

The overwhelming conclusion of this debate has been simple: inner commitment is a better motivator of performance than external rewards, such as bonuses. Consequently, in order to truly encourage high performance, leaders should focus on building people's inner commitment. Most of what has been written and said so far, however, has been about motivating people to perform and achieve results. What about motivating people to change behavior? It may not sound different to motivating them to perform, and it may not *be* that different. But there *are* some differences and they *are* important. Over the course of the next two chapters we are going to find out what those differences are.

Moreover, for all that has been written and said, it seems that motivating people to change remains a key and significant challenge for managers. As the survey that we reported in Chap. 1 showed, only 28% of managers say they feel confident they can do it. They are probably right to feel this way, too. After all, as the resolutions made every new year's eve demonstrate, initial interest and good intentions are one thing, but sustainable motivation and commitment to change are quite another.

In this chapter we are going to look at *inner commitment*—what researchers would call *intrinsic motivation*. That is, motivation that is fueled not by any external rewards but by internal feelings. It is the motivation to act in a certain way purely because we find that behavior in some way fulfilling.

For example, one of your authors regularly goes to the gym, not because he is paid to, but because he finds the activity enjoyable in itself. We will look at why this type of motivation is important, and what exactly managers can to do to build and reinforce it to help support behavior change. In Chap. 4, we will consider what researchers call *extrinsic motivation* and the science of reward and punishment.

Why Intrinsic Motivation Is Important

The reason writers and academics have been championing the importance of intrinsic motivation is simple and compelling. Over the long run, individuals who have more of it tend to outperform people who are driven more by extrinsic factors, such as rewards. Performance, productivity, and sheer enjoyment of work have all been found to be greater in people with higher levels of intrinsic motivation (Grant 2008; Froiland 2011; Kanfer and Ackerman 1989), as have related behaviors such as initiative and concentration (Thomas and Velthouse 1990; Blais et al. 1993). In fact, the most recent *meta-analytic* studies—ones that look at the results of hundreds of other, independent pieces of research—have found that motivation accounts for 24% of a person's performance levels (Johnson et al. 2014). So regardless of anything else, intrinsic motivation seems to be something that we should be trying to encourage in everyone.

This appears to hold true for behavior change, too. People with higher levels of intrinsic motivation for particular behaviors have been shown to be more able both to do those things in the first place and then to sustain them over time (Ryan et al. 2008; Ryan and Connell 1989). For example, a recent study looked at employees' acceptance of a new IT system in a firm. The business wanted to go paperless and to give up all the old handwritten forms. The researchers found that people who had a higher level of internal motivation to use IT were more likely to change their behavior and use the new system than those who did not have much internal motivation for it (Mitchell et al. 2012).

This is not to say that external rewards and things like praise and punishment do not work. Indeed, as we show in Chap. 4, they can be powerful and important tools to help people change behavior. But in general, over the long haul, intrinsic motivation is more likely to help us sustain change over time. It keeps us going longer.

There is a catch here, though, because although there is simplicity to external motivators like rewards—in that they are essentially something that you "do" to people—creating intrinsic motivation can be a lot more complex and much harder work. Fortunately, there's a recipe we can follow.

A Recipe for Intrinsic Motivation

The recipe for intrinsic motivation comes from cognitive psychology and is something psychologists call *self-determination theory* (Deci and Ryan 2010). Like all family recipes, it has evolved a bit over time. In the 1970s and 1980s, when it was first articulated, it suggested that everyone everywhere has three inner needs that must be satisfied for them to feel motivated. Think of them as the necessary ingredients: *autonomy, competence*, and *relatedness*. Autonomy is the feeling that we have a choice in what we do and are not being controlled by others. Competence is the idea that we need to believe in our ability to do something. And relatedness is the sense that we are connected to and supported by other people.

As we will see, the evidence for the importance of these three is strong, and they are now widely accepted as essential for building intrinsic motivation. Over the years, our understanding of them has changed a bit, of course. Competence has become more about challenge and mastery, while relatedness has been recast as more about having some connection to what you are doing and a sense of purpose, as well as being connected to people. So, to reflect these changing ideas about them, we are going to call our ingredients *autonomy, mastery*, and *connection* (see Fig. 3.1).

First, we will consider each in turn, explaining what it means, why it is important, and what you can do to build it in other people. Then, we will look at two techniques you can use to work out which ingredients are the most valuable for different people and thus the ones you need to focus on in order to help them change.

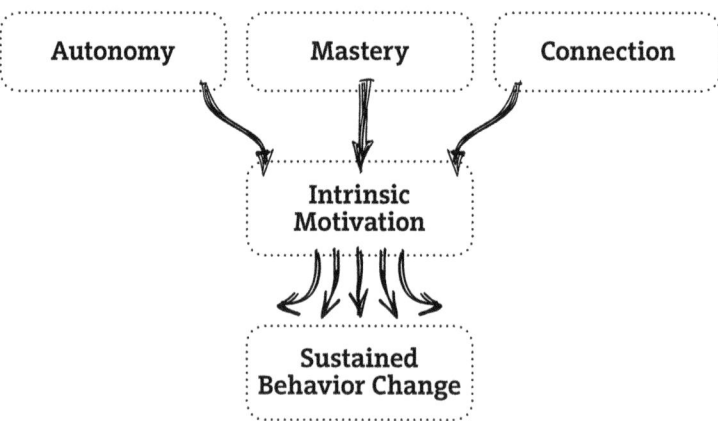

Fig. 3.1 Three ingredients for intrinsic motivation

Autonomy

Perhaps the single most important ingredient for feeling intrinsically motivated to do something is autonomy. It is the sense of being in control and having a choice. People with high levels of autonomy have been found to be more able to sustain effort, perform well, and achieve their goals (Fernet et al. 2012). They are more likely to enjoy what they do and find it satisfying (Deci et al. 1989). And they are more likely to succeed in their new year's resolutions, to act on new ideas, and to be able to achieve changes such as quitting smoking or losing weight (Berg et al. 2001; Williams et al. 1996, 2006).

managers have a vital role to play in ensuring that people feel autonomous

Critically, managers have a vital role to play in ensuring that people feel autonomous. Of course, both broader organizational and even societal culture play a role in how autonomous people feel, but the impact of a manager is more immediate and significant. And your role here as a manager is particularly important when you need people to do something—when it is you or the organization asking for change, rather than the individual initiating it (Gagné et al. 2000)—because you need to do so in a way that still leaves people feeling that they have a choice. So how do you do it?

Autonomy Technique #1: Involve People

One simple way of making sure that people have a sense of control is to involve them in the process of setting goals. The idea is that by doing so, you can make the goals feel more significant for them and increase their sense of ownership of those goals. When the change is being driven by individuals, this will come automatically, but when it is you or the organization driving the change it requires some work. Fortunately, there has been a lot of research into how best to achieve this and there are three simple things you can do:

- **Ask for feedback**. Simply asking people for their feedback and opinions about a proposed change has been shown to improve their willingness to act—as long as they believe you are genuinely listening to what they say.
- **Seek out implementation ideas**. If a change or goal is being set by you or the organization, then ask people for their ideas on how to implement it. This kind of involvement has been shown to increase people's willingness

to take on organization-led changes, since it helps them feel that they are part of the process (Sims 2002).
- **Check if people are ready**. Asking people if they are ready to change can be a useful way of both making people feel heard and getting their views on what the challenges to implementing a change may be. One useful way of doing this is to ask rating scale questions. For instance, "On a rating scale of 1 to 10, how ready are you to do this?" Or, "On a rating scale of 1 to 10, how able do you feel to make this happen?" This gives you more information than a response of "fairly ready," and it gives you a structure within which to ask follow-up questions, such as, "So what would it take for you to be a 9 or even a 10?"

Autonomy Technique #2: Get the Tone Right

The key is to talk to people, but it is vital that you talk to them in the right way. Research shows that a behavior change goal that is assigned or driven by a manager can be as effective as one chosen by an individual, as long as the manager is respectful, polite, and genuinely listens to what the individual has to say (Latham et al. 1988). In other words, the tone of the conversation has to be right. Specifically, there are five things you can do here:

- **Mean it**. This one is critical. If you are to set a constructive tone, you need to mean it. If you approach a situation thinking that you absolutely need to change how someone behaves, that controlling intention is likely to come across in the way you speak and how you phrase things. Conversely, if you view what you are doing as helping someone to develop, that will come across, too.
- **Be clear**. Be clear about what the change involves. Discuss the benefits, as well as acknowledging any costs to the individual of changing their behavior (for example, effort or time).
- **Be curious**. Ask people what they think and how they feel about the behavior change.
- **Ask, don't tell**. If you or the organization are initiating the change, then avoid using controlling language such as, "Do this…" Instead, ask them, say you need their help.
- **Sidestep resistance**. Someone who resists change is effectively providing you with information about the factors that reduce their intrinsic motivation to change behavior. If you find yourself arguing or even just disagreeing, in effect you are confronting and dismissing this resistance rather than

sidestepping it and listening to what it is telling you. Sidestepping resistance, then, is about information gathering and the easiest way to ensure you are doing it is to make sure you are asking questions. "What do you mean by that? Tell me more about it" By asking questions like this you can ensure that people feel their concerns have been heard and that you understand what the factors are that may influence how successful or sustained the change is likely to be. And once you know the factors, you may be able to do something about them.

Autonomy Technique #3: Offer Choice

If someone feels they have a choice, they will have a greater sense of autonomy. A review of 42 studies that together involved 23,000 people found that reminding people of their autonomy made it much more likely that they would agree to a request such as donating to charity, signing a petition, or paying a stranger's bus fare (Carpenter 2013). In one experiment in a French shopping mall, only 10% of people gave to charity when asked. Yet when researchers added, "You are free to accept or refuse," the proportion shot up to nearly 50%. So reminding people that they are in control and have a choice can help build their motivation to do something. And there are three ways you can accomplish this:

- **Tell them they have options**. As the studies above showed, simply adding a phrase such as "It's up to you how you do it" or "You're free to choose" reminds people that they have options and so increases their sense of autonomy. This is actually an example of a behavioral economics technique called *nudging* and we will return to look at more techniques like this in Chap. 10.
- **Create options**. In some situations people do not really have much option about what they do—for example, a situation in which you, as their manager, just *need* them to start behaving in a certain way. Even then, although the change in *what* they do is being driven by you, you can still make sure they feel they have options about *how* they go about it. So talk with people and try to help them understand what those options are. And, importantly, even if you enter the conversation with a clear view of what their options are, avoid immediately stating them and instead invite people to come up with suggestions of their own.
- **Provide guidelines**. Choices alone are not always helpful. We will look at the science of how people make choices later on in the book in Chap. 10,

but for now it is useful to know that people find choices easier to make when they have information and guidelines to help them. So, where possible, help people navigate their choices.

Hobson's Choice

The chair hit the window with enough force to smash the glass. Two minutes into a therapy session, it was quite a statement to make. The chair did not land anywhere, mind you. It just hung there, its legs supported by the iron bars that crisscrossed the now broken window. Fury across his face, the man who had thrown the chair strode to the door, intent on storming out in a flurry of expletives. Suddenly, though, he stopped, and the look of frustration and confusion spreading across his face showed why. He had remembered where he was and that the door before him was locked as tight as any door could be. Making a dramatic exit is not easy in a prison.

This was the challenge that one of your authors faced when working as a therapist in a prison facility. Few people really want to attend therapy in a prison, and of those who do, fewer still genuinely want to change. Neither of those facts made the challenge any easier: how to make the man stay and participate. The solution, as it turned out, was to give him a choice when he thought he had none.

"If you want to leave, you can. I'll have the door opened. But this is what is going to happen. You'll be reported and you'll have to face the consequences. They won't be serious, but they'll be a hassle. You could also just stay, but sit and sulk and not take part. As long as you don't stop anyone else participating then I'm fine with that, too. No one can force you to take part. But you won't enjoy yourself, you'll get bored and nothing about your life will change. But stay and participate, and something might change. At the very least, you won't be so bored and you'll be out of your cell. It's up to you, though. What do you want to do?"

It was not much of a choice, admittedly. But it was a choice, and it was *his* choice. And when he sat back down and eventually even apologized, it was a choice he genuinely owned.

Helping people feel a sense of autonomy, then, is possible and can be achieved even when there are some very real limits on what the choices are. And research has shown that it is a vital ingredient for building and reinforcing intrinsic motivation. It is, however, one of three ingredients and on its own is often not enough.

Mastery

This one is straightforward: people tend to be more motivated to perform a task or change a behavior when they feel able to do so (Deci and Ryan 1985). And they tend to perform tasks better and enjoy them more when they feel competent. The research on this is clear and there is no real argument.

Where there has been some debate, though, is around whether feeling challenged is more important than feeling competent. The suggestion from some researchers is that tougher goals and challenging changes are more motivating than easy ones, since they require people to work harder to achieve more (Locke and Latham 2006). They thus provide a greater sense of growth and becoming more accomplished. For example, one recent study showed that people who saw their work goals as difficult experienced greater increases in job satisfaction and feelings of success over a three-year period than people who saw their goals as easy (Elliot and Harackiewicz 1994). And this seems to be true for people in a range of different roles: from engineers and scientists to loggers and unionized hourly workers (Latham and Locke 2006).

Yet challenge may not always be helpful. In more complex or broad tasks, or in situations in which the precise behavior change required is not clear, a sense of competence may be more important for creating intrinsic motivation than a sense of challenge (Seijts and Latham 2001). This is the case, for example, when motivating someone to become a "better leader" or a "better influencer." Likewise, some people are not particularly motivated by achieving goals, so making them feel challenged may not be useful. This mix of competence and challenge is why we like the term *mastery*, since it seems to convey a bit of both. With these caveats in mind, let's look at what you can do to help foster a sense of mastery in people.

Mastery Technique #1: Reinforce people's Sense of Competence

One of the easiest ways to ensure people feel competent to do something is to clarify and remind them of what they can do. We are going to look at this topic in more depth in Chap. 6, but for now two things are important:

- **Emphasize strengths**. One simple thing you can do is acknowledge the strengths that someone has that you think will help them to change. Convey your confidence in them, too, by telling them you think they can do it. For example: "I'm confident you can do this. You're flexible and clever, and you've got great interpersonal skills. All that we're talking about

now is using these skills in a more considered way, so that you can influence other people more effectively."
- **Give praise where it is due.** This one is rather complex. As we will see in Chap. 4, some people seem to respond better to criticism than praise. But, as a rule, if people do something good, then tell them. This applies particularly to novices—people at the start of their careers or new to something—for whom positive feedback can help to instill confidence in their ability to succeed (Ryan and Deci 2000).

Mastery Technique #2: Position Change as Challenge

The other basic technique you can use to create a sense of mastery is to bring challenge to the surface—to help people to see what they are doing as an interesting challenge rather than a change. Just what type of challenge most motivates people will depend upon the individual, but there are a number of things you can do to make sure that they feel the right amount and type of challenge for them:

- **Ask about challenge.** One of the first and most important things you should do is to ascertain how people feel about challenge. You are looking for two things here: how much they enjoy challenge, and what types of challenges they like most. For the first, you can employ rating scale questions again: asking, "On a scale of 1 to 10 how much do you enjoy challenge?" tends to yield more information than simply asking "How much do you enjoy challenge?"

To determine types of challenges, you are specifically looking for whether people are motivated more by achieving goals or by the sense of developing and learning. If it is the former, you can frame the behavior change as a challenge toward a specific goal or target. If it is the latter, you can express the behavior change as the challenge to learn a new skill or develop themselves in some way.

This may sound simplistic, but you would be surprised at how powerful it can be and how often it is overlooked. We tend to jump straight to solutions, goals, and targets. Yet just asking people how they feel about challenge ensures that change can be positioned in a way that appeals to what intrinsically motivates them.

- **Appeal to people's sense of pride.** If you think that someone might not respond well to any challenge, there is one final card you can play. Describing a behavior change as a matter of pride—be it being the best, refusing to fail, or simply doing something as well as it can be done—can be a powerful motivator (Katzenbach 2003). It works with both individuals and teams and can be particularly useful for fostering commitment to a change in a group of people. For instance, consider Susan, a call center leader we once worked with, who was trying to introduce some new customer service standards into a group that had historically been resistant to change. We suggested that she mention the word *pride* as often as possible. So she deliberately and repeatedly started talking about her sense of pride in being part of such an experienced team that knew so much about delivering the best customer service possible. And she clearly positioned the changes she was asking people to make as a matter of pride for them all and a way of staying ahead of the competition. It was simple stuff, but it worked.

Like autonomy, then, having a sense of mastery is important for intrinsic motivation. One final ingredient remains: connection.

Connection

In the original *self-determination theory* of motivation, the last piece of the motivation puzzle was called *relatedness*. In recent years, however, psychologists have begun talking about it more in terms of whether you feel some sense of *connection* to what you are doing and whether you can see some purpose in it.

For example, in 2005, the economist Dan Ariely conducted an experiment into how the perceived purpose of a task affected people's willingness to work. He asked participants to assemble some simple Lego toys—as many of them as they felt motivated to make. For one group of participants, he made the task "purposeful" by displaying the completed toys while they carried on making more. Now that may not sound particularly purposeful, and it wasn't. But compared to what happened with a second group, it was incredibly purposeful. For the second group, every time they finished making a toy, Ariely would dismantle it in front of them while they made the next toy. Unsurprisingly, the participants in the first group made more toys than those in the second (Ariely et al. 2008). Being able to see some purpose in what we are doing matters.

Ariely's experiment is one of many that have looked at the impact of things like purpose on how motivated we feel. Indeed, since the 1980s there has been a flood of books urging leaders to be more transformational, inspirational, or visionary and to infuse people with a sense of purpose. Even the US military is getting in on the act. Written orders now begin with a "Commander's Intent" that spells out the purpose behind an order. The issue has come even more to the forefront in recent years, with the suggestion that having a clear sense of purpose is more important to younger generations than older ones (Poswolsky 2014). But what does this mean for the average manager trying to motivate someone to change an aspect of their behavior? What do you actually have to do?

The answer lies in the original ideas about connection and its importance for intrinsic motivation. It may have been expanded by concepts such as purpose in recent years, but in its original conception it is about how connected people feel to both goals and other people. We believe that although purpose is a commendable concept, the current emphasis on it may be inadvertently unhelpful. It can conjure up images of higher motives of making the world a better place and leave leaders unclear about how to make them happen. Helping people feel *connected* to what they are doing and why they are doing it, by contrast, is a more pragmatic business. So let's look at what you can do to foster this sense of connection.

it is about how connected people feel to both goals and other people

Connection Technique #1: Establish why

The first thing you need to do here is establish why change matters to individuals. How you do this depends on whether the other person is driving the behavior change or you are.

- **Ask people why.** When people come to you asking for help in changing a behavior or improving some aspect of their performance, start by asking, "Why? Why do you want to change this? What will happen if you change? And what would happen if you didn't?" Asking this may seem counterintuitive. But you would be surprised at how often people do not have much of an answer beyond, "I think it will help." This may sound reasonable, yet it is a sign that you need to work on improving their sense of connection to the change by exploring why it matters to them and what the consequences and benefits of changing will be.

- **Tell people why**. When you or your organization is asking someone to change, the person needs to fully understand what is expected of them, and why they need to do it. For all we have said about the importance of autonomy, a behavior change goal that is set by a manager can be just as motivating as one that is chosen by an individual, as long as the rationale and benefits of the change are clear (Brown and Leigh 1996; Kahn 1990). People just need to feel that the change is important and relevant for them. So tell them, and help them understand why. Just be careful not to make too many assumptions about what may be motivating to others, as one of the easiest mistakes to make here is to assume that what motivates you will also motivate others.

Connection Technique #2: Make It Personal

One way to ensure that a person feels personally connected to a change or goal is to make sure it feels significant to them (Hackman and Oldham 1975). It is one thing to say, "This is important for the business." It is quite another to say, "This is important for us." Consider an executive we recently coached. He had repeatedly received feedback that he needed to improve his political skills, but had never done anything about it because he did not believe it was important. It was only when we helped him understand what the impact was on his ability to get other people to support his initiatives, and on his capacity to generate promotion opportunities for himself, that he became intrinsically motivated to do something about it.

Connection Technique #3: Get Practical

Although it may seem counterintuitive for a section dealing with "getting practical," we need to pause for a second to think about philosophy—and one particular philosopher, Ludwig Josef Johann Wittgenstein. He was an Austrian-British philosopher who wrote a great deal about language and meaning. Perhaps surprisingly for a philosopher, Wittgenstein was very pragmatic and he came up with a simple and useful definition of whether something is meaningful. He said that in order for something that someone says to us to be meaningful for us, we have to know how to go on from it—what to do next. If we say, "Hello" to you, you know how to respond. But if we say, "Green packets rise unhappily," most people (including us!) will not have a clue how to respond, other than asking what on earth we mean. It is meaningless because we do not know how to respond to it.

We can apply this to how we speak with people about changes or goals. To ensure they are meaningful, we need to make sure that people know how to go on—that they understand what to do next. So if someone tells you they would like help to change—whether it is to become more flexible, less aggressive, or a better presenter—a good question to ask is whether they know how to go on and what to do next.

The practicalities of knowing how to go on are a critical element for motivation. Knowing what to do next and how to make a change helps people believe that they *can* make that change. And it is why every book on how to set goals emphasizes the importance of being specific about the actions people are going to take—because it is through being specific that they show people how to go on.

Using the Recipe

What we have here, then, is a recipe for creating intrinsic motivation. Create autonomy, emphasize mastery, and ensure connection. It is pretty simple, powerful, and proven by years of research (see Fig. 3.2).

So far, we have described the key ingredients and suggested some ways to build each one. To make the most of these techniques, though, you need to know which ones are most relevant for each individual. Ideally, if we had the

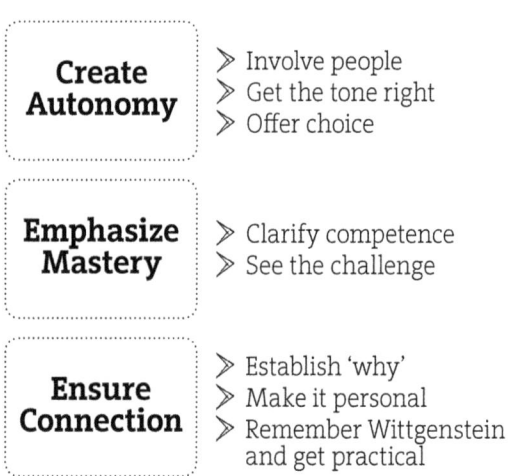

Fig. 3.2 Techniques to build intrinsic motivation

time, we would go through each of the three key ingredients, trying out each technique one by one. But life is rarely ideal. We only have so much time and we often need to know which one(s) to hone in on.

Different People, Different Tastes

The challenge is that which of the three key ingredients is most relevant will vary between people, as will what each of the three means to them. Autonomy may not be as important for one person as it is for another. And what makes one person feel connected may not motivate someone else at all.

In studying such differences between people, researchers have found a number of important factors to consider, including culture, role, age, and gender.

Culture

People in individualistic cultures tend to be more intrinsically motivated by mastery—and, specifically, challenge—than people in collectivist cultures (Locke and Latham 2002).

For example, one study found that in Singapore people tend to set moderate rather than difficult goals—possibly because being part of a group rather than distinguishing oneself is more central to people's well-being (Kurman 2001). This does not mean that challenge cannot be motivating in collectivist cultures, but rather that, for many people in them, tasks that are positioned as team or group challenge are more likely to be intrinsically motivating than challenges specific to individuals.

Similarly, there has been some research to suggest that for people from Asian collectivist cultures, autonomy may be less important. In a study examining the importance of choice, Anglo Americans were more intrinsically motivated when they were allowed to choose the task to be performed, while Asian Americans were more intrinsically motivated when the choices were made for them by a trusted authority figure or peers (Iyengar and Lepper 1999). Similar findings about the relative lower importance of autonomy have also been found in other collectivist cultures such as those found in India, Turkey, and Morocco (Radhakrishnan and Chan 1997).

Culture Makes a Difference

When one of your authors moved to the US and attended his son's first baseball game, he was amazed at the lines of parents standing beside the pitch, screaming encouragement with all their might, while their little six-year-old was trying to hit the ball. "Let's go Daniel! You can do it, put a little muscle into it." And within a few weeks, he had joined the choir of encouragement, hurling positive vibes across the pitch at full volume. A few years later he moved to Germany and, on attending his son's first soccer practice, had a moment of real shock and insight into cultural differences. For, like the American parents, the German ones were also standing at the side of the pitch and also urging the kids onward. But they were not yelling positive encouragement. They were shouting every time their kids failed to hit the ball, criticizing them, coaxing them, and challenging them to do better. Culture makes a difference.

Role

There has been some research showing that autonomy may not be as important for people in nonmanagerial roles (Gagné et al. 1997). There is also some evidence to suggest that connection may be more important for part-time workers than full-time workers.

Age

Likewise, there is a suggestion that both autonomy and connection may be more important for younger workers (Ginnodo 1989). For instance, in one study of nearly 15,000 people, Millennials (those born between 1980 and 1995) were found to place far greater value on being able to control what they did and how they did it than the older generations (Finn and Donovan 2013).

Gender

Finally, there is evidence to suggest that women may place greater importance on aspects of competence than men (and, specifically, feeling appreciated). Men, meanwhile, appear to place greater value on some elements of connection—such as feeling that work is interesting—than women (Wiley 1997). So when trying to motivate women to change, emphasizing competence and using praise may work better than emphasizing challenge. And when trying to motivate men, making sure they understand why the change is important may be critical.

These are some of the broader factors that can influence what people find intrinsically motivating. However, we need to be careful with research findings like these because, while broader cultural and demographic differences may exist, the most important aspects are the individuals you work with and what matters to them personally. Sitting across from a young Singaporean male manager, you may be able to guess which factors are more likely to be important for him, but you cannot make assumptions and have to check.

Two Models for Profiling People

So, in addition to recommending that you consider the broader issues of culture, role, age, and gender, we want to introduce two simple models that you can use to explore how people are different and what matters to them.

Model #1: Career Concept Model

The career concept model provides a way to understand how people's views about their careers can affect what intrinsically motivates them (Driver 1979; Brousseau 1984). It distinguishes between four types of career profiles: *expert*, *linear*, *spiral*, and *transitory*.

- **Expert**. People with this kind of career style see their choice of career as being made for a lifetime. They are committed to their occupation and motivated by a desire to go in-depth and be an expert in their field.
- **Linear**. Those with this career style focus on upward movement (such as through an organization's hierarchy), with only rare changes in the types of role undertaken. The higher up in an organization they go, and the more influence they have, the more successful they feel.
- **Spiral**. In this career style, people strive for mastery, but also make additional career moves beyond their original career choice. They are motivated by variety and broadening their horizons. And each new career choice builds on past choices in order to allow them to develop new skills.
- **Transitory**. This style of career involves frequent changes of organizations and types of role, with variety and a sense of independence being the key motivators.

The first step in using this model is to ask people what career success looks like for them and identify which of the four profiles they most fit. Take a minute now and think about yourself—about which profile describes your career to date.

Questions you could use to investigate other people's profiles include:

- How would you describe your career so far?
- What has driven you to make the career choices you have made?
- What led you to move from <any role in their career> to the next role?

Having done this, you can then draw some tentative conclusions about what kinds of things are most likely to intrinsically motivate them. We say "tentative" because you need to check to see if what we expect does indeed apply to each individual. Figure 3.3 shows the most common intrinsic motivators for each of the different profiles.

The usefulness of this model lies in the fact that it can help you, as a manager, to quickly draw some conclusions about what might motivate others. And it can help others think about whether a particular change they wish to make is really something that they will be able to remain motivated about over time.

For instance, consider Ava, a manager we worked with who had received some negative feedback about her project management skills and was being sent on a training course. By briefly asking her about her career background we were able to see that she had had a *spiral* career path to date. This meant that she was unlikely to be motivated by the trainer's passion for deep expertise in project management and there was a risk that she would not use the skills being taught. This was exacerbated by the fact that she felt she had been ordered to do the training and had no choice about it. Using the career

Fig. 3.3 Likely key intrinsic motivators for each profile

concept model, we were able to understand that breadth of expertise and freedom to choose were important for her and so outlined the benefits of training in terms of these two intrinsic motivators. We positioned the training as an option and emphasized that project management would be another "string to her bow," which would open up greater options for her in future. This was a simple rephrasing of the benefits, but it worked because it was based on an understanding of her key intrinsic motivators.

Model #2: Promotion and Prevention

The second model for helping us understand the differences between people comes from cognitive psychology. It suggests that, when it comes to any new situation or change, we can approach things in one of two ways: *promotion* or *prevention*. Someone who adopts a promotion approach plays to win; someone who adopts a prevention approach plays so as not to lose. A promotion-focused person is more likely to take chances, seize opportunities, and be creative. A prevention-focused person, meanwhile, hates to make mistakes, tends to be more thorough and is likely to be a better planner. Most people are a mix of the two, yet most will also tend more toward one than the other (Halvorson and Higgins 2013). Think about yourself: are you more promotion focused or prevention focused?

This model is relevant for us because people with a promotion focus tend to be intrinsically motivated by different types of things than people with a prevention focus (see Fig. 3.4).

The utility of this model lies in its simplicity. It is easy to understand and even easier to apply. Say you are trying to help motivate an employee to be more creative. If they are more promotion focused, you can emphasize the challenge and opportunities. Yet, if they are more prevention focused, you are probably better off emphasizing the dangers of not innovating.

Like the career concept model, the promotion and prevention model enables us to apply what we know about intrinsic motivation. It helps us to help others better understand what is important to them and what is most likely to motivate them. And it helps us to understand how best to present and phrase changes so they have the best chance of succeeding.

In our experience, and we suspect yours, people in businesses tend to jump all too quickly to solutions. Operating in time-pressured environments with strict deadlines, managers often help people identify a change that can be made and then, frequently without breathing space, move on to make that change. This model helps us pause and check whether a potential change

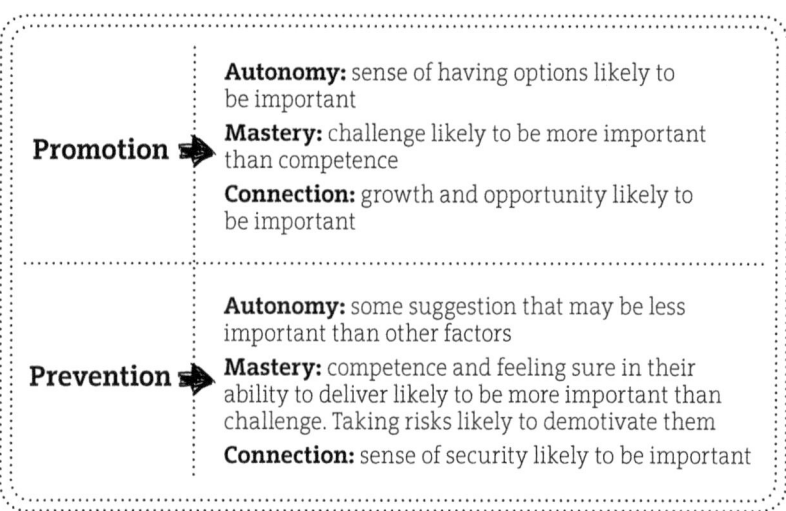

Fig. 3.4 Intrinsic motivators for promotion- and prevention-focused people

really does appeal to someone's inner drivers, and thus whether it has a good chance of succeeding.

Just One Side of the Story

At the beginning of this chapter we said that the overwhelming consensus of writers and academics is that inner, intrinsic commitment is the most powerful and sustainable type of motivation. And there is no doubt in our minds that this recent focus on intrinsic motivation has been and remains useful. If people do not feel intrinsically motivated to change, then the change is less likely to succeed, particularly in the long term. So, in this chapter, we have shown the practical steps you can take to build and reinforce people's intrinsic motivation for change.

We also noted at the start of this chapter that most of what has recently been written about motivation has focused more on motivating people to perform, rather than to change behavior. For the most part, the things that motivate people to perform are the same as the things that motivate them to change. But this is not always true and one notable and important exception here is the use of *extrinsic* motivators—external incentives such as rewards and punishments. Listening to some recent commentators, you might believe that these rewards and punishments should be avoided wherever possible. Yet, as

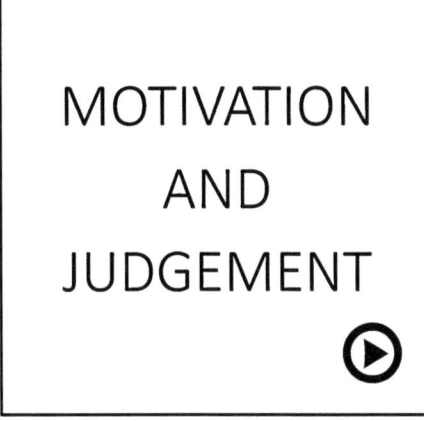

Fig. 3.5 The Effect of motivation on judgement (▶ https://doi.org/10.1007/000-ak1)

we will see, while this may be somewhat true for motivating performance, when it comes to motivating change it is just not so. As critical as intrinsic motivation is, it is just one side of the story and, to fully understand motivation, we need to understand the role of extrinsic motivators.

For brief reflections on the content of this chapter, new to the second edition, see Video Fig. 3.5.

Key Questions to Ask Yourself

1. On a rating scale of 1 to 10, how strongly does the behavior change appeal overall to the individual's intrinsic motivation?
2. What would the rating be for how strongly the change appeals to each of the three elements of intrinsic motivation: autonomy, mastery, and connection?
3. Does the individual have a sense of autonomy, choice, and involvement in the change process?
4. What can you do to highlight competence, progress, and challenge?
5. Does the individual know how to go on—what to do next—and understand the relevance and importance of the change for them?
6. How might the individual's culture, age, role, and gender affect their intrinsic motivation for this change?
7. How might the individual's career concept and personality affect their intrinsic motivation for this change?

Further Resources

- Daniel H. Pink (2009). *Drive: The Surprising Truth about What Motivates Us*. New York: Riverhead Books. Also available as a brief video summary on YouTube.
- Dan Ariely (2012). *What makes us feel good about our work?* TED talk available from www.TED.com with subtitles in different languages.

References

Grant, A.M. (2008). Does intrinsic motivation fuel the prosocial fire? Motivational synergy in predicting persistence, performance, and productivity. *Journal of Applied Psychology*, 93(1), 48.

Froiland, J.M. (2011). Parental autonomy support and student learning goals: A preliminary examination of an intrinsic motivation intervention. *Child and Youth Care Forum*, 40(2), 135–49.

Kanfer, R. and Ackerman, P.L. (1989). Motivation and cognitive abilities: an integrative/aptitude-treatment interaction approach to skill acquisition. *Journal of Applied Psychology*, 74(4), 657.

Thomas, K.W. and Velthouse, B.A. (1990). Cognitive elements of empowerment: an "interpretive" model of intrinsic task motivation. *Academy of Management Review*, 15(4), 666–81.

Blais, M.R., Brière, N.M., Lachance, L., Riddle, A.S., and Vallerand, R.J. (1993). L'inventaire des motivations au travail de Blais. *Revue Québécoise de Psychologie*, 14(3), 185–215.

Johnson, D.W., Johnson, R.T., Roseth, C., and Shin, T.S. (2014). The relationship between motivation and achievement in interdependent situations. *Journal of Applied Social Psychology*. doi: https://doi.org/10.1111/jasp.12280.

Ryan, R.M., Patrick, H., Deci, E.L., and Williams, G.C. (2008). Facilitating health behaviour change and its maintenance: interventions based on self-determination theory. *The European Health Psychologist*, 10(1), 2–5.

Ryan, R.M. and Connell, J.P. (1989). Perceived locus of causality and internalization: examining reasons for acting in two domains. *Journal of Personality and Social Psychology*, 57(5), 749.

Mitchell, J.I., Gagné, M., Beaudry, A., and Dyer, L. (2012). The role of perceived organizational support, distributive justice and motivation in reactions to new information technology. *Computers in Human Behavior*, 28(2), 729–38.

Deci, E.L. and Ryan, R.M. (2010). Self-Determination. *Corsini Encyclopedia of Psychology*, 1–2.

Fernet, C., Austin, S., and Vallerand, R.J. (2012). The effects of work motivation on employee exhaustion and commitment: an extension of the JD-R model. *Work & Stress*, 26(3), 213–29.

Deci, E.L., Connell, J.P., and Ryan, R.M. (1989). Self-determination in a work organization. *Journal of Applied Psychology*, 74(4), 580.

Berg, M.B., Janoff-Bulman, R., and Cotter, J. (2001). Perceiving value in obligations and goals: wanting to do what should be done. *Personality and Social Psychology Bulletin*, 27(8), 982–95.

Williams, G.C., McGregor, H., Sharp, D., Kouides, R.W., Lévesque, C.S., Ryan, R.M., and Deci, E.L. (2006). A self-determination multiple risk intervention trial to improve smokers' health. *Journal of General Internal Medicine*, 21(12), 1288–94.

Williams, G.C., Grow, V.M., Freedman, Z.R., Ryan, R.M., and Deci, E.L. (1996). Motivational predictors of weight loss and weight-loss maintenance. *Journal of Personality and Social Psychology*, 70(1), 115.

Gagné, M., Koestner, R., and Zuckerman, M. (2000). Facilitating acceptance of organizational change: the importance of self-determination. *Journal of Applied Social Psychology*, 30(9), 1843–52.

Sims, R.R. (2002). Employee involvement is still the key to successfully managing change. In S.J. Sims and R.R. Sims (Eds.), *Changing the Way We Manage Change* (pp. 33–54). Westport, CT: Quorum Books.

Latham, G.P., Erez, M., and Locke, E.A. (1988). Resolving scientific disputes by the joint design of crucial experiments by the antagonists: application to the Erez–Latham dispute regarding participation in goal setting. *Journal of Applied Psychology*, 73(4), 753.

Carpenter, C.J. (2013). A meta-analysis of the effectiveness of the "but you are free" compliance-gaining technique. *Communication Studies*, 64(1), 6–17.

Deci, E.L. and Ryan, R.M. (1985). *Intrinsic Motivation and Self-determination in Human Behavior*. New York: Plenum Press.

Locke, E.A. and Latham, G.P. (2006). New directions in goal-setting theory. *Current Directions in Psychological Science*, 15(5), 265–8.

Elliot, A.J., and Harackiewicz, J.M. (1994). Goal setting, achievement orientation, and intrinsic motivation: a mediational analysis. *Journal of Personality and Social Psychology*, 66(5), 968.

Latham, G.P. and Locke, E.A. (2006). Enhancing the benefits and overcoming the pitfalls of goal setting. *Organizational Dynamics*, 35(4), 332–40.

Seijts, G.H. and Latham, G.P. (2001). The effect of distal learning, outcome, and proximal goals on a moderately complex task. *Journal of Organizational Behavior*, 22(3), 291–307.

Ryan, R.M. and Deci, E.L. (2000). Intrinsic and extrinsic motivations: classic definitions and new directions. *Contemporary Educational Psychology*, 25(1), 54–67.

Katzenbach, J. (2003). Pride: a strategic asset. *Strategy & Leadership*, 31(5), 34–8.

Ariely, D., Kamenica, E., and Prelec, D. (2008). Man's search for meaning: the case of Legos. *Journal of Economic Behavior & Organization*, 67(3–4), 671–7.

Poswolsky, A.S. (2014, April). 4 tips to help millennials find meaningful work. *Fast Company*. Retrieved August, 12, 2014, from http://goo.gl/OGcIjz.

Brown, S.P. and Leigh, T.W. (1996). A new look at psychological climate and its relationship to job involvement, effort, and performance. *Journal of Applied Psychology*, 81(4), 358.

Kahn, W.A. (1990). Psychological conditions of personal engagement and disengagement at work. *Academy of Management Journal*, 33(4), 692–724.

Hackman, J.R. and Oldham, G.R. (1975). Development of the job diagnostic survey. *Journal of Applied Psychology*, 60(2), 159.

Locke, E.A. and Latham, G.P. (2002).Building a practically useful theory of goal setting and task motivation: a 35-year odyssey. *American Psychologist*, 57(9), 705.

Kurman, J. (2001). Self-regulation strategies in achievement settings: culture and-gender differences. *Journal of Cross-Cultural Psychology*, 32, 491–503.

Iyengar, S.S. and Lepper, M.R. (1999).Rethinking the value of choice: a cultural perspective on intrinsic motivation. *Journal of Personality and Social Psychology*, 76(3), 349.

Radhakrishnan, P. and Chan, D.K. (1997). Cultural differences in the relation between self-discrepancy and life satisfaction: examining personal and parental goals. *International Journal of Psychology*, 32, 387–98.

Gagné, M., Senecal, C.B., and Koestner, R. (1997). Proximal job characteristics, feelings of empowerment, and intrinsic motivation: a multidimensional model. *Journal of Applied Social Psychology*, 27(14), 1222–40.

Ginnodo, W.L. (1989). How to build employee commitment. *National Productivity Review*, 8(3), 249–60.

Finn, D. and Donovan, A. (2013). *NextGen: A Global Generational Study*. New York: PwC. Retrieved August 12, 2014, from http://goo.gl/y65tb.

Wiley, C. (1997). What motivates employees according to over 40 years of motivation surveys. *International Journal of Manpower*, 18(3), 263–80.

Driver, M.J. (1979). Career concepts and career management in organizations. In C.L. Cooper (Ed.), *Behavioral Problems in Organizations* (pp. 79–139). Englewood Cliffs, NJ: Prentice-Hall.

Brousseau, K.R. (1984). Job-person dynamics and career development. *Research in Personnel and Human Resources*, 2, 125–54.

Halvorson, H.G. and Higgins, E.T. (2013). Do you play to win—or to not lose? *Harvard Business Review*, 91(3), 117–20.

4

Extrinsic Motivation: Using Reward and Punishment

Permeating every society and every culture, every business and every household, there is a fundamental behaviorist idea about behaviors and how to change them: the *law of effect* (Thorndike 1898). It is the belief that if you reward certain behaviors you will get more of them, and if you punish certain behaviors, you will get less of them. This belief is so basic that it should not sound controversial to you. And if you want proof, just ask any parent or dog owner and they will tell you: when it comes to encouraging behaviors, sweets and treats work.

That would make a great chapter summary, too, if it were not for one small problem. According to many recent headlines, rewards do not work nearly as well as people think. But is this right and does it apply to motivating people to change behaviors? In this chapter, we are going to find out. We will look at the science of *extrinsic motivation*—the use of motivators that you apply to people. For managers, this means positive things like money, prizes, praise, and recognition, as well as negative things such as criticism and punishment. You can find specific examples in Figs. 4.1 and 4.2.

Supplementary Information The online version contains supplementary material available at https://doi.org/10.1007/978-3-031-29340-5_4. The videos can be accessed individually by clicking the DOI link in the accompanying figure caption or by scanning this link with the SN More Media App.

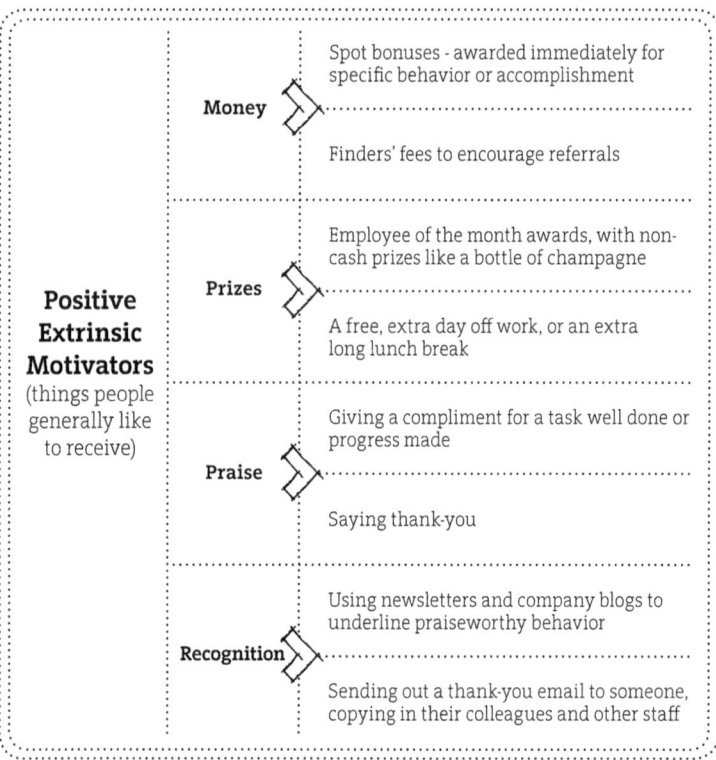

Fig. 4.1 Positive extrinsic motivator

Should You Use Rewards?

We are going to look at when and how extrinsic motivators can be used to help people change behavior. But before we look at *how* to use them, we first need to check whether you should, because if many of the headlines are to be believed, you should not be using them at all. So we will begin with four key criticisms leveled at extrinsic motivators, checking the evidence for each to see whether the warnings aimed at it are really warranted. As we will see, navigating the research is not always easy, since the subject tends to be quite emotive. People seem to be either very vocally in favor of extrinsic motivators or equally passionately against them. So it is time for a reality check.

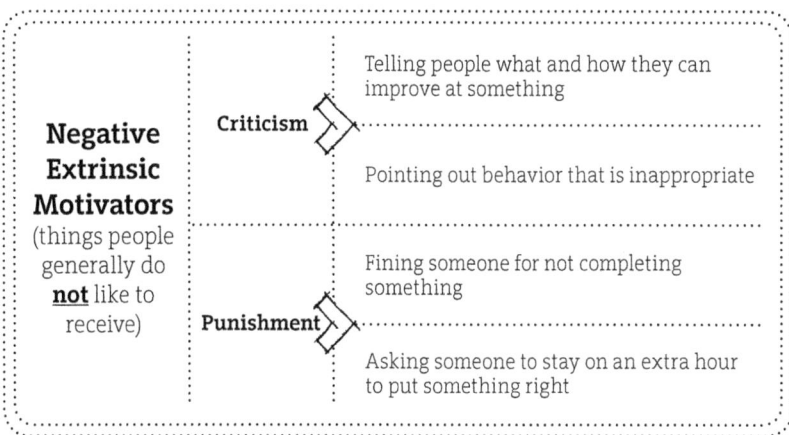

Fig. 4.2 Negative extrinsic motivators

Criticism #1: Money Does Not Motivate

Most of the research on extrinsic motivators has focused on monetary rewards and on whether paying people more and awarding bonuses will result in higher performance levels. We are interested more in whether money can help motivate people to change behavior, but let's start with this broader issue.

It is certainly true that some studies have shown that pay-for-performance and bonuses do not produce better performance from either individuals or organizations (Bonner and Sprinkle 2002a; De Waal 2013). Indeed, an influential *Harvard Business Review* article declared that there were over two dozen studies showing that people who expect to receive a reward for completing a task do not perform as well as those who expect no reward (Kohn 1993). However, it is also true that there are even more studies showing that pay-for-performance schemes and bonuses *can* improve performance (Rynes et al. 2004a; Locke et al. 1980; Guzzo et al. 1985; Stajkovic and Luthans 1997; Currall et al. 2005). Indeed, some figures suggest that introducing such schemes can increase organizational productivity between 30% and 50% (Schneider et al. 2003). So, given these two very different pictures of whether money motivates people, what should we believe?

The answer is that we can believe both. Focusing employees on objectives and performance levels through financial rewards *can* help motivate people to higher levels of performance. Yet it is also true that money does not always work. Financial rewards appear to be most able to motivate people doing less complex tasks and at lower pay levels (Ariely et al. 2009a). And money is generally better at motivating people to greater levels of effort and quantity of work than at improving quality (Jenkins Jr et al. 1998; Bonner and Sprinkle 2002b). This is why some tasks—such as creative or design tasks—seem to respond less well to financial rewards. There is also research to show that once bonuses reach a certain level, making them even bigger does not produce better performance (Rynes et al. 2004b; Ariely et al. 2009b). Finally, it seems that financial incentives appeal more to some people than to others: they seem to be more important to extroverts, for instance, and individuals with high internal needs for achievement (Stewart 1996; Harrison et al. 1996; Trank et al. 2002; Trevor et al. 1997; Turban and Keon 1993).

Even with these caveats, it is clear that the claims that money cannot motivate people are overstated. There are certainly limits to what money can do, but this is not reason enough to abandon financial rewards altogether. Our toolkit needs all the tools it can muster. Moreover, whatever the issues with pay-for-performance and bonuses, we are primarily interested in whether money can help motivate people to change specific behaviors and perform particular tasks. And on that point, there seems to be enough research to suggest that it can. Cash rewards have repeatedly been shown to increase the success of behavior change initiatives such as helping individuals stop smoking, increasing the amount of exercise people get, and dietary behaviors (Gneezy et al. 2011; Lynagh et al. 2013). So, as a broad statement, we can reject this first criticism of extrinsic motivators. But we should not get too excited, because the idea that they may not work is not the biggest criticism aimed at them. There's something worse—the suggestion that using rewards may actually decrease motivation.

Key Lesson

Money can help motivate people to change behavior, but should probably not be the first or only tool we use.

Criticism #2: Rewards Kill Intrinsic Motivation

In recent years, a growing number of high-profile pieces of research have shown that introducing external rewards can sometimes lower intrinsic motivation (Weibel et al. 2010; Deci and Ryan 2000; Frey and Jegen 2001a; Fehr and Falk 2002; Irlenbusch and Sliwka 2003; Falk and Kosfeld 2006; Gneezy and Rustichini 2000). In other words, by offering a reward, you may reduce how much people enjoy a task.

The technical term for what happens is *crowding out* (Frey and Jegen 2001b). The idea is that the introduction of external rewards crowds out and reduces other motives for undertaking a task. For example, if your daughter enjoys studying or works diligently and you want to encourage her further, you might introduce a regular reward for her hard work. That certainly sounds reasonable. Unfortunately, studies have consistently shown that by doing so you are likely to both decrease her enjoyment of the task and eventually reduce her effort, too (Pink 2009).

There is strong evidence that where people already have a high level of intrinsic motivation, then the introduction of external rewards can be downright unhelpful. Yet, just as with the effectiveness of financial rewards, some commentators have latched on to these findings and made more of them than perhaps they should, because, in some circumstances, external rewards can *increase* intrinsic motivation.

An example of this is *pro-social* rewards, in which you reward people with money to give to their charity of choice (Anik et al. 2013). Similarly, you can reward someone by investing in something they are interested in, for example, through a budget for them to attend a development course. There is also evidence showing that praise and criticism, if offered with information about how to improve performance, can improve feelings of autonomy and thus intrinsic motivation (Cameron and Pierce 1994; Deci 1971; Swann Jr and Pittman 1977). It is simply wrong, then, to suggest that rewards always kill intrinsic motivation. On the contrary, if used correctly, rewards can boost intrinsic motivation.

Key Lesson

If you are going to offer a reward for a task that is already enjoyed, do so carefully. And remember that rewards are most effective when they reinforce what intrinsically motivates people.

Criticism #3: External Motivators Can Have Negative Side Effects

This third criticism is hard to deny, because external motivators do not always have the desired effect. For instance, there is enough evidence to show that when strong financial rewards are in place, sooner or later someone will cross ethical boundaries to earn them. There is also evidence that the pay inequality that can result from bonus schemes may fuel turnover (Grant and Singh 2011), and that solely basing bonuses on individual performance can reduce collaboration (Solmon and Podgursky 2000). Furthermore, rewards and punishments of any sort run the risk of focusing people on the specific targets or behaviors being rewarded or punished, at the expense of other factors that may be important (Bahrick et al. 1952; Mc Namara and Fisch 1964). This is one of the criticisms leveled at banks during the recent financial crisis—rewarding short-term results compromised long-term sustainability and governments had to step in with bailouts.

Yet, as before, although all of these concerns are warranted and there is research to show that all of these side effects *can* occur, they are not inevitable. For example, fast-food retailer Prêt à Manger is a strong believer in teamwork and collaboration, but it also likes to motivate people to individual achievement. Its solution is a special kind of reward. When employees are promoted or pass training milestones, they receive financial vouchers. But instead of keeping them, they have to give the vouchers to colleagues—to the people who helped them along the way (Clifford 2011a).

As another example, take the most common negative side effect associated with external motivators: the presumed harmful effects of criticism. There is certainly evidence to suggest that criticism *can* reduce performance, harm confidence levels, and decrease intrinsic motivation (Arvey and Ivancevich 1980a). But it does not always.

As with rewards, the way individuals respond to criticism depends on three things: the individual, the situation, and how the criticism is delivered. For example, although novices respond better to praise, people who are more experienced or experts actually seem to improve their performance more after criticism (Finkelstein and Fishbach 2012). Criticism may also work better than praise in situations where people are close to achieving a goal. In one study, researchers found that while positive feedback motivated dieters who had just started trying to change their weight, negative feedback was better at motivating those who were close to their weight-loss goal.

Finally, in terms of how to deliver criticism, it works best when it is followed by specific advice about what people can do to improve. Indeed, this is one of the key reasons criticism sometimes helps people improve more than praise does. When we criticize, we tend to follow it up with a suggestion for what people can do about it. But when we praise, we tend to be less specific. We say things like, "That was great," or "I really liked the way you ran that meeting." If we approached praise more like we do criticism, we might say something like, "The way you ran that meeting—being clear at the start about the structure, allowing sufficient time for each section, and making sure that discussions did not go over time—was really useful." And when we do this, praise is far more likely to improve performance.

While this third criticism is based on solid fact, and there are genuine causes for concern, it is not sufficient to make us stop using extrinsic motivators altogether. It merely shows us that we need to be clever about how and when we use them.

Key Lesson

Extrinsic motivators are more risky to use than intrinsic ones, and can have negative side effects. But almost all of them can be managed with some thought and planning.

Criticism #4: Rewards and Punishments Do Not Last

A further common criticism of extrinsic motivators is that they do not have long-term effects. If we adopt a behavior to gain a reward, we tend to cease the behavior when the reward is withdrawn. Similarly, if we stop a behavior to avoid a punishment, we may restart it once the threat of punishment passes. The fear, then, is that we can inadvertently create a situation in which we become dependent upon using an external motivator to keep a behavior change going.

There is something intuitively compelling about this criticism. After all, if your employer stopped paying you, would you carry on going to work? There is also a lot of evidence to support the criticism. With behavior changes such as losing weight, increasing exercise by going to the gym, and stopping smoking, studies have repeatedly shown that once a reward is removed, the behavior change stops. People start gaining weight again, give up on the gym, and go back to smoking (Paul-Ebhohimhen and Avenell 2008; Volpp et al. 2009; Volpp et al. 2008).

This research has been criticized, though, for not rewarding people enough or stopping the rewards too soon. Some studies show that if you repeat rewards enough times, the behavior change *can* remain once the reward is removed (Charness and Gneezy 2009). The suggestion is that you do not have to continue rewarding forevermore—you only need to do it long enough for a behavior to become a habit or routine. There is still a degree of debate about this, but the key difference between the studies finding that the effects of rewards can last and those finding that they do not seems to be the involvement of other factors (De Silva 1998a). In other words, it often takes more than a reward or punishment to help establish a habit.

For instance, rewarding people for going to the gym is more likely to work if they are also able to develop a social network there—something that can appeal to people's need for connection and thus their intrinsic motivation

(Babcock and Hartman 2010). Similarly, criticism and punishments such as a reduction in bonus are far more likely to work if they are paired with a clear explanation of why they are being used and concrete suggestions for what could be done to avoid them next time.

We will look at how to build habits in more depth in Chap. 8, but for now we can conclude that there is something to this criticism: rewards and punishments are prone not to have lasting effects, especially if they are used on their own as the only incentives to change behavior. But—and this is the important bit for us—there are things you can do to help make sure that they do last, such as using them enough and pairing them with something else.

Key Lesson

One-off rewards are unlikely to work, and both rewards and punishments need to be combined with other motivators to stand the best chance of working.

How to Use Rewards

It seems that while each of these four key criticisms is based on genuine concerns, some have been overstated and none of them is reason enough not to use extrinsic motivators.

So having established that we *should* consider extrinsic motivators as a key tool at our disposal, the question now is how best to use them. When should we use them? Who with? And which rewards or punishments should we use—or, in other words, what works best?

When to Extrinsically Motivate People

There are four basic rules to give guidance on when to use rewards (see Fig. 4.3).

When to Reward Rule #1: Support Intrinsic Motivation

Strange as it may sound, the trick to making extrinsic motivation work is to think first about its opposite—intrinsic motivation. Ask yourself: what is someone's basic intrinsic motivation for changing a behavior? In many cases, using the model of autonomy, mastery, and connection, you will be able to identify something. In some situations, this intrinsic motivation will be enough. An individual may be a great salesperson and strongly internally

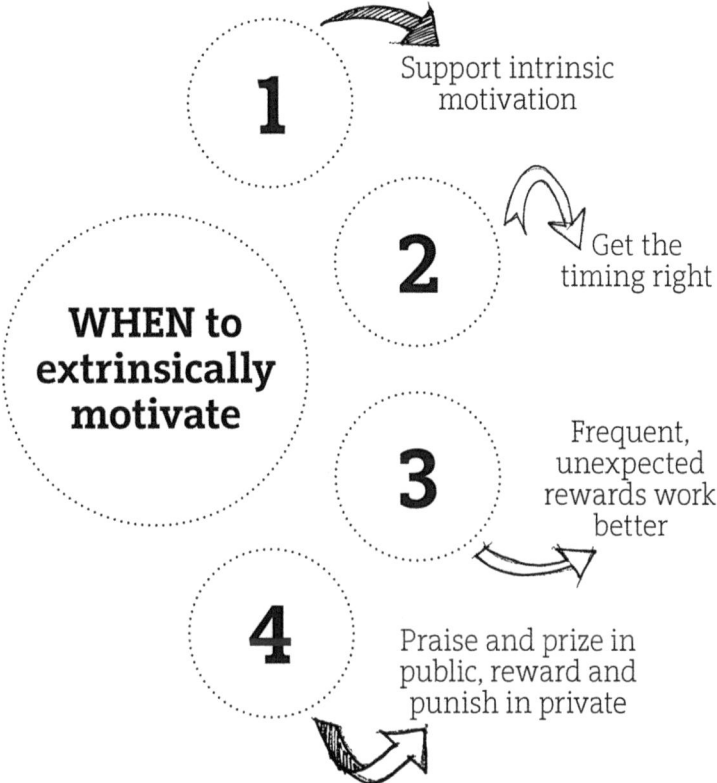

Fig. 4.3 Four rules for when to extrinsically motivate

motivated to improve, so simply pointing out that a change in how they sell would be able to help them achieve greater mastery will be sufficient to motivate them to do it.

Other times, though, people's intrinsic motivation may need a helping hand, and that is when extrinsic factors can be useful. It may be that the required change is simply unpleasant. Perhaps you need people to complete paperwork regularly. In this case, a reward may help. Alternatively, one of your authors' employers encourages people to fill in certain administrative forms by imposing small fines if they are not submitted on time. To make this seem less punitive, however, all money collected from fines goes to charity.

Sometimes, the change needed may be enjoyable, but it may require the boost of an additional motivator. This is when we have to tread carefully. It is vital that any extrinsic motivators we use emphasize the aspect of the change that a person enjoys. An example here would be rewarding someone who enjoys a particular task with extra resources so they can do it even more. Another example would be sometimes delegating making presentations to someone who enjoys doing them. You do not have to offer any kind of reward, but if a lot of work is involved or you want to make sure that they do the presentations as well as possible, then you could suggest that if they do well, you will give them further opportunities to present, and perhaps at more senior-level meetings.

When to Reward Rule #2: Get the Timing Right

Some of the earliest research into rewards over 100 years ago showed that timing is critical. In studies on animals such as rats and dogs, it was found that providing a reward or punishment immediately after a behavior occurs is far more effective than doing so sometime later. And this seems to hold true when humans are trying to change their behavior, too. This is why if you are going to offer bonuses, "spot bonuses," which are given the moment a particular behavior occurs, tend to be more effective than end-of-year awards. Going back to food retailer Prêt à Manger, top executives there are given a set number of "Wow" cards each year, with scratch-off rewards like £10 or an iPod, to hand out to employees who they see acting in a way they want to reward (Clifford 2011b).

Timing is also important for verbal motivators such as praise and criticism. Offering constructive criticism immediately can help fix errors in real time for more efficient learning (Corbett and Anderson 1989). And prompt praise and criticism are particularly important for someone who is new to a task. Praise helps reinforce confidence, while criticism can ensure people do not build up bad habits (Knoblauch and Brannon 1981).

That said, there are exceptions. If someone is extremely busy, stressed, or in a bad mood, it is probably not the best time to offer constructive criticism (Eyal et al. 2009). And there is also evidence that if a task is something that someone believes they are already good at, it may be better to wait until after they have completed it to offer feedback (Clariana 1999; Corno and Snow 1986).

When to Reward Rule #3: Offer Frequent, Unexpected Rewards

In what was at the time the largest study ever conducted on workplace satisfaction, a 1999 Gallup survey showed—unsurprisingly—that frequent praise was associated with higher workplace satisfaction (Robison 2006a). There is also something here for people trying to change behavior. As a rule, frequent praise is more effective at boosting confidence and making people feel rewarded and positive toward a task than less frequent praise (Robison 2006b). However, there is a caveat, because if praise becomes so frequent that it is expected, it loses some of its power. People become immune to it.

The makers of slot machines have known this for a long time. If they program a machine to payout at fixed intervals—say once every ten pulls of the lever—people are less likely to carry on playing than if the machine pays out on a random schedule. And what is really interesting is that this is true even if the random schedule means less frequent payouts (say once every 12 times on average). In the same vein, some research has shown that when we contract with someone to give them a reward when they achieve a certain target, the rewards are less effective than if we give them an unexpected reward (Amabile et al. 1986).

In terms of behavior change, this means that if you have the resources to offer a monetary reward or prize if someone achieves a change, you should do it unexpectedly rather than agreeing beforehand that if they achieve a certain target they will receive it. And go easy with the praise: yes it is important, but if you praise the same person for the same thing every day, then sooner or later, the only thing they will notice is when you stop giving it.

When to Reward Rule #4: Praise and Give Prizes in Public, Reward and Punish in Private

Praise and prizes are strong motivators, and every time you offer them you have the opportunity to double up and offer an additional extrinsic motivator for free: public recognition. So, if you are going to praise someone and other people happen to be in earshot, deliver your praise so the other people can hear. Likewise, if you are going to give out prizes such as an employee of the month award, do it so that everyone knows who won.

Not all rewards are better off given in public, though. Bonuses for achieving targets are better made in private in order to avoid anyone becoming envious. And although it can sometimes be tempting to make a public example of someone when they break a rule, punishments are best delivered in private. The punishment will usually be sufficient on its own, and heaping on public shame tends only to destroy intrinsic motivation. This is particularly so in more collectivist cultures in which personal reputation and "face" are highly valued.

Who to Extrinsically Motivate, and How

Having looked at when to use extrinsic motivators, the second issue we need to consider is the person or people involved. Just as different people are intrinsically motivated by different things, people vary in how they react to rewards and punishments. And in looking at how people differ, research has focused on three key types of differences: cultural, personality, and experience (see Fig. 4.4).

Who to Reward Rule #1: Consider Culture

There has been a lot of research into the effect of culture on the impact of extrinsic motivators, and the findings are clear: culture matters. You need to adapt how you go about providing rewards and punishment according to the culture you are in. If you do not, they could have the opposite effect than the one you intended. Some of the key findings here include:

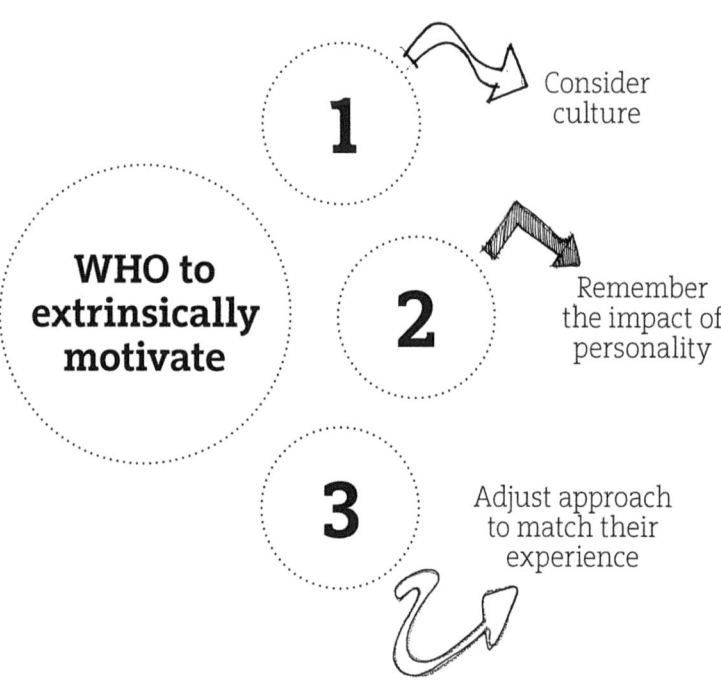

Fig. 4.4 Three rules for who to extrinsically motivate

- **Help people save face in face-saving cultures.** Saving face—making sure people do not feel that their reputation or standing with colleagues has been damaged when you criticize or punish them—can be important in some cultures. Examples include East Asian cultures, such as Japan and Vietnam, and Middle Eastern ones, such as Saudi Arabia. In many Middle Eastern cultures, criticism tends to be made carefully and in private. And in Japan, managers sometimes need to provide implicit nonverbal feedback, rather than explicit comments. In one study, one of the biggest complaints cited by Americans working in Japan under a Japanese manager was the lack of explicit feedback (Masumoto 2004). There is a flipside to this face-saving equation, too. Public praise can be more motivating in these cultures than in countries where saving face is less important, such as the US and parts of Europe.
- **Aim praise and criticism at groups in collectivist cultures.** People in collectivist cultures, such as China, tend to seek individual feedback less than those in individualistic cultures, such as the US (Chen et al. 1998; Morrison et al. 2004). They also tend to prefer it and accept it more when it is depersonalized (Van de Vliert et al. 2004). So, if you are working in a collectivist culture, focus on team behavior wherever possible. And if you need to hone in on individual behavior, try to make it about the issue rather than the individual. You can do this by saying things like, "*We* have an issue here. How can we make *this* work better?" rather than, "You did this wrong—next time do it this way."
- **People in hierarchical cultures respond best to hierarchical feedback.** One other way that cultures can differ is in the degree to which they are hierarchical. And there is evidence to suggest that in strongly hierarchical cultures, such as the Philippines, Malaysia, and Nigeria, people appreciate and listen more to feedback from superiors. In cultures that are less hierarchical, meanwhile, such as Sweden, Finland, and the Netherlands, people seem equally accepting of feedback from both superiors and peers (De Luque and Sommer 2000). This means that in low hierarchy cultures, managers are more able to openly use feedback from individuals' peers to help change their behavior or improve their performance. In more hierarchical cultures, managers can still use such feedback, but they may need to collect it from others and then position it as coming from themselves.

Who to Reward Rule #2: Remember the Impact of Personality

Personality has many different aspects, and most simple rules about "do this with this type of person" are prone to being oversimplifications. However, one such rule that research suggests *is* fairly reliable is linked to the difference between *promotion*-focused and *prevention*-focused people. You may remember we introduced this concept in Chap. 3. Someone who adopts a promotion approach plays to win and is more likely to take risks; whereas someone with a prevention approach plays in order not to lose and to avoid risks. Most people are a mix of the two, yet most also tend more toward one than the other.

One simple rule for applying extrinsic motivators is to align how you apply them to these two basic personality types. With promotion-focused people, emphasizing the benefits and rewards of changing a behavior is likely to be more effective than creating clarity on what will happen should they fail. With prevention-focused people, however, emphasizing the risk associated with not changing behavior is likely to be more effective (Van-Dijk and Kluger 2004; Cadsby et al. 2007).

Who to Reward Rule #3: Adjust Approach to Match People's Level of Experience

The final simple rule is to remember that novices and experts tend to react differently to extrinsic motivators. There are two dimensions to this:

- With people who are beginning to learn or develop at something, concentrate on positive feedback and praise. With more experienced people or those fairly close to particular goals, try to use more constructive criticism, as well as praise.
- Similarly, with people embarking on a change, try to be more directive in your feedback, giving specific advice to them about how they could improve. With those who have already gone some way toward changing a behavior, still give feedback about how their performance could be better, but rather than giving direct advice, ask them what they think they could do about it. Research indicates that while novices can benefit from direct suggestion, experts tend to act on feedback more readily if they feel a sense of ownership over the solutions.

What to Extrinsically Motivate People With

How do you decide which rewards or punishments to use? A critical part of the answer to this question lies in who you are using the motivators with. And general rules are hard to give, since every situation is different. That said, four clear rules do stand out (see Fig. 4.5).

What to Reward Rule #1: Praise First, Money Last

When we think of rewards, we tend to think of tangible things like money and prizes. Yet when thinking about which rewards to give, we are better off starting with the intangibles: praise and recognition. They are free to give and can be just as powerful as financial rewards. Indeed, there is some evidence that they can be more effective than money (Mueller and Dweck 1998). And if you are going to use financial rewards, try using non-cash prizes wherever possible, since they can be more effective than cash in many situations. As a rule, money should be a last resort.

Fig. 4.5 Four rules for what to extrinsically motivate people with

What to Reward Rule #2: Punishments Should Be Rare, Collaborative, and Predictable

Punishments are dangerous motivators to use, because they can have all sorts of negative unintended consequences. Handled poorly, they can impact confidence, trust, and intrinsic motivation. As a rule, you should always try a reward first. Sometimes, though, punishments are necessary. In the example we gave above of administrative paperwork not being completed, the business had tried rewarding those who did it with praise and public recognition. An e-mail was sent out each week naming those who had done it and thanking them. But a large proportion of people still did not complete the forms, so punishment was the last resort.

The first thing the business did was to involve its staff in deciding what the punishment should be. They set it as a problem that needed solving and then asked people for suggestions: "What punishment can we use that will make a difference?" Then, to make sure the chosen punishment of a fine worked, the business ensured that everyone understood:

- When forms needed to be completed. Why the forms were important.
- What the punishment for noncompletion would be, and when it would be applied.
- That people would receive a warning before the punishment was applied.
- That there would be no exceptions and, no matter what the excuse or reason, the punishment would always be applied.

Finally, to ensure the punishment was seen as fair, the business followed through, and always applied the same punishment for everyone, consistently, whenever the rules were broken.

By involving people in selecting the punishment and explaining the reasons for it, the business was effectively trying to improve people's intrinsic motivation for the task. They were appealing to people's sense of autonomy by giving them ownership of the punishment and emphasizing that they had a choice and a chance to avoid it. So in order to use punishments effectively and possibly even to boost intrinsic motivation, think rare, collaborative, and predictable (Arvey and Ivancevich 1980b).

What to Reward Rule #3: Align Solutions to the Situation

This one is less obvious and involves the use of the promotion versus prevention focus we mentioned earlier. Not only can you think of people in terms of whether they are promotion or prevention focused but you can also think about behaviors that way, too. For instance, behaviors such as creativity and sales can be thought of as promotion focused, while behaviors that improve health and safety can be thought of as prevention focused.

To illustrate the importance of this, consider a firm that specializes in the design and manufacture of aircraft. In a continuing effort to improve safety, the management team decided to offer a bonus to everybody if a particular safety target was reached. To their surprise, however, the bonus offer did not seem to make much difference to safety rates. The reason for this, they realized, was that whereas preventing accidents is a prevention-focused task, bonuses are a promotion-based motivator. What they needed instead was a motivator that would put people into a prevention-focused mindset. So they repositioned the bonus as something to be lost if safety standards were not met, rather than as something to be gained if standards were met. And sure enough, safety rates improved.

It is important, then, to consider not only whether the individual trying to change their behavior is promotion or prevention focused, but also the nature of the behavior they are trying to change.

What to Reward Rule #4: Be Fair and Consistent

A number of years ago, one of your authors worked as a psychotherapist in prisons. To his surprise, he discovered that the prison officers who were disliked the most were not the harsh or even brutal ones, but the inconsistent ones—the ones who were not seen as treating people fairly. And in the same vein, no one likes an unfair reward or punishment. So one final basic rule is to make sure that whatever extrinsic reward you offer is fair. Now obviously what people see as fair varies, but we can do a few things to help ensure that what we do is considered as equitable as possible:

- **Give evidence.** Explain what you are doing, showing why a reward or punishment is warranted. Make sure people understand why you are doing it.
- **Be consistent.** Whether it is rewards or punishments, make sure you provide them consistently, treating all people the same.

- **Make sure the behavior is controllable.** If you are going to reward or punish a behavior, ensure that it is something that the individual feels able to control.

Perceived Fairness

A few years ago, a colleague of ours was invited to appear at a conference as a keynote speaker and to chair a panel discussion. He was paid for his appearance, and paid well. However, he noticed that the other members of the panel received gifts from the host, while he did not receive anything. Now he knew, intellectually, that he had been paid, whereas the panel members had not been and the gifts were token thank-yous to them. But emotionally, he felt cheated because he felt as if he was missing out. The moral of the story? When giving gifts do not think about what you think is fair, consider what the receivers and witnesses of the gift will perceive as fair.

Bringing Intrinsic and Extrinsic Together to Change Behavior

We have covered a lot different techniques over the past two chapters—first on how to build intrinsic motivation and now on using extrinsic motivators. Where should you start, though, and how do you bring these two pieces of the motivation puzzle together? The answer is to begin with what people want, because everyone wants something.

> *begin with what people want, because everyone wants something*

Consider Phil. He was an MBA graduate in his late 20 s, hired into a financial analysis role. During the interview he had appeared a little quiet, but the recruiters had put that down to normal candidate nerves and had not thought much more about it. As it happened, that proved to be a mistake.

It took a year for things to come to a head. Phil was not only quiet but also extremely shy. We were told he was fine interacting on a one-to-one basis, but silent to the point of absence in group situations. He was not building close relationships or giving people confidence that he fitted in. For example, he had been repeatedly told that people at the firm did not wear ties, but he still did so. And although his work was of a good quality, he was passive and reactive in how he approached it—doing what was asked of him, but never taking the initiative.

To make matters worse, Phil had been mismanaged. These issues had been recognized for a while, but no one had said anything to him. Now, a senior

VP had heard about Phil and made a decision: Phil was to "shape up, or be shipped out."

When asked for our advice on how to motivate someone who appeared disengaged, we suggested finding out three things: how Phil believed things were going; what he would change about his role or situation if he could; and what he wanted from his work. What we were looking for in his answers was a lever for change—a hook to hang things on, something that Phil cared about to which we could relate the change required. For example, if he was ambitious we could position the change as being about improving his prospects. If he just enjoyed the analysis his job involved, then we could position the change as helping him be a better expert. Whether you plan to work on building intrinsic motivation or to employ extrinsic motivators, the first step is find out what people care about.

In this case, we suggested that Phil's manager use the career concept model outlined in Chap. 3 to better understand Phil's intrinsic motivation.

When the manager first saw the model, his immediate guess was that Phil was most interested in an *expert* career. Yet, on speaking with Phil, the manager discovered that he was deeply ambitious and that he saw his career as progressing in a *linear* way. Using this as an indication that autonomy and mastery would likely be particularly important for Phil, we recommended that the manager:

- Be completely open with him about his situation, involve him in brainstorming solutions, and try to offer him a choice of options.
- Give him feedback about the strengths that he brought to the role and try to position all changes as ways to make him even better at what he did.

We also suggested that the manager think about Phil in terms of the promotion focus and prevention focus model. Realizing that he was predominantly prevention focused, we recommended that the manager position the situation more as being about avoiding being "shipped out" than about any potential benefits of "shaping up." And given that there was an obvious punishment waiting for Phil if things did not improve, we asked the manager to set out clear criteria and timelines so that Phil understood exactly what he had to do and by when. To balance this, we recommended that the manager also think about using a more positive extrinsic motivator. In particular, since many of the behaviors required would be new to Phil, we recommended that he received frequent feedback about his progress, and praise wherever due, especially at the start.

With all of this, we were trying to build a package of motivators that could help support Phil in his development. Ultimately there were other aspects to this package, but ensuring his motivation was a key foundation and it was all built upon the simple question: "What do you want?"

Beyond Motivation

It is true that if we wind the clock back ten years, the focus tended to be predominantly on extrinsic motivators, at the expense of promoting people's intrinsic motivation. So we have much to thank people like Dan Pink and Dan Ariely for, with their passionate support for the power of intrinsic motivators. But we must not let the pendulum swing too far.

> *extrinsic motivators* can *help to motivate people in the short term*

Is intrinsic motivation more powerful than the use of extrinsic factors? Over the long run, yes it probably is, and as a source of motivation it is almost always longer lasting. But extrinsic motivators *can* help to motivate people in the short term—something that is particularly important when people are trying to change behavior. Sometimes they just need help to get started and during the early days of trying out a new behavior, until it becomes a habit or a standard part of their routine. So the longevity of the motivation is not always so important.

Moreover, whatever your thoughts about extrinsic motivators, whether you are a committed skeptic or an ardent fan that uses them wherever possible, the fact is that they are a tool that managers have at their disposal. To ignore them seems unwise. Behavior change is a tough business and frankly we need every tool we can get our hands on.

In the past two chapters, we have tried to provide a comprehensive set of techniques you can use to help motivate people to change. It is a critical part of the context for change, and, if you get it wrong, it can cause any behavior change initiative to fail. The old adage is true: one way or another—through intrinsic interests or extrinsic rewards—people have to want to change.

Yet motivation is only the first piece of the puzzle. No matter how powerful motivators are, they can only help so much, and this is why research shows that they work best as part of a broader package designed to support behavior change (De Silva 1998b). This brings us to the next factor in our MAPS model for change, because wanting to change is one thing, being able to is quite another.

4 Extrinsic Motivation: Using Reward and Punishment

Video Fig. 4.1 Could delayed feedback be best? (▶ https://doi.org/10.1007/000-ak2)

For brief reflections on the content of this chapter, new to the second edition, see Video Fig. 4.1.

Key Questions to Ask Yourself

1. How do the extrinsic motivators you are using support and play to what intrinsically motivates the individual?
2. Might the individual's culture, experience level, and personality impact the effectiveness of the extrinsic motivators you are using? How many different nonmonetary rewards are you using?
3. Are you getting the timing and frequency of rewards and punishments right?
4. Will employees feel that the distribution and handling of rewards and punishments are fair and consistent?

Further Resources

- Adrian Gostick and Chester Elton (2009). *The Carrot Principle: How the Best Managers Use Recognition to Engage their People, Retain Talent, and Accelerate Development.* Cambridge: The Free Press.
- The Freakonomics podcast on praise and criticism: When is a negative a positive? Available as an audio download from http://goo.gl/3jRWr9, or a written transcript from http://goo.gl/ahtEOS.

References

Thorndike, E.L. (1898). Animal intelligence: an experimental study of the associative processes in animals. *Psychological Monographs: General and Applied*, 2(4), i–109.

Bonner, S.E. and Sprinkle, G.B. (2002a). The effects of monetary incentives on effort and task performance: theories, evidence, and a framework for research. *Accounting, Organizations and Society*, 27(4), 303–45.

De Waal, A. (2013). Do bonuses work? *Human Capital Media*. Retrieved 13 August, 2014, from http://humancapitalmedia.com/item/do-bonuses-work.

Kohn, A. (1993). Why incentive plans cannot work. *Harvard Business Review*, 71, 54–63.

Rynes, S.L., Gerhart, B. and Minette, K.A. (2004a). The importance of pay in employee motivation: discrepancies between what people say and what they do. *Human Resource Management*, 43(4), 381–94.

Locke, E.A., Feren, D.B., McCaleb, V.M., Shaw, K.N., and Denny, A.T. (1980). The relative effectiveness of four methods of motivating employee performance. *Changes in Working Life*, 363(1), 388.

Guzzo, R.A., Jette, R.D., and Katzell, R.A. (1985). The effects of psychologically based intervention programs on worker productivity: a meta-analysis. *Personnel Psychology*, 38(2), 275–91.

Stajkovic, A.D. and Luthans, F. (1997). A meta-analysis of the effects of organizational behavior modification on task performance, 1975–95. *Academy of Management Journal*, 40(5), 1122–49.

Currall, S.C., Towler, A.J., Judge, T.A., and Kohn, L. (2005). Pay satisfaction and organizational outcomes. *Personnel Psychology*, 58(3), 613–40.

Schneider, B., Hanges, P.J., Smith, D.B., and Salvaggio, A.N. (2003). Which comes first: employee attitudes or organizational financial and market performance? *Journal of Applied Psychology*, 88, 836–51.

Ariely, D., Gneezy, U., Loewenstein, G., and Mazar, N. (2009a). Large stakes and big mistakes. *The Review of Economic Studies*, 76(2), 451–69.

Jenkins Jr, G.D., Mitra, A., Gupta, N., and Shaw, J.D. (1998). Are financial incentives related to performance? A meta-analytic review of empirical research. *Journal of Applied Psychology*, 83(5), 777.

Bonner, S.E. and Sprinkle, G.B. (2002b). The effects of monetary incentives on effort and task performance: theories, evidence, and a framework for research. *Accounting, Organizations and Society*, 27(4), 303–45.

Rynes, S.L., Gerhart, B., and Minette, K.A. (2004b). The importance of pay in employee motivation: discrepancies between what people say and what they do. *Human Resource Management*, 43(4), 381–94.

Ariely, D., Gneezy, U., Loewenstein, G., and Mazar, N. (2009b). Large stakes and big mistakes. *The Review of Economic Studies*, 76(2), 451–69.

Stewart, G.L. (1996). Reward structure as a moderator of the relationship between extraversion and sales performance. *Journal of Applied Psychology*, 81(6), 619.

Harrison, D.A., Virick, M., and William, S. (1996). Working without a net: time, performance, and turnover under maximally contingent rewards. *Journal of Applied Psychology*, 81(4), 331.

Trank, C.Q., Rynes, S.L., and Bretz Jr, R.D. (2002). Attracting applicants in the war for talent: differences in work preferences among high achievers. *Journal of Business and Psychology*, 16(3), 331–45.

Trevor, C.O., Gerhart, B., and Boudreau, J.W. (1997). Voluntary turnover and job performance: Curvilinearity and the moderating influences of salary growth and promotions. *Journal of Applied Psychology*, 82(1), 44.

Turban, D.B. and Keon, T.L. (1993). Organizational attractiveness: an interactionist perspective. *Journal of Applied Psychology*, 78(2), 184.

Gneezy, U., Meier, S., and Ray-Biel, P. (2011). When and why incentives (don't) work to modify behavior. *Journal of Economic Perspectives*, 25(4), 191–210.

Lynagh, M.C., Sanson-Fisher, R.W., and Bonevski, B. (2013). What's good for the goose is good for the gander. Guiding principles for the use of financial incentives in health behaviour change. *International Journal of Behavioral Medicine*, 20(1), 114–20.

Weibel, A., Rost, K., and Osterloh, M. (2010). Pay for performance in the public sector—benefits and (hidden) costs. *Journal of Public Administration Research and Theory*, 20(2), 387–412.

Deci, E.L. and Ryan, R.M. (2000). The "what" and "why" of goal pursuits: human needs and the self-determination of behavior. *Psychological Inquiry*, 11(4), 227–68.

Frey, B.S. and Jegen, R. (2001a). Motivation crowding theory: a survey of empirical evidence. *Journal of Economic Surveys*, 15(5), 589–611.

Fehr, E. and Falk, A. (2002). Psychological foundations of incentives. *European Economic Review*, 46(4), 687–724.

Irlenbusch, B. and Sliwka, D. (2003). Incentives, decision frames, and motivation crowding out-an experimental investigation. Bonn: Institute for the Study of Labor (IZA).

Falk, A. and Kosfeld, M. (2006). The hidden costs of control. *The American Economic Review*, 96(5), 1611–30. .

Gneezy, U. and Rustichini, A. (2000). A fine is a price. *Journal of Legal Studies*, 29(1), 1–17

Frey, B.S. and Jegen, R. (2001b). Motivation crowding theory: a survey of empirical evidence. *Journal of Economic Surveys*, 15(5), 589–611.

Pink, D.H. (2009). *Drive: The Surprising Truth about What Motivates Us.* New York: Riverhead Books.

Anik, L., Aknin, L.B., Norton, M.I., Dunn, E.W., and Quoidbach, J. (2013). Prosocial bonuses increase employee satisfaction and team performance. *PlOS one*, 8(9), e75509.

Cameron, J. and Pierce, W.D. (1994). Reinforcement, reward, and intrinsic motivation: a meta-analysis. *Review of Educational Research*, 64(3), 363–423.

Deci, E.L. (1971). Effects of externally mediated rewards on intrinsic motivation. *Journal of Personality and Social Psychology*, 18(1), 105

Swann Jr, W.B. and Pittman, T.S. (1977). Initiating play activity of children: the moderating influence of verbal cues on intrinsic motivation. *Child Development* 48, 1128–32.

Grant, A. and Singh, J. (2011). The problem with financial incentives — and what to do about it. Wharton, University of Pennsylvania whitepaper. Retrieved on August 12, 2014, from http://goo.gl/wHC6UB.

Solmon, L.C. and Podgursky, M. (2000). *The Pros and Cons of Performancebased Compensation*. Santa Monica, CA: The Milken Family Foundation.

Bahrick, H.P., Fitts, P.M., and Rankin, R.E. (1952). Effect of incentives upon reactions to peripheral stimuli. *Journal of Experimental Psychology*, 44(6), 400.

Mc Namara, H.J. and Fisch, R.I. (1964). Effect of high and low motivation on two aspects of attention. *Perceptual and Motor Skills*, 19(2), 571–8.

Clifford, S. (2011a, August). Would you like a smile with that? *The New York Times*. Retrieved on August 12, 2014, from http://goo.gl/vLv4Qy.

Arvey, R.D. and Ivancevich, J.M. (1980a). Punishments in organization: a review, propositions, and research suggestions. *The Academy of Management Review*, 5(1), 123–32.

Finkelstein, S.R. and Fishbach, A. (2012). Tell me what i did wrong: experts seek and respond to negative feedback. *Journal of Consumer Research*, June 2012 (published online July 26, 2011).

Paul-Ebhohimhen, V. and Avenell, A. (2008). Systematic review of the use of financial incentives in treatments for obesity and overweight. *Obesity Reviews*, 9(4), 355–67.

Volpp, K.G., Troxel, A.B., Pauly, M.V., Glick, H.A., Puig, A., Asch, D.A., and Audrain-McGovern, J. (2009). A randomized, controlled trial of financial incentives for smoking cessation. *New England Journal of Medicine*, 360(7), 699–709.

Volpp, K.G., John, L.K., Troxel, A.B., Norton, L., Fassbender, J., and Loewenstein, G. (2008). Financial incentive–based approaches for weight loss: a randomized trial. *Jama*, 300(22), 2631–7.

Charness, G. and Gneezy, U. (2009). Incentives to exercise. *Econometrica*, 77(3), 909–31.

De Silva, S. (1998a). *Performance-Related and Skill-Based Pay: An Introduction*. Geneva: International Labour Office.

Babcock, P. and Hartman, J. (2010). Exercising in herds: treatment size and status specific peer effects in a randomized exercise intervention. Unpublished paper.

Clifford, S. (2011b, August). Would You Like a Smile With That? *The New York Times*. Retrieved on August 12, 2014, from http://goo.gl/vLv4Qy.

Corbett, A.T. and Anderson, J.R. (1989). Feedback timing and student control in the LISP intelligent tutoring system. In D. Bierman, J. Brueker, and J. Sandberg (Eds.), *Proceedings of the Fourth International Conference on Artificial Intelligence and Education* (pp. 64–72). Amsterdam: IOS Press. Mason, B.J. and Bruning, R. (2001). *Providing Feedback in Computer-based Instruction: What the Research Tells Us.* Center for Instructional Innovation, University of Nebraska–Lincoln: 14. Retrieved August 12, 2014, from http:// goo.gl/zzkE7Q.

Knoblauch, C.H. and Brannon, L. (1981). Teacher commentary on student writing: the state of the art. *Freshman English News,* 10(2), 1–4.

Eyal, T., Fishbach, A., and Labroo, A. (2009). *Effects of Feedback on Goal Pursuit.* Unpublished Manuscript, University of Chicago.

Clariana, R.B. (1999, February). Differential memory effects for immediate and delayed feedback: A delta rule explanation of feedback timing effects. Paper presented at the Association of Educational Communications and Technology annual convention, Houston, TX.

Corno, L. and Snow, R.E. (1986). Adapting teaching to individual differences among learners. In M.C. Wittrock (Ed.), *Handbook of Research on Teaching* (3rd edn., pp. 605–29). New York: Macmillan.

Robison, J. (2006a). In praise of praising your employees. *GALLUP Business Journal,* November 9.

Robison, J. (2006b). In praise of praising your employees.

Amabile, T.M., Hennessey, B.A., and Grossman, B.S. (1986). Social influences on creativity: the effects of contracted-for reward. *Journal of Personality and Social Psychology,* 50(1), 14.

Masumoto, T. (2004). Learning to "do time" in Japan: a study of US interns in Japanese organizations. *International Journal of Cross Cultural Management,* 4, 19–37.

Chen, Y.R., Brockner, J., and Katz, T. (1998). Toward an explanation of cultural differences in in-group favoritism: the role of individual versus collective primacy. *Journal of Personality and Social Psychology,* 75, 1490–502.

Morrison, E.W., Chen, Y., and Salgado, S.R. (2004). Cultural differences in newcomer feedback seeking: a comparison of the United States and Hong Kong. *Applied Psychology: An International Review,* 53, 1–22.

Van de Vliert, E., Shi, K., Sanders, K., Wang, Y., and Huang, X. (2004). Chinese and Dutch interpretations of supervisory feedback. *Journal of Cross-Cultural Psychology,* 35, 417–35.

De Luque, M.F.S., and Sommer, S.M. (2000). The impact of culture on feed-back-seeking behavior: an integrated model and propositions. *Academy of Management Review,* 25, 829–48.

Van-Dijk, D. and Kluger, A.N. (2004). Feedback sign effect on motivation: is it moderated by regulatory focus? *Applied Psychology,* 53(1), 113–35.

Cadsby, C.B., Song, F., and Tapon, F. (2007). Sorting and incentive effects of pay for performance: an experimental investigation. *Academy of Management Journal*, 50(2), 387–405.

Mueller, C.M. and Dweck, C.S. (1998). Praise for intelligence can undermine children's motivation and performance. *Journal of Personality and Social Psychology*, 75(1), 33–52.

Arvey, R.D. and Ivancevich, J.M. (1980b). Punishment in organizations: a review, propositions, and research suggestions. *Academy of Management Review*, 5(1), 123–32.

De Silva, S. (1998b). *Performance-Related and Skill-Based Pay: An Introduction*. Geneva: International Labour Office.

5

Ability

The second factor in our MAPS model for change is *ability*. Of all the factors in the model it is probably both the most straightforward and the one you are already most familiar with. In fact, it tends to be dealt with as part of the basic two-step method people use. This is therefore going to be a brief chapter, because—to be honest—there is not that much to say. What there is to say, however, *is important*. And along the way, we are going to show you some techniques that may be new to you and cover some research that you may not have heard before.

Typically, when people talk about ability with regard to behavior change, they mean one of two things:

- Whether a person is capable of change of any sort.
- Whether they are capable of performing a specific new behavior that they are trying to adopt.

We are not going to talk here about the first of these—their ability to change and learn in general—because the whole book is about this. We believe that, given the right circumstances, pretty much *everyone* is capable of changing and learning in general, and this book is about how to create the right circumstances. What we are going to consider briefly, though, is whether

---

Supplementary Information The online version contains supplementary material available at https://doi.org/10.1007/978-3-031-29340-5_5. The videos can be accessed individually by clicking the DOI link in the accompanying figure caption or by scanning this link with the SN More Media App.

people are actually capable of performing the specific behavior that they are trying to adopt.

Three Elements of Ability

Usually when managers talk about people's ability to take on a new behavior, they mean one or all of three things:

1. **Opportunity**. Whether someone's role provides the opportunity to perform the new, desired behavior.
2. **Capability**. Whether someone has the necessary skills and knowledge to perform the behavior.
3. **Resources**. Whether someone has the physical resources required to learn and perform the new behavior—any equipment, time, and money they may need.

With each of these three elements of ability, your role as a manager is to perform the standard two-step method. You first have to identify what is required and whether the person has it, and you then need to resolve the issue and bridge any gaps. For example, for someone trying to improve their presentation skills, you should:

1. Check whether they have an opportunity to practice and actually make some presentations and, if not, find them some opportunities.
2. Check what specific aspects of presentations skills they need to improve and how they can achieve this.
3. Check whether they have the time for any training that may be required and secure the necessary budget.

Aspects relating to opportunity and resources can be critical—let's face it, if the necessary time and money are not available, the change is probably not going to happen. But these aspects also tend to be straightforward to resolve. Capability issues, however—the skills and knowledge people need to develop in order to be able to perform a new behavior—can be a little trickier. So in this chapter, we focus on capability issues in particular and look at some techniques that can help you identify and resolve them.

Identifying Capability Issues

It is usually fairly obvious what new skills and knowledge will be required in order for someone to learn and adopt a new behavior. Defining what these new required capabilities are is typically part of the goal-setting and action-planning processes that all behavior change should include.

Your best tool here is simple curiosity

Your best tool here is simple curiosity—the ability to question everything. By asking questions and digging beneath the surface of issues, you can create greater clarity about what—if any—capability shortfalls exist. Taking the presentation skills example, what was it about presentations the person found difficult? What made them think they were not good at presentations and needed to improve? What feedback had they received? What did they see as the key skills required for doing great presentations, which of these did they think they possessed, and which did they need to develop? Had they tried to improve before, and if so, what happened? Alternatively, for a different—perhaps more positive—approach to this same issue, see the "Basing change on ability" box.

Basing Change on Ability

Rather than looking for capability gaps, it can sometimes be helpful to focus on what people *can* do. Take Jia: an HR executive in a large multinational. When we met her, she was desperate for help. For over five years she had been given the feedback that she was very strong and inspirational in one-to-one and small group interactions, but not at all effective in interacting with large audiences. She had been to special training sessions and worked with a coach who specialized in public speaking. However, feeling that none of this support was working and that she was not getting any better, her anxiety had only increased and her self-confidence had fallen even further.

So when we met her, rather than focus on what she found difficult, we asked her about her ability—about what she *could* do well. We focused on the one-to-one and small group settings that she had been told she was good in, and asked what it was that she did that enabled her to be effective in these situations. She became curious about this herself, sought feedback on it from others, and came to the conclusion that it was her ability to "read" the immediate feedback people were giving her in those situations and her capacity to then respond to that. In large audiences, she did not have this feedback and so was robbed of a key skill.

Having established her ability, though, it was then a relatively simple process to help her find ways of maintaining her access to feedback in a large audience. We worked, for example, on techniques for interacting with just a few members of the audience that she could keep eye-contact with and so get feedback from. By refocusing the issue on what she *could* do, it helped reinforce Jia's self-confidence and gave her a way forward that was based on strengths she already had.

Unfortunately, there will be times when it is not obvious what—if any—capability gaps exist. This is often the case when people come to you seeking advice about how to change, and especially when they are not completely clear about which specific behaviors they want to change. When this happens, we have two classic techniques from systemic psychotherapy that can help you create greater clarity about what—if any—capability issues exist. Each technique can help both you and the person trying to change behavior to look at things from a different angle and obtain a new perspective on them.

The objective of using these techniques is to become completely clear about what behavior the person is trying to change and what skills and knowledge they should have in order to succeed. From there a decision about how to proceed and resolve any issues can be made.

Identifying Technique #1: Rating Scale Questions

This is a simple, but powerful technique that we mentioned briefly in Chap. 3. It can be used in a wide variety of situations and is excellent at helping you to break issues down into smaller components and to clarify exactly what needs to happen.

As their name suggests, rating scale questions are all about numbers. They thus often work well with people who are more numerically inclined. They involve a few simple steps. First, you ask someone to create a rating scale on which 1 is the worst the issue could be and 10 is the best it could be. You ask them to describe and define these ends of the scale, often in detail. So, for example:

> "Imagine a rating scale where 1 is the worst anyone could ever be in terms of being a presenter. What would that be like? How would they behave? Now think about what a 10 would be like: what sorts of behavior would that involve?"

Next, you ask the person where they currently are on the scale. Again, you get them to describe their situation in detail. Then, you ask them what one point higher on the scale would look like—what they would have to change, learn, or develop to be rated just a little higher. So, if they had initially rated themselves a 6, you would ask them about what they would have to do to be rated as a 7. A quicker way into the technique is to skip the first step and jump straight into something like:

> "Imagine a rating scale where 1 is the worst anyone could ever be in terms of being a good presenter, and 10 is the best anyone could be. How would you rate yourself today?"

You can then use the same follow-up question:

> "What would you need to do more or differently to be rated just one point—or even just one half-point—higher on the scale?"

And you can follow that up with:

> "And what would you need to learn, change, or develop to be able to do that?"

Rating scale questions provide you with a way to help someone become more specific about what needs to change and how they can change it. After an individual has tried to do something to change their behavior, for example, you can return to the question by asking:

> "Where are you on the scale now?"

Identifying Technique #2: The Miracle Question

Like rating scale questions, the *miracle question* helps people to think about how things could be different. It is usually most effective when there is a general or vague issue and you are finding it difficult to clarify what needs to change. For example, we recently used this technique with an individual who said that she wanted to be better at "influencing people," but was not clear in her own mind about what this meant. In its generic form, the question goes like this:

> "Let me ask you a strange question. Imagine I had a magic wand, or that a miracle happened overnight. Imagine that you woke up tomorrow morning and things were different. The issue was gone and things were better. How would you know? What would be different? What would be the first thing you noticed?"

So, with an individual who wanted to be a better influencer, for example, you could ask:

> "If you woke up tomorrow and a miracle had happened so that, overnight, you became a brilliant influencer, what would be different? What would you be able to achieve? What would you be doing differently?"

Notice how we started the original question with the phrase, "Let me ask you a strange question." This is a simple device that can be used when you are unsure how your query will be received. It sets the question up so that someone is less likely to reject or dismiss it.

People's initial response is often to say that they do not know. Give them time, though, and keep probing and they often develop a quite detailed answer. Through follow-up questions, you can help them to become gradually more specific about what the miracle would look like and thus what needs to change. For example, you could ask:

> "Why do you think you haven't been able to make this change before? What has prevented you?"

And:

> "What would enable you to make this change now?"

Resolving Capability Issues

Almost every behavior change involves the acquisition of a new skill of some sort. If you want to be more concise, that is a skill. If you want to learn to speak up more in meetings, that is a skill. And if you want to be a better networker, that is a skill, too. The solution here is typically straightforward: having identified the skill or knowledge that you need, you learn it, through teaching, training, or practice.

Sometimes, however, it is not so straightforward. There may be a lot to learn, or someone may have difficulty learning what they need to. In rare situations, this may be because they really *are* unable to. They may simply not be bright enough or quick enough to do something. But in most cases, there will be a way around this, and there are two techniques in particular that we find useful. You can make the behavior change easier, so that it does not require new skills or knowledge. Or you can try to remove any blockers that exist to people learning.

Resolving Technique #1: Making Change Easier

divide the behavior change goal into a series of smaller, easier steps

You may have heard this technique referred to as *proximal goals, simple habits,* or *baby steps,* and as a technique it has been gaining in popularity in recent years. The principle is simple. To make change easier, you divide the behavior change goal into a series of smaller, easier steps that do not require big leaps in ability. The idea is to make big changes easier by edging toward them, rather than trying to accomplish them in one giant leap.

For any project managers reading this, it probably sounds like standard practice: you break up complex jobs into smaller and simpler tasks, and then aim for them, one by one. And, indeed, the role of development plans is essentially to do precisely this and map out a way toward an objective. Yet you may be surprised at how often people overlook this step and do not question whether a behavior change goal can be made easier.

For example, getting better at strategic thinking is a common and big objective. One way to make it easier is to split it up into smaller objectives that gradually broaden people's business awareness and develop their ability to apply this knowledge. The first steps could thus look like this:

- Become well read about developments in my industry.
- Produce a monthly e-mail for my team explaining these developments and their relevance to our firm and what it is trying to achieve.
- Become well read about developments in another industry.
- Produce an e-mail for my team explaining these developments, the similarities to our industry, and any lessons to be learned for us.

One thing to be clear about here is that this is *not* the same as setting easy goals. It is about making big goals feel easier by splitting them up into smaller chunks. Yes, it may take longer this way, but it is better to make sure you reach your goals slowly than not at all. It is a simple, but powerful technique. And it underlines a key mantra of this book: you absolutely, positively, completely *need* good goals because, without them, change is not going to happen, no matter how much effort you put into creating a positive context for it.

This, then, is your first option for resolving capability issues: make the goals easier. But what do you do if it does not work? What do you do if someone does not seem able to learn the skills they need to change?

Resolving Technique #2: Uncovering Blockers

We are optimistic people, so we always approach any behavior change attempt from the starting point that the person trying to change is capable of it. But what if they are not? What do we do then?

A number of years back, we worked with Tim, a business leader who time and time again had been given feedback that he was too direct and too quick to challenge others' thinking. In many businesses this would have been seen as a strength, but not in his firm. There, creating consensus and being a team player were seen as critical to success. Tim had climbed the corporate ladder into increasingly large roles because he produced results. But now, near the top of the firm, he had been told that he would not progress any further unless he changed his style.

Tim had been at the company his whole career and, although he was strongly ambitious, he was loyal to the firm and so his first instinct on being told this was not to leave, but to try to change his behavior. And try he did. Again and again. He asked for feedback, he went on courses and he hired a coach. Yet whatever he did, sooner or later he ended up reverting to his old behavior. For two years, he repeatedly tried and failed to change, until eventually he came to us.

What we did was to look at *why* he had been failing. In particular, we looked for blockers, or what some commentators have referred to as *competing commitments* (Kegan and Lahey 2001, 2009). These are conscious or unconscious goals or beliefs that people may have, which can get in the way of their learning a new behavior or changing an existing one. With Tim, one of the questions we asked was *why* he challenged other people's thinking and why he thought it was necessary to do so. And when we did this we uncovered that saying what you believe and being prepared to challenge other people was something that Tim's father had instilled in him as a child almost as a value—as something that he *should* always do. For Tim, not being direct and challenging other people was akin to dishonesty.

This unconscious belief, which he had never really thought about before, was a competing commitment, a deeply held value that stopped him from changing his behavior. We talked with Tim about different ways of looking at it: about how challenging people less overtly could still fit with this fundamental value, that he would still be challenging, just more gently. And for a while he tried this and it seemed to help, to the extent that his boss was commenting on how much he had changed. A year later, though, we received an e-mail out of the blue from Tim saying that, with much regret, he had left the firm. He had succeeded in sustaining his "less challenging" style, but he had never really reconciled himself with it, never felt comfortable with it, and so had eventually decided that he wanted to be somewhere he could behave in a more direct and challenging way.

We realize that this is an example of a failed behavior change. It is also an example of what you have to do when confronted by someone who seems unable to learn the new skills they need in order to change. Dig a little deeper and go looking for competing commitments.

Why Deliberate Practice Is Important

In 2008, the journalist Malcolm Gladwell wrote a book called *Outliers* (Gladwell 2008). Even if you have not read the book, you may have heard of one of the chapter titles and key ideas from it: "The 10,000 hours rule." This is the idea that it takes roughly 10,000 hours of practice to achieve mastery in a field, say to become an expert violinist or a professional golfer. And it is a *lot* of time. Assuming you practice for six hours a day, every single day, without any holidays or time off, it is over four and a half years of your life of solid practice. Every. Single. Day.

The message in this is that if you are willing to put in the time, you can become good at something. If you are only five feet tall, chances are that you will never be a professional basketball player. But you can be good at it—you can learn the skills and master them—even if you will never quite be able to score a slam dunk. And yes, some people may be born with amazing hand–eye coordination and so be capable of achieving levels of ball catching that you and we will never be able to achieve. But, in general, the message in Gladwell's book is that innate talent is overrated and that practice and sheer hard work can get you a long, long way.

Gladwell was right, too, but he missed one important aspect that has subsequently led to a lot of sometimes heated debate. One of Gladwell's inspirations for his book and that specific chapter was a 1993 paper written by Anders Ericsson, a professor at the University of Colorado, called "The Role of Deliberate Practice in the Acquisition of Expert Performance." (Ericsson et al. 1993) However, Ericsson was not pleased by what he read in Gladwell's book and in 2012 he wrote a rebuttal paper called "The Danger of Delegating Education to Journalists." What upset Ericsson was that Gladwell had missed one very significant element of his research: that *how* you practice can be as important as, or even more important than, the amount of practice you have. In other words, some types of practice lead to much better performance than others, and to achieve real mastery, you need to do more than just show up.

The type of practice that Ericsson's research showed is most effective is what he calls *deliberate practice*. This involves:

- Repeatedly practicing a skill.
- Rigorously assessing your performance.
- Receiving specific feedback about how you performed and how you can improve.
- Identifying which aspects of your performance you can improve that will have the biggest impact on your overall performance.
- Acting on the feedback given to you and deliberately working on the weakest elements of your performance.
- Continuing your practice at increasingly challenging levels.

This all points to something that you, as a manager, can do to help someone learn a new skill. You can make sure that when they practice it, what they are doing *will* actually help them improve. You can make sure that their performance is genuinely evaluated and that they receive specific feedback about how they can get better. It is simple stuff, but it is essential.

Moving Beyond Ability

One of your authors once spent a summer cutting down trees, earning a little extra cash to see him through university. After a few days, he felt like he had mastered the technique—essentially three or four simple cuts with a chainsaw. And then he learned a lesson: that cutting down trees is easy and not that difficult to master, right up to the point when things go wrong—when a tree catches on another, or falls slightly the wrong way. And then, all of a sudden, felling trees can become a much more complex job that requires someone with a bit of experience who knows what they are doing.

This sums up how we feel about ability, too. It does not really matter, right up to the moment someone does not have it, at which point it matters more than anything else. It is the easiest part of the MAPS model, and it is also the easiest part to take for granted or to forget. But our biggest learning about ability is *never* to take it for granted and never to forget it.

We said this would be a short chapter, and it has been. By and large, making sure that people are able to change is a straightforward business. But your task, as a manager and as someone creating a context for change, is always to approach it with curiosity, always to question it, and never to be too time-pressured to dig a little deeper.

For brief reflections on the content of this chapter, new to the second edition, see Video Fig. 5.1.

THE IMPORTANCE OF HARD KNOWLEDGE ▶

Video Fig. 5.1 The importance of hard knowledge (▶ https://doi.org/10.1007/000-ak3)

Key Questions to Ask Yourself

1. Does the person have sufficient opportunity to perform and practice the desired behavior?
2. Are there any physical resources lacking that could limit the progress of the behavior change?
3. What skills and knowledge might the individual need to succeed in this behavior change? Do they have these already, or will they need to learn them?
4. Have you agreed on a set of proximal goals that will act as a successful pipeline to the ultimate desired behavior?
5. Are there any competing commitments or psychological blockers that could impede the change process?

Further Resources

- Geoffrey Colvin (2008). *Talent is Overrated*. London: Portfolio. A summary video is also available on YouTube.
- Dan Coyle's TEDx talk on Growing a Talent Hotbed, also available on YouTube.

References

Kegan, R. and Lahey, L.L. (2001). The real reason people won't change. *Harvard Business Review*, November 2001, 85–92.

Kegan, R. and Lahey, L.L. (2009). *Immunity to Change: How to Overcome it and Unlock Potential in Yourself and Your Organization*. Boston: Harvard Business Press.

Gladwell, M. (2008). *Outliers: The Story of Success*. New York: Little, Brown and Co.

Ericsson, K.A., Krampe, R.T., and Tesch-Römer, C. (1993). The role of deliberate practice in the acquisition of expert performance. *Psychological Review*, 100(3), 363.

6

Psychological Capital: Believing You Can Succeed

For the past few decades, psychologists have been studying a cluster of personal qualities and characteristics that have become known as *psychological capital*. They are the inner resources you need to succeed at almost everything, and certainly professionally. They include believing you can succeed (having self-confidence and optimism) and having the inner strength to see things through (having willpower and resilience). Each of these qualities is an important part of a person's inner context for change. And each is capable of significantly affecting how likely someone is to succeed in changing their behavior.

the inner resources you need to succeed at almost everything

For the past few decades, psychologists have been studying a cluster of personal qualities and characteristics that have become known as *psychological capital* (see Fig. 6.1). They are the inner resources you need to succeed at almost everything, and certainly professionally. They include believing you can succeed (having self-confidence and optimism) and having the inner strength to see things through (having willpower and resilience) (Luthans et al. 2007). Each of these qualities is an important part of a person's inner context for change. And each is capable of significantly affecting how likely someone is to succeed in changing their behavior.

Supplementary Information The online version contains supplementary material available at https://doi.org/10.1007/978-3-031-29340-5_6. The videos can be accessed individually by clicking the DOI link in the accompanying figure caption or by scanning this link with the SN More Media App.

Fig. 6.1 Psychological capital

Psychological capital, then, is the third critical factor in our MAPS model for change. Over the next two chapters, we will explore what you as a manager can do to ensure that someone has the self-confidence, optimism, willpower, and resilience that they need to change behavior. Before we do this, however, we first need to pause and answer an important fundamental question that may already have occurred to some readers:

"Isn't this all just positive psychology phooey?"

Why Psychological Capital Is Critical

There is a basic fault here, a deep trench that separates your two authors. One is an optimist, who believes that being positive is good and desirable. The other, well, let's just say he is not like that. And for him, writing a chapter about concepts like self-confidence and hope is an uncomfortable experience. It brings out the cynic in him.

The cause of his cynicism is a movement called *positive psychology* that emerged in the late 1990s. The psychologist most publicly associated with this is Martin Seligman. Believing that psychology had historically been too focused on the more "negative" sides of life, such as mental illness, Seligman campaigned for a more positive approach: the study of how to make people happy and their lives fulfilling. On the back of this work, an avalanche of popular self-help books emerged, all claiming that being positive is a good thing. And while the debate about positivity is not yet over, we do not want to claim that it is not generally a good thing. But the cynical reader might wonder whether this chapter is just another part of this avalanche and only about helping people feel good about themselves.

Although it is possible that by following the advice in this chapter you might inadvertently help someone to feel good about themselves, it is absolutely *not* what it is about. It is about whether people have the self-confidence they need to take on the challenge of changing their behavior. It is about whether they will persevere, put in the necessary effort, and, when necessary, adapt their approach in order to succeed. And it is about whether they have the resilience required to cope with setbacks and challenges.

These things are crucial for two main reasons. First, they have been shown to be connected to a whole host of work-related outcomes, such as job performance, work satisfaction, and organizational citizenship behaviors, as well as lower levels of things like absenteeism and stress (Avey et al. 2010a, 2011; Luthans et al. 2011). More importantly for us here, they have also been shown to be critical foundations for behavior change (Strecher et al. 1986a; Avey et al. 2010b). Those people who are more confident they can change, and are more able to persevere and cope with setbacks, are also more likely to succeed in changing their behavior.

Second, research shows that these elements of psychological capital can be changed and improved (Luthans et al. 2006, 2008; Luthans 2012). Of particular interest for us here are the studies showing what exactly contributes to people's levels of psychological capital. Unsurprisingly, individual factors such as personality and self-esteem have been found to be relevant, the single biggest predictor of how much psychological capital people have is not personal characteristics but their manager's behavior and the type of work environment they create (Luthans et al. 2014).

So not only is psychological capital essential for change, but you—as a manager—are uniquely positioned to increase employees' levels of psychological capital, and thereby improve their chances of being able to change their behavior (see Fig. 6.2). Far from being phooey, psychological capital is important and practical and something that you can affect.

So let's consider in more detail the two sides of psychological capital—believing you can succeed and having the inner strength to see things through. Let's look at how they are relevant and what you, as a manager, can do to build them. We are going to begin in this chapter with self-confidence and optimism, before moving on to the inner strengths of willpower and resilience in Chap. 7.

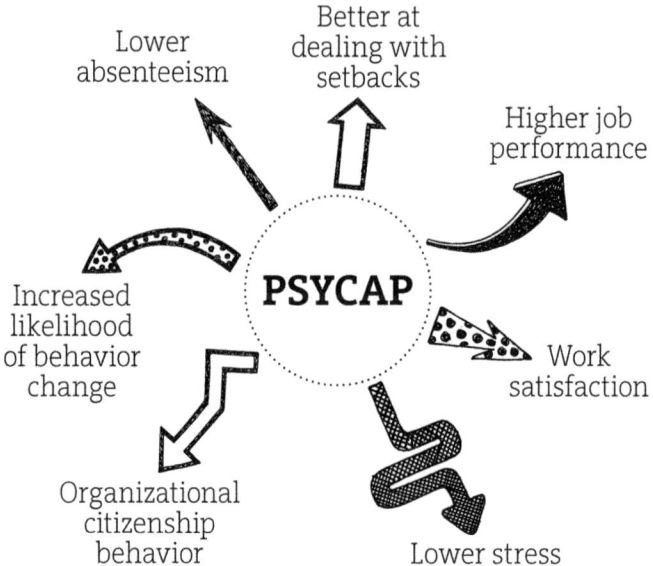

Fig. 6.2 The benefits of psychological capital

Believing You Can Succeed

Henry Ford, the great American industrialist and founder of the Ford Motor Company, once said, "Whether you think you can or think you can't, you are right." He had a point. In fact, Ford was referring to what psychologists sometimes call the *Galatea effect*. It is the idea that if you believe you can do something and have high expectations of yourself, you are more likely to do well.

One of the best known examples of this comes from intelligence tests. Your ability obviously has a pretty large impact on how well you do on these tests, but research shows that how well you *believe* you will do also has an impact. You may be really bright, but if you do not believe you can do well on a test, you probably won't. In other words, believing in yourself is not just a fluffy concept: it genuinely and significantly affects how well you are able to perform tasks and learn new things.

We are now going to look at two overlapping, but slightly different, ways in which people can believe in themselves: self-confidence and optimism. The most researched of these is self-confidence.

Self-Confidence

If you read about self-confidence, you will see it called by different names. Researchers, for example, often use the term *self-efficacy*. This has a very specific and slightly different meaning. While s*elf-confidence* refers to people's level of trust in their abilities, *self-efficacy* is their level of trust in their ability to do a particular thing. It is therefore possible for someone to have low self-confidence in general, but high self-efficacy for a particular task. Yet although the two terms are slightly different, for our purposes they mean basically the same thing.

Moreover, whatever it is called, the good news for you as a manager is that people's confidence in their ability to change behavior can be improved—and when it is, their likelihood of success also improves. People with higher levels of self-confidence have been found to work harder and persist longer when they encounter difficulties (Schunk and Ertmer 2000; Gist et al. 1991). As a result, they are more likely to achieve behavioral changes such as losing weight, stopping smoking, and quitting drugs (Bandura 1982; Strecher et al. 1986b). And in terms of developing themselves at work, people with greater self-confidence have been shown to be more likely to react positively to training, engage with online training, and learn both practical skills and complex interpersonal skills such as negotiation tactics (Salas and Cannon-Bowers 2001).

The even better news for you is that, as we have seen, managers' behavior and the type of work environment they create can significantly affect their direct reports' levels of confidence (Walumbwa et al. 2011). Indeed, a strong line of research dating back nearly 40 years suggests that there are four levers, or techniques, you can use here to support people's self-confidence: mastery, modeling, persuasion, and even people's physiological state (Bandura 1977a).

Self-Confidence Technique #1: Guided Mastery

There is a simple rule: success builds confidence; failure undermines it. Just as a sense of mastery can improve people's intrinsic motivation, it is also essential for self-confidence. Indeed, having some success at a task is the single best way of improving self-confidence about doing it. This is why so many training courses try to incorporate an element of practice: they are trying not only to build people's skill level but also their confidence in doing something. The name of this approach is *guided mastery (*Bandura 1986*)*. First, you make sure someone knows what to do and how to do it. Then you give them opportunities to practice. This means that if you, as a manager, are helping someone adopt a new behavior you should:

- Make sure they understand what they need to do, by giving them instructions, training, or coaching.
- Make sure to start simply and slowly work up to more complex matters when you are explaining things to them.
- Make a plan with them about how and when they will be able to practice the new behavior.
- Ask them about how confident they feel (using a rating scale question as outlined in Chap. 5) and in which situations they would feel most and least confident about the new behavior. Help them think through what they can do to support themselves and the new behavior in situations in which they think they will feel less confident.
- Use the suggestions from Chap. 5 on how to make tasks easier. Ensure that the action plan includes some subgoals—first steps or first attempts that are easier to complete and thus boost confidence.
- Provide feedback about how well they are doing and what they need to do to improve even more. Emphasize that they are making progress and make sure that you attribute this progress to them.

These simple steps do not take much effort—they can be accomplished through a simple and usually brief conversation—but they can be important in helping people change behavior. It does not matter how confident you think someone seems, take the time to ask them how confident they feel and how they intend to practice and master the new behavior.

Locus of Control

A concept closely related to self-confidence is *locus of control* (LOC). It is the degree to which people believe that what happens to them is in their power to control (Rotter 1966). People with an *internal* LOC believe that when things go well it is because they have done something well. People with an *external* LOC, however, believe that when things go well it is because of luck or because of what other people have done for them. The differences between people with an internal and an external LOC have been much researched, with some of the most interesting findings being:

- People with an external LOC respond less well to working with a manager who has a participative leadership style.

- People with an internal LOC are more concerned with information in making decisions than with the social demands of these situations (Phares 1976).
- Behavior change is likely to last longer in individuals with internal LOC (Lambert and Bergin 1994).
- People with external LOC are more likely to respond well to external motivators such as rewards (Baron and Ganz 1972).

Some researchers believe that LOC is basically the same as self-confidence, others think it is different. Either way, when you try to support people's confidence in their ability to do something, you are effectively trying to increase their internal LOC.

Self-Confidence Technique #2: Modeling

In 1967, a study of how to help children of around 10 years old to improve their reading ability made an interesting discovery (Cloward 1967). The study looked at whether these 10-year-olds could learn from older children, aged 15 or 16. They found that the younger children's reading improved most when the older kids they were paired with were of the same gender and ethnicity. In other words, the younger children were more likely to learn something when the older children were physically similar to them. These findings have been replicated many times since. They apply to adults as well as children and to all sorts of different behaviors. Seeing people similar to ourselves succeed through their own sustained effort raises our belief that we, too, have the ability to master the activity (Bandura 1977b, 1997). And this is particularly true for those who are learning or trying to practice a new skill or behavior.

The opportunity here for you when trying to help someone change behavior is to help them identify role models. For instance, if someone wants to improve their influencing skills, help them identify someone they can observe who is great at it. In fact, the other person does not even need to be great at it. They just need to be better and to have improved because the objective is not to showcase perfection but to make progress seem attainable.

Likewise, if you are trying to help a group of people improve how they do something, highlight the progress of one or two key role models in the group. And, importantly, make sure that any role models you use are as similar as possible to the person or people who are aiming to change their behavior. The more similar the model in terms of age, gender, physical characteristics, education, status, and experience, the more effect there will be on developing confidence.

There is also a second type of modeling. The great golfer Jack Nicklaus once said that he never hit a shot, not even in practice, without first having a very clear picture of it in his head. These days, visualizing a task before doing it is a technique taught to many of the world's best sportspeople. For an example, go to YouTube and type in "Cristiano Ronaldo free kick." Ronaldo is one of the best soccer players of his generation and is famous for having improved his ball-kicking technique through visualization. Observe his stance and concentration before he steps up to take a free kick. It is the same every time. One of his trainers has described how he taught Ronaldo to give each corner of the goal a different color. When practicing his kicks, Ronaldo would then call out the color for the part of the goal he was aiming for, and mentally visualize himself kicking the ball there before actually stepping up to take the kick (Winter 2013).

This may sound strange for the workplace, and some people do not feel comfortable with mental visualization—which is fine. But the evidence for its impact on people's confidence in their ability to see through an act or behavior is clear. So, next time you are attempting to help a call-center operator deal with difficult callers more effectively, try asking them to rehearse the conversation in their heads. Or if you are supporting someone to improve their presentation skills, suggest they repeatedly rehearse in their minds how they want it to go. The technique may not suit everyone or every behavior, but it is used by people who are among the best in their field worldwide and it could help someone you manage.

Self-Confidence Technique #3: Persuasion

Telling people they are good at something cannot make them good at it. But reminding them what they are capable of and expressing belief in their ability to master something *can* make them more likely both to put in the effort to do it and then to sustain that effort if problems arise. Indeed, research has shown that regardless of how good people genuinely are at a task, telling them that they are above or below average at it can affect their level of confidence in the task, how they approach it and how well they ultimately perform it (Bouffard-Bouchard 1990).

"You are experts. Behave like it."

Many years ago, when starting in a new role managing a team of learning and development specialists, one of your authors was struck by the team's lack of confidence and became concerned about how this affected the way they engaged with their business customers. His message to them was simple, but proved to have a profound affect: "You are experts. Behave like it." Simply expressing confidence in his people in this way helped them to feel more confident and thereby affected how they approached their stakeholders.

The technical term for this phenomenon is the *Pygmalion effect*. Essentially, the higher the expectations we place on people and the more we tell them we believe in them, the better they tend to do. Perhaps unsurprisingly, the opposite—called the *Golem effect*—is also true: when we tell people that we do not think they are going to do well, they tend not to.

Over the years, many studies have been conducted showing the Pygmalion and Golem effects at play in various settings. One of our favorites dates back to 1995 (Eden and Zuk 1995). A number of naval cadets were split into two random groups. One group was told that, based on test results, it was believed they would be able to overcome seasickness and perform well in rough seas. The other group was not told anything. And at the end of the experiment, those who had been told they would cope better reported less sickness and showed higher performance levels than their comrades who were not told anything. That's how powerful the Pygmalion effect is. It can even help overcome physical, biological reactions.

Part of your role in helping support people's attempts to change their behavior is to make use of the Pygmalion effect and boost their confidence by expressing your confidence in them. In order to be effective in persuading people that they can do something:

- Use phrases such as "I know you can do this" or "You are better at this than you think you are." You do not want to use these phrases all the time, since people may begin to see them as inauthentic, but occasional statements like this can have a big impact.
- Ask people who are new to something or who obviously lack confidence to name what strengths and abilities they are bringing to the task or new behavior. It will help remind them what they are good at. If they are unsure, tell them what strengths you think they are bringing to it. Give positive feedback and praise whenever you see them doing something well.
- Publicize achievements. When someone achieves something notable, announce it to the broader team.

- Ask people about a time in the past when they succeeded in changing their behavior in some small way. Help them remember how they did it and to identify what strengths or qualities enabled them to change.

The Circle Technique

Sometimes, people can find it hard to remember that progress is possible. They can come to see themselves as stuck or incapable of achieving things. In this situation, you can try the *circle technique* (Visser 2013).

Draw two circles on a large piece of paper or whiteboard: an inner circle and an outer circle. Ask the person to write down in the inner circle what they have already achieved, either directly on the paper or whiteboard, or using Post-it Notes. This can be in general—what they have achieved in their career to date—or in terms of how much progress they have made toward a specific goal. Then, ask them to write down what they still need to achieve in the outer circle. This can be done for teams or individuals.

People are often surprised at everything that has already been achieved, which can in turn boost their confidence. And, as a bonus, it can also help people become clearer about what they need to do next.

Self-Confidence Technique #4: Physiological States

Sometimes, the behavior change that people are trying to achieve can evoke anxiety in them. Helping someone improve their public speaking ability or learn to deal with conflict are classic examples of this. A challenge for many people in these cases is coping with what their own body is doing to them. People who experience extremely sweaty palms, a racing heartbeat, or even a change in how their voice sounds prior to giving a talk may begin to worry about their ability to do it well. A little anxiety can help us feel alert—"psyched up"—and as if we are at the top of our game. But if we feel too little or too much tension, it can be difficult to feel confident. And in this vein, tiredness, illness, and stress have all been found to reduce people's self-confidence.

Although using a person's physiological state as a lever for improving their self-confidence is probably the weakest of the four levers and will not be relevant to all behavior changes, it can be effective with some people in some situations. Bearing this in mind, here are some things you can try to help people who may be suffering from anxiety about their ability to do something:

- Always enquire if they feel anxious about something, and if they do, ask them how they physiologically experience that anxiety. Before you can help people, you need to be clear that they have an issue with it.
- Try reassuring them that some anxiety can be a useful performance enhancer, that the symptoms will pass, and remind them that they have the skills they need to achieve what they are trying to do.
- Suggest they practice deep breathing and other techniques for managing the physiological symptoms of anxiety (for example, see the section on *mindfulness* in Chap. 7).
- Help them think about their body language and their stance. For example, putting your hands to your face in some way or hiding your hands in pockets are both what are called "low-power poses" and can make you look and feel less confident. But if you stand and behave as if you are confident, research suggests that this can help you to genuinely feel this way. In fact there is evidence that high-power poses can result in higher levels of testosterone and lower levels of cortisol—a hormone profile that is associated with increased self-confidence (Carney et al. 2010; Sherman et al. 2012; Mehta et al. 2008; Mehta and Josephs 2010).

Anything that can help someone reduce the physical symptoms of anxiety can be useful. But remember that what works for one person may not work for another. Everybody has to find their own way of coping with it.

Improving Self-Confidence: An Example

So far, we have covered four levers, or techniques, that you can use to help someone improve their self-confidence. You do not always have to use all of them, of course, and which will be most relevant will depend on the individual you are working with. Consider the following example. A senior leader in the retail banking sector—let's call him Jim—was trying to help one of his direct reports, a regional manager called Frank, to be more proactive in pushing sales in his area. Jim felt that Frank was fairly reactive to the market, and although he was always conscientious and competent in developing plans, when asked to do so, he did not tend to initiate these plans or come to Jim with ideas. Jim had mentioned this to Frank during his end-of-year appraisal and the local HR representative had helped Frank write a development plan, which specified actions to be taken and timelines.

This may not immediately sound like an issue of self-confidence, but by talking with Frank, Jim had identified that the reason he failed to proactively generate ideas was an anxiety about how they would be received and an underlying lack of confidence. Indeed, when Jim asked him, "On a rating scale of 1 to 10, how confident do you really feel about developing these kinds of strategic initiatives?" Frank had rated his self-confidence as low as 4. Indeed, Jim felt certain that the problem was more due to Frank's lack of confidence than to any lack of capability.

Jim's first move was to check Frank's development plan to make sure there were some quick and easy wins on it—things that Frank would be able do fairly simply and that could be used to help boost his confidence. Next he expressed his confidence in Frank, telling him he thought it was just a confidence issue, not one of ability. He pointed out times when Frank had been creative in solving problems and how he had always been one of the top-performing regional managers. In one of their regular weekly meetings, he took some time to ask Frank about the strengths he brought to the task and could use in developing strategic initiatives. And he set up additional monthly meetings—just 15 minutes each—so the two of them could review Frank's progress against his development plan. He also invited HR to those meetings so that there was a public element to it and successes could be more widely acknowledged when they occurred. These were all simple steps, but they had one clear purpose—to support Frank's self-confidence and thereby his attempts to become more proactive in developing strategic initiatives. They worked, too. When we met Jim six months later, he reported that Frank had responded well and was beginning to show much more proactivity and creativity in his approach to the market.

Improving Self-Confidence Key Facts

- Self-confidence is the most studied and possibly the most powerful way to improve psychological capital.
- Boosting people's self-confidence can also increase their internal locus of control (LOC).
- The four main levers, or techniques, for improving self-confidence are mastery, modeling, persuasion, and managing physiological states.

Optimism

The second element of believing you can succeed is optimism—the degree to which you view and interpret the things that happen in your life in a positive way. It has not been as widely researched as the other elements, nor as widely applied in the workplace, but it is worth paying attention to. The research that does exist shows that in roles as varied as sales agents and factory workers, employees with higher levels of optimism perform better and show high levels of resilience (Seligman 1998).

As mentioned already, the psychologist most associated with optimism is Martin Seligman. For him, being optimistic is important because of the types of conclusions that it leads people to draw. Generally speaking, optimists take credit for good events—drawing strength from them—and distance themselves from bad ones, while pessimists tend to do the opposite (Goldsmith and Matherly 1988; Lyubomirsky et al. 2006). For instance, optimists tend to interpret bad events as being only temporary ("I'm tired"), whereas pessimists are likely to interpret them as being more permanent ("I'm all washed up and finished"). The opposite is true for good events, which optimists see as having more permanent causes and consequences ("I'm talented"), whereas pessimists view them as more temporary ("I worked hard on this one").

There are similar differences in the way that optimists and pessimists generalize events. When things go wrong, optimists often draw specific conclusions ("This part of the project has not gone well"), whereas pessimists make more generalized ones ("The whole project is messed up"). Again, the opposite is true for good events.

The importance of optimism when it comes to behavior change is that people who possess it are more likely to be able to cope with setbacks and sustain change. There are limits, however, since too much optimism can also be a bad thing. People who are overoptimistic often underestimate risks and tend not to prepare sufficiently for setbacks. Fortunately, although optimism has not been studied much, how to improve it has been, and in fact there are just two simple techniques you need to know about.

Optimism Technique #1: Managing Cognitive Distortions

Psychologists use the phrase *cognitive distortions* to describe the thinking tendencies that Seligman described. They are ways of thinking that lead us to interpret what is happening in our lives in unhelpful ways. A large number of different cognitive distortions have been described by psychologists, but some of the most relevant for us here are:

- **Overgeneralization**. This involves coming to a general conclusion based on a single incident or a single piece of evidence. For example, as a result of something bad happening only once, someone might expect it to happen over and over again.

- **Personalization**. This is the tendency to see things in too personal a way. For instance, someone may see other people's reactions to them as being about them, rather than about how the other people are feeling. Or if something goes wrong, their first impulse may be to blame themselves.
- **All-or-nothing thinking**. This involves seeing things in a "black-or-white" way, without any middle ground or shades of gray. For example, some individuals with this cognitive distortion have to be perfect, or else they feel like a failure. Or they may perceive situations in simple "either/or" categories, with no gradations in between.

Your role as a manager trying to help others change their behavior in some way is to help them notice when they are falling foul of these cognitive distortions. It really is as simple as that. Sitting down with someone and saying, "I notice that sometimes you tend to overgeneralize and I worry that when you get a setback it seems to hit you harder. What do you think? Do you notice that in yourself?" Then, if they do recognize it, you can suggest that they try to keep a close eye on how and when they are generalizing and offer to point it out if you see them doing it again.

Managing cognitive distortions like these is not easy. Optimism or pessimism tends to be deeply ingrained in us. But helping someone understand their tendency toward optimism or pessimism less as a permanent personality trait that they cannot change and more as a changeable behavior can be liberating and give them a way of managing it.

Optimism Technique #2: Reinforcing True Self-Concept

In 2013, researchers at the University of Missouri made a really interesting research finding (Vess et al. 2014). They gathered a group of participants and asked half of them to write down five words that described who they really were, their true self-concept. They then induced a feeling of failure in the whole group by giving them a test and telling them afterwards that they had done very poorly in it. They found that the participants who had written down the words describing who they were—who had effectively reminded themselves of their self-concept—were less likely to experience strong negative feelings about the test result than the other group. Moreover—and importantly for our purposes—any negative feelings they had tended to be more specific to the test ("I really messed that up") rather than generalized to themselves more broadly ("I'm useless at these tests").

For us, this means that helping people remember who they really are is a good way of helping them to be more optimistic in interpreting events. An example of how we have used this technique is with a team that was trying, as a group, to become more assertive in their dealings with internal stakeholders and customers. Aware that they were inevitably going to experience both successes and failures as they tried to change their behavior, we asked them to write down words that described who they were and what they were good at. We then had the words typed up and laminated on small cards that they could carry around with them. We reminded them that changing their approach with customers would not always be easy and that it was essential not to give up when setbacks occurred, but to remember what they were trying to achieve and who they really were.

Improving Optimism Key Facts

- Optimism has been less studied than the other elements of psychological capital, but it has been shown to impact both job performance and people's ability to change their behavior.
- Optimism is a way of thinking, and although it tends to be deeply ingrained, it is a behavior that—like any other—can be changed.
- Central to improving someone's ability to think optimistically is to help them identify and understand their cognitive distortions.
- Helping people to remember who they really are and the strengths they bring can help them remain optimistic when things go wrong.

Only Half the Story

Self-confidence and optimism—the two elements of believing in yourself that we have looked at here—are both important for ensuring that people are psychologically well equipped to change their behavior. Some behavior changes may be so small and simple that self-belief may not be that necessary or important. For many behavior changes, though, self-belief can be a hidden but critical foundation. You may not notice its impact when it is there, but if it is absent, it can become a potential blocker of change. The good news for managers is that, as we have seen, self-belief can be boosted and supported. It is, though, just half the story of psychological capital. We will look at the other half—the inner strength to see things through and cope with setbacks—in Chap. 7.

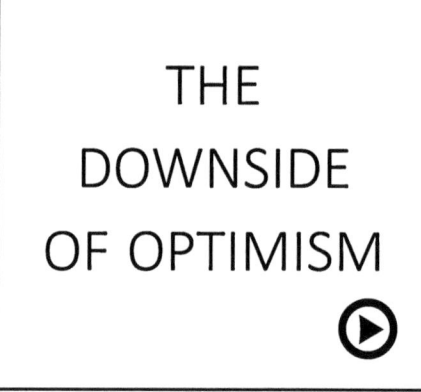

Video Fig. 6.1 The downside of optimism (▶ https://doi.org/10.1007/000-ak4)

For brief reflections on the content of this chapter, new to the second edition, see Video Fig. 6.1.

Key Questions to Ask Yourself

1. On a rating scale of 1 to 10, how self-confident is the individual in general?
2. On the same scale, how confident are they that they will be able to change their behavior?
3. Is there anything concerning the behavior change that they are worried about?
4. Are they usually optimistic, or less so? How could this affect how they feel about the behavior change?

Further Resources

- Teresa Amabile and Steven Kramer (2008). *The Progress Principle.* Boston: Harvard Business Review Press. Alternatively, there is a shorter article called "The Power of Small Wins" that was published in *Harvard Business Review* in 2011. A summary TEDx video is also available on YouTube.
- Fred Luthans, Carolyn Youssef, and Bruce Avolio (2006). *Psychological Capital: Developing the Human Competitive Edge.* New York: Oxford University Press

References

Luthans, F., Youssef, C.M., and Avolio, B.J. (2007). *Psychological Capital*. New York: Oxford University Press.

Avey, J.B., Luthans, F., and Youssef, C.M. (2010a). The additive value of positive psychological capital in predicting work attitudes and behaviors. *Journal of Management*, 36, 430–52.

Avey, J.B., Reichard, R.J., Luthans, F., and Mhatre, K.H. (2011). Meta-analysis of the impact of positive psychological capital on employee attitudes, behaviors and performance. *Human Resource Development Quarterly*, 22, 127–52

Luthans, F., Youssef, C.M., and Rawski, S.L. (2011). A tale of two paradigms: the impact of psychological capital and reinforcing feedback on problem solving and innovation. *Journal of Organizational Behavior Management*, 31(4), 333–50.

Strecher, V.J., DeVellis, B.M., Becker, M.H., and Rosenstock, I.M. (1986a). The role of self-efficacy in achieving health behavior change. *Health Education & Behavior*, 13(1), 73–92.

Avey, J.B., Luthans, F., and Youssef, C.M. (2010b). The additive value of positive psychological capital in predicting work attitudes and behaviors. *Journal of Management*, 36(2), 430–52.

Luthans, F., Avey, J.B., Avolio, B.J., Norman, S.M., and Combs, G.M. (2006). Psychological capital development: toward a micro-intervention. *Journal of Organizational Behavior*, 27(3), 387–93.

Luthans, F., Avey, J.B., and Patera, J.L. (2008). Experimental analysis of a web-based training intervention to develop psychological capital. *Academy of Management Learning and Education*, 7, 208–21.

Luthans, F. (2012). Psychological capital: implications for HRD, retrospective analysis, and future directions. *Human Resource Development Quarterly*, 23(1), 1–8.

Luthans, B.C., Luthans, K.W., and Avey, J.B. (2014). Building the leaders of tomorrow: the development of academic psychological capital. *Journal of Leadership & Organizational Studies*, 21(2), 191–9.

Schunk, D.H. and Ertmer, P.A. (2000). Self-regulation and academic learning: Self-efficacy enhancing interventions. In M. Boekaerts, P.R. Pintrich, and M. Zeidner (Eds.), *Handbook of Self-Regulation* (pp. 631–49). San Diego, CA: Academic Press.

Gist, M.E., Stevens, C.K., and Bavetta, A.G. (1991). Effects of self-efficacy and post-training intervention on the acquisition and maintenance of complex interpersonal skills. *Personnel Psychology*, 44(4), 837–61.

Bandura, A. (1982). Self-efficacy mechanism in human agency. *American Psychologist*, 37(2), 122.

Strecher, V.J., DeVellis, B.M., Becker, M.H., and Rosenstock, I.M. (1986b). The role of self-efficacy in achieving health behavior change. *Health Education & Behavior*, 13(1), 73–92.

Salas, E. and Cannon-Bowers, J.A. (2001). The science of training: a decade of progress. *Annual Review of Psychology*, 52(1), 471–99.

Walumbwa, F.O., Cropanzano, R., and Goldman, B.M. (2011). How leader– member exchange influences effective work behaviors: social exchange and internal– external efficacy perspectives. *Personnel Psychology*, 64(3), 739–70.

Bandura, A. (1977a). Self-efficacy: toward a unifying theory of behavioral change. *Psychological Review*, 84(2), 191–215.

Bandura A. (1986). *Social Foundations of Thought and Action: A Social-Cognitive View*. Englewood Cliffs, NJ: Prentice-Hall.

Rotter, J.B. (1966). Generalized expectancies for internal versus external control of reinforcement. *Psychological Monographs*, 80 (Whole No. 609).

Phares, E.J. (1976). *Locus of Control in Personality.* Morris-town, NJ: General Learning Press.

Lambert, M.J. and Bergin, A.E. (1994). The effectiveness of psychotherapy. In A.E. Bergin and S.L. Garfield (Eds.), *Handbook of Psychotherapy and Behavior Change* (4th edn., pp. 143–89). New York: John Wiley & Sons.

Baron, R.M. and Ganz, R.L. (1972). Effects of locus of control and type of feedback on the task performance of lower-class black children. *Journal of Personality and Social Psychology*, 21(1), 124–30.

Cloward, R.D. (1967). Studies in tutoring. *The Journal of Experimental Education* 36(1), 14–25.

Bandura, A. (1997). *Self-Efficacy: The Exercise of Control*. New York: Freeman.

Bandura, A. (1977b). *Social Learning Theory.* Englewood Cliffs, NJ: Prentice-Hall

Winter, H. (2013, August). The secrets behind the development of Real Madrid's Cristiano Ronaldo, revealed by Rene Meulensteen. Retrieved on August 12, 2014, from http://goo.gl/Rb4esC.

Bouffard-Bouchard, T. (1990). Influence of self-efficacy on performance in a cognitive task. *Journal of Social Psychology,* 130, 353–63.

Eden, D. and Zuk, Y. (1995). Seasickness as a self-fulfilling prophecy: raising self-efficacy to boost performance at sea. *Journal of Applied Psychology*, 80(5), 628.

Visser, C. (2013, November 2). The progress focused circle technique. Video retrieved from http://goo.gl/huUDLk.

Carney, D.R., Cuddy, A.J.C., and Yap, A.J. (2010). Power posing brief nonverbal displays affect neuroendocrine levels and risk tolerance. *Psychological Science*, 21, 1363–8.

Sherman, G.D., Lee, J.J., Cuddy, A.J., Renshon, J., Oveis, C., Gross, J.J., and Lerner, J.S. (2012). Leadership is associated with lower levels of stress. *Proceedings of the National Academy of Sciences*, 109(44), 17903–7.

Mehta, P.H., Jones, A.C., and Josephs, R.A. (2008). The social endocrinology of dominance: Basal testosterone predicts cortisol changes and behavior following victory and defeat. *Journal of Personality and Social Psychology*, 94, 1078–93.

Mehta, P.H. and Josephs, R.A. (2010). Testosterone and cortisol jointly regulate dominance: evidence for a dual-hormone hypothesis. *Hormones and Behavior*, 58, 898–906.

Seligman, M.E.P. (1998). *Learned Optimism*. New York: Pocket Books. Luthans, F., Avolio, B., Walumbwa, F., and Li, W. (2005). The psychological capital of Chinese workers: exploring the relationship with performance. *Management and Organization Review*, 1, 247–69.

Goldsmith, R.E. and Matherly, T.A. (1988). Creativity and self-esteem: a multiple operationalization validity study. *The Journal of Psychology*, 122(1), 47–56.

Lyubomirsky, S., Tkach, C., and DiMatteo, M.R. (2006). What are the differences between happiness and self-esteem? *Social Indicators Research*, 78(3), 363–404.

Vess, M., Schlegel, R.J., Hicks, J.A., and Arndt, J. (2014). Guilty, but not ashamed: "true" self-conceptions influence affective responses to personal shortcomings. *Journal of Personality*, 82(3), 213–24.

7

Psychological Capital: Willpower and Resilience

The world famous Oscar-nominated actor Will Smith once explained his success in this way:

> *The only thing that I see that is distinctly different about me is I'm not afraid to die on a treadmill. I will not be outworked, period. You might have more talent than me, you might be smarter than me, you might be better than me in nine different ways. But if we get on the treadmill together, one of two things is going to happen: You're getting off first, or I'm going to die. It's really that simple.* (Cited in Foster 2013)

True Grit

Whether you call it determination, perseverance, or sheer stubbornness, the inner strength and steel to keep going and not quit is a key component of psychological capital. The psychologist Angela Lee Duckworth calls it something else: grit (Duckworth et al. 2007). Studying what makes the difference between people who achieve their goals and those who do not, Duckworth has discovered that high levels of grit can predict:

- The trainees most likely to graduate from the US Military Academy at West Point.

Supplementary Information The online version contains supplementary material available at https://doi.org/10.1007/978-3-031-29340-5_7. The videos can be accessed individually by clicking the DOI link in the accompanying figure caption or by scanning this link with the SN More Media App.

© The Author(s), under exclusive license to Springer Nature Switzerland AG 2023
N. Kinley, S. Ben-Hur, *Changing Employee Behavior*,
https://doi.org/10.1007/978-3-031-29340-5_7

Fig. 7.1 The inner steel to see things through

- The rookie teachers in tough inner city neighborhoods most likely to still be in their jobs after their first year of teaching.
- The children most likely to win spelling bee competitions.
- The salespeople most likely to keep their jobs and do well.

Whatever we call it, it is clear that the ability to persevere can be essential, both to success in general and when trying to change behavior. In this chapter, we are going to look at two key ingredients that people need to possess in order to have the inner steel to see things through: willpower and resilience (see Fig. 7.1).

Willpower

Essentially, willpower is the capacity to exercise self-control: the ability to start, continue, or stop doing something. When it comes to changing behavior, this usually means the ability to carry on changing it. In many respects, willpower is like self-discipline. And, indeed, most of the research on the topic has focused on how people manage to *not* do things: how they manage to not smoke, gamble, binge on food, use drugs, or express their anger inappropriately.

The bad news about willpower is that we do not have an endless supply of it. To demonstrate this, the psychologist Mark Muraven asked one half of a group of people to relax, and the other half to do something rather strange. He asked them to *not* think of a white bear. That may sound simple enough, but you try it. Whatever you do, do not think of a white bear. For most people, once you've been told *not* to think of something, it is almost impossible not to. It takes a lot of self-control.

After five minutes of this, Muraven told his participants that they would next be having a driving test, but that they could have a glass of beer or two beforehand if they wanted. The results were surprising. The people who had been using their self-control trying not to think of a bear drank more beer than those who had just been relaxing (Muraven et al. 2002). They simply had less self-control left. Other studies that have asked people to wait before eating some cake have found similar results. Individuals asked to expend some self-control by waiting five minutes before eating some cake, subsequently ate more than people told they could eat the cake immediately (Baumeister et al. 1998). So using self-control on one task reduces the amount we are able to use on a subsequent task. It seems we only have so much self-control to go around.

That's the bad news. The good news, though, is that people can improve and strengthen their willpower and, as a manager, you are ideally placed to help them. We have already seen that improving intrinsic motivation will increase the length of time that people will persist with a behavior change. But there are five other techniques you can use, too.

Willpower Technique #1: Care About People

Not only do people have a limited supply of willpower, but it is also rather like a delicate crop: It needs the right conditions to flourish. Tiredness, hunger, or stress can all reduce levels of willpower (Muraven and Baumeister 2000). So one easy thing you can do when trying to help someone change behavior is to encourage them to look after themselves. If they look tired, tactfully mention it and point out how it can affect their willpower and perseverance. This is why managers who care about their people and take the time to notice how they are tend to be able to encourage higher levels of performance from them in the long run. Care feeds willpower.

Tiredness, hunger, or stress can all reduce levels of willpower

Caring does not always merely mean expressing concern, either. It can be more pragmatic. One of your authors once worked with a manager, Alicia, who was trying to develop her ability to say no to new work that was not a core part of her objectives. Alicia did not like to say no to anyone, and the busier and more stressed she became, the less able she was to exercise some control and turn down additional requests. Noticing that there was one weekly meeting in particular that seemed to result in these extra requests, your author worked with Alicia to have the meeting moved from its slot late on Friday afternoon to a morning time at the beginning of the week. It was when Alicia was least stressed and tired each week and so more able to enter the meeting with a clear head and focus on saying no to requests that were not priorities.

Willpower Technique #2: Practice

Care stops willpower from waning, but the best way to increase someone's overall level of willpower is practice (Oaten and Cheng 2006a, b, 2007; Gailliot et al. 2007). They need to practice exercising their will, showing self-control and being self-disciplined. The trick is to choose something small and simple. For example, daily willpower exercises such as keeping a daily diary of food intake, maintaining good posture for an hour a day, or using your non-dominant hand (e.g., deliberately using your left hand if you are normally right-handed) have all been found to help people stop smoking (Muraven 2010a, b; Muraven et al. 1998). So, if someone is having trouble seeing through a behavior change, get them to practice their willpower. One of your authors had success with this technique with someone who was trying to stop putting off certain tasks, simply by asking him to send your author a text message once every hour. The discipline of doing this helped him to become firmer in making sure he did not keep procrastinating.

Willpower Technique #3: Stop Renegade Attention

In order to achieve a goal, focus is necessary (Kirschenbaum 1987). When someone fails to stay focused on a behavior change they are trying to achieve, the result is that they usually forget to do the new behavior. It becomes lost in the busy-ness of the day. This is also an increasing problem at work, since people across functions, industries, and continents are all reporting that they feel as if their jobs are becoming busier every year. Some researchers have referred to the tendency to become distracted as *renegade attention* (Baumeister et al. 1994). And when it comes to stopping renegade attention, three things in particular seem to work.

First, adding structure to the behavior change can help—always doing it in a particular place or at a particular time. The often quoted example here is the manager who wants to become better at walking the floor and getting out from behind the desk and speaking with people. The best way to ensure this happens is to set a specific time every day to do it. That way, the chances of becoming distracted and forgetting to do it are far less. It is a powerful technique, and we will return to it when we look at how to build habits in Chap. 8.

The second and third things people can do to stop renegade attention are to learn techniques called *self-talk* and *mindfulness*. Although each of them is a fairly simple approach, they have both generated a massive amount of research and have whole books dedicated entirely to them. So to do them justice here, we have separated them into separate sections and included them as the last two of our five techniques. It is worth remembering, however, that although each has a variety of uses, our main interest in them here is as powerful tools to stop renegade attention and thereby boost willpower.

Willpower Technique #4: Self-Talk

What you say to yourself is important. To many readers, that may sound like an odd statement. After all, in many cultures, talking to yourself is associated with madness. (There is an old joke that says, the first sign of madness is talking to yourself, the second is answering back.) Yet there is an amazing amount of research to show that most people talk to themselves quite frequently, either out loud or quietly in their heads. For example, before starting a big challenge, they might take a deep breath, exhale, and then quietly say to themselves, "OK. You can do this."

Interest in this kind of activity and its impact upon us has only really taken off in the last 20 years or so. It has probably become most associated with the "positive thinking" or positive psychology movement, mentioned briefly in Chap. 6. Walk down the self-improvement aisle of any bookshop and you will find book upon book all proclaiming the importance of thinking positive thoughts and saying positive things to yourself. The titles urge you to "self-talk your way to success" or promise to show how to "kiss negative thinking goodbye." So, should you urge the same for the people whose behavior you are trying to change?

There is no doubt that many of these books have genuinely helped people and that the origins of this movement lie in good and solid experimental research. But the problem with them is that they tend to oversimplify the subject and too often the advice boils down to "Say nice things to yourself." And this *is* a problem because, as it turns out, saying nice things to yourself is not always what you need.

Much of the research in this area has been conducted with sportspeople. And time and again, these studies have shown that self-talk can enhance both the self-confidence and performance of many athletes (Hatzigeorgiadis et al. 2004; Miles and Neil 2013; Hamilton et al. 2007; Landin and Hebert 1999). Although interesting, these findings raise three questions:

1. What types of self-talk are effective?
2. How does it help?
3. How exactly can we use this to help people change behavior?

The first important finding is that one basic way of thinking about self-talk is to distinguish between positive self-talk (which includes positive statements about yourself) and negative self-talk (which involves negative or critical statements). And, broadly speaking, the finding here is that—unsurprisingly—positive statements help you feel better about yourself and negative ones, well, they don't. As we have already mentioned in Chap. 6, boosting confidence can be important, so getting people to think about whether their self-talk is positive or negative, and then encouraging them to make more positive statements, is a worthwhile activity that can support behavior change.

There is another way to think about self-talk, though, which is perhaps of more interest to us. Researchers have also distinguished between *instructional* self-talk, which involves reminding yourself of information or talking yourself through choices, and *motivational* self-talk. Someone preparing for an important presentation, for example, might say to themselves, "OK. Step 1, make introductions. Step 2, etc.," which is instructional self-talk. Or they could say to themselves, "You've done this before, you can do it today," which is motivational self-talk. Studies have shown that instructional statements are more able to boost performance on tasks involving skill or technical expertise, whereas motivational self-talk is more effective for tasks that are about strength or endurance (Theodorakis et al. 2000; Hatzigeorgiadis et al. 2004). So for most work-related activities, instructional self-talk may well be more helpful.

Things become really interesting when we consider how instructional self-talk helps, because research shows that it boosts performance by increasing focus and attention (Landin 1994). In other words, it stops renegade attention. And as techniques go, instructional self-talk is not only one of the most powerful but also one of the quickest and easiest. No wonder it is so popular. So next time you are helping someone think about how to change their behavior and it involves a task that can be broken down into steps, help them think about what those steps are and then suggest that they say these steps to themselves—either out loud or in their heads—before starting the activity.

Consider Max, a leader we were helping who felt he did not make a good impact in team meetings. After talking to Max, we suggested he identify a small routine of mini-actions to help make speaking up in a firm manner easier for him: things like sit up straight, take a deep breath, speak slowly, and begin with a standard opening line, such as "What I think is important here…" Although this was useful, what really helped Max was suggesting that he repeat these steps to himself in his mind at the beginning of each meeting and just before speaking. It focused him, stopped him from thinking negative thoughts at those times, and reminded him what he needed to do.

Willpower Technique #5: Mindfulness

The final way to stop renegade attention and boost willpower is to develop the ability to notice when your attention is wandering. The problem for many people is that they can become so immersed in events or tasks that they forget to do something that they wanted to. The solution here—the ability they need to develop—is something called *mindfulness*, an attention-training technique that in the past five years has increasingly grabbed the headlines and been the subject of considerable research.

Many of these headlines stem from the fact that mindfulness has been associated with an amazing array of benefits (up to and including improved immune system functioning) (Pace et al. 2009; Davidson et al. 2003). If you believed them all, you could be forgiven for thinking that it was a cure for almost everything. Amidst all the hype, however, mindfulness *has* been consistently shown to produce two benefits in particular: an increased capacity to focus and maintain attention, and an improved ability to manage stress and pressure (Chiesa et al. 2011; Irving et al. 2009; Roeser et al. 2013; Jha et al. 2007; Sedlmeier et al. 2012). And this has been shown for groups of people as diverse as doctors, teachers, and US Marines.

You will find almost as many definitions of mindfulness as there are books on the subject, but most people agree that it consists of two key skills:

- **Attention control**. The ability to focus and sustain your attention on a particular object or task and to ignore distractions.
- **Self-reflexivity**. The ability to stand back and be aware of what and how you are thinking and feeling as you are actually doing it, in the moment. It is being able to reflect on how you act, but doing so *while* you are acting rather than afterwards. For example, instead of feeling anxious and reacting unconsciously to that anxiety, you would be aware that you are anxious and so more able to control your reaction to it.

Self-Reflexivity

A core skill that all trainee psychotherapists are taught is self-reflexivity. When a client is speaking to them, therapists need to do more than merely listen. They also need to be able to constantly reflect on both how the conversation is going ("Why are they saying that? And why are they saying it now?") *and* how they are reacting to what the client is saying ("How do I feel about that? And how is that changing how I react to them?").

It is not a skill reserved for therapists, however. It can be a handy technique for anyone, especially as a way of managing difficult conversations. Next time you are involved in a conversation and feel that it is becoming stuck, or that it is steadily spiraling out of control and toward an argument, try this simple piece of self-reflexivity. Pause. And then ask yourself—and then the other person—"Is this conversation going the way I/we wanted it to? Assuming we both did not start out wanting an argument, why is it happening this way?" By pausing and asking yourselves this, you can then discuss how you would like the conversation to go and what you can do to stop it escalating into an argument.

Both attention control and self-reflexivity can be vitally important for behavior change, since they can help people stay focused on what they are trying to do, and help them become aware of when they are losing sight of this before it is too late. So what can you do as a manager to help someone develop these skills?

Controlling attention is arguably the easier skill to learn and there is only one basic technique you need to know about. It is simply practicing focusing your attention on specific things, such as your breathing, particular objects, or certain sounds. Try it: It is surprisingly hard to block out all thoughts other than the one thing you are focusing on. Instead, your mind tends to wander. Put a pencil on a desk and stare at it and, sooner or later, you will probably start focusing on the desk instead. Or try concentrating on the sound and physical motion of your own breathing without hearing and pay attention to the sounds of the people, cars, or even weather around you.

So the key technique here essentially involves practicing and thereby strengthening your attention muscles. Studies show that in order to get better at it, you should do it every day and in increasing amounts. Start with a minute a day and work your way up to 15 minutes. It does not take long, and you can even do it sitting at your desk, but it can have a surprisingly big impact on your ability to control your attention.

Self-reflexivity, by contrast, is typically taught through two techniques. The first involves helping people to practice reflecting on things. For example, after a meeting, ask someone how it went, why they think it went that way, and how they feel about that. Or our favorite question, "What thoughts or ideas were going through your head then?" The idea behind this is that by getting better at reflecting on things after they have happened, people will also increase their ability to reflect on things *as* they are happening.

The second main technique for improving self-reflexivity is self-check-in. This means getting people to "check-in" with themselves to see how they are feeling at particular moments. For example, suggest to someone that before a meeting they reflect on, "How am I feeling about this meeting and what do I want to happen in it?" Or that every time they open an e-mail they pause for a second and ask themselves how they feel in general, how they feel about the e-mail, and what they want or expect from it. All it takes is a second or two, but it is excellent practice.

These, then, are simple and quick techniques for improving mindfulness. Although the techniques are simple, doing them is not always easy, so you need to emphasize to people that it takes practice. Indeed it takes months and years, rather than days and weeks, to develop mindfulness. But it is undoubtedly worth it and is possibly the single best technique for developing all aspects of psychological capital.

Improving Willpower Key Facts

- People have only limited amounts of willpower. When they use it, it takes time to replenish it.
- Willpower is like a muscle and, like any other muscle, it becomes weaker when people are tired, hungry, or stressed. But it can also be strengthened through practice.
- A significant part of willpower is staying focused, and two of the main techniques for helping do this are self-talk and mindfulness.

Resilience

The second key ingredient people need to possess in order to have the inner steel to see things through is resilience. Consider this example.

We must confess, we can't remember his name. But then his name was not what was memorable about him. He was 16 years old and on the verge of being sent to prison for a petty theft crime. Like many persistent young offenders, the boy had himself been a victim, and in his case his background was particularly dark. His early years were a long list of truly horrid experiences: He was a victim of physical, sexual, and emotional abuse. Yet there he sat, intelligent, articulate, and cheerful. Defensive, hurt, and angry, without a doubt. But also with an amazing ability to bounce back from setbacks. What really stuck in your authors' minds was not his name, but his resilience—the fact that, despite all life had thrown at him, he kept on coming back for more.

Resilience is the ability to cope with adversity and sometimes even grow stronger from it (Luthans 2002). Since changing behavior almost always involves setbacks of some sort, being able to move on from them is critical. Most of the research in this area has been drawn from work with adolescent children who have succeeded despite great personal difficulties (Masten 2001). However, there is an increasing body of work that demonstrates that resilience is just as important in the workplace (Luthans et al. 2005; Luthans and Youssef

2007). This research shows that resilient people are more likely to succeed in their goals and that what really characterizes them is their ability to develop new or alternative ways of doing things when they face difficulties and failures (Youssef and Luthans 2007). They find a way around the inevitable challenges their work involves.

As you might expect, there is considerable evidence showing that resilience is largely created and determined by people's early childhood experiences. Yet there is also clear evidence that people can improve and grow it, and three techniques in particular stand out: promoting a growth mindset, self-compassion, and planning for problems (Werner 1993).

Resilience Technique #1: Promote a Growth Mindset

There is compelling research coming from work with academic students that shows that the way they think about learning—their beliefs and assumptions about it—can have a big impact on how they cope with the challenges inherent in it. Professor Carol Dweck of Stanford University has led the research in this area (Morehead 2012; Dweck 2006). She has found that children who are told, "You are smart" or "You are great at that" tend to develop the belief that their intelligence and talents are set, like fixed traits. However, children who are told things like, "You are really improving at that" tend to develop the understanding that their abilities and competence grow through their hardwork—what Dweck calls a *growth mindset*. Looking at the ability of these two types of children to deal with setbacks, it is those who have a growth mindset who seem the most capable of dealing with setbacks. They see failures as an opportunity to grow, as much as anything else.

For managers, there is the same opportunity here as for parents. To help your people develop greater resilience, try promoting a growth mindset in them. If you see them working hard and improving as a result, make sure you comment on it and praise them for it. And when they make a mistake, notice how they work to put it right and ask them afterward what they learned from it. It may sound simple—and it is—but it emphasizes to people that they are continually learning and developing.

There is a more advanced way of helping people develop a growth mindset, too. Next time you see someone respond to a setback with a *fixed mindset*—a response that includes the idea that they failed or made a mistake because they simply are not good at something—try the following:

- Set up a meeting with them—15–20 minutes when you will not be disturbed.
- Ask them about the event and tell them you noticed them respond in this fixed way.
- Ask them to reflect on exactly what happened in that and similar events, focusing in particular on what they *say* to themselves. Most people have a kind of inner conversation with themselves. For example, they may say something like, "I knew that was going to go wrong. I'm just not good at it. I should have off-loaded it for someone else to do." Now it may be that they do indeed have limited skills in the area concerned and it may be that they really should have off-loaded the task that went wrong to someone else. But what is important here, and what you are trying to uncover, is the unhelpful self-talk and beliefs. Following this process and questioning people's self-talk may feel a bit unusual if you have not done it before, but it can be a powerful way to help people reflect on how they react and help them to understand how they can react differently in future.
- Help them to grasp the idea that although they may not be good at something, they *can* improve. Once you have asked what they say to themselves when things go wrong, you can then ask how they could and should respond to themselves. You may need to suggest responses here to help them, such as "Look, this is not easy. It takes time to learn. Yes, next time look for more support, but every time you do this, you get better."
- Finally, help them to reflect on the fact that they have a choice about how they respond: They can do so negatively or constructively.

Resilience Technique #2: Cultivate Self-Compassion

Perfectionism, which includes some degree of self-criticalness, has been shown to be a strong driver of achievement (Witcher et al. 2007; Baker and McNulty 2011). But there are limits. Too much self-criticism is not healthy for either the soul or performance levels. And in recent years, researchers have begun to explore this in their studies and to identify one of the core components of resilience as self-compassion: the ability to forgive yourself when things go wrong. This is emphatically *not* the same as letting yourself off the hook or lowering your standards. It is the ability to move on and stop berating yourself when things go bad. This is particularly important when trying to achieve specific goals, such as a behavior change, with studies showing that people who have higher levels of self-compassion are more likely to achieve these goals (Breines and Chen 2012a). In fact, studies have found that, far from lowering their standards, self-compassionate people are more likely to see their weaknesses and mistakes as changeable and are thus more likely to work to improve them and avoid making similar mistakes in the future (Breines and Chen 2012b).

So, when you see people being too hard on themselves, try helping them to become more self-compassionate. The two key ways of doing this are by comforting them or by assisting them to become more objective about themselves. The first of these is simply a matter of saying, "Don't be so hard on yourself" or "Don't worry about it so much. Setbacks happen to everyone, no matter how successful they seem to be from the outside." The second option involves asking them to reflect on whether they would be as hard in their criticism if it were someone else and—if not—what they would say to another person who experienced the same setback.

Resilience Technique #3: Plan for Problems

Whether or not someone has a naturally strong ability to cope with setbacks, there is something you can do to help prepare them for when things go wrong: Make a plan. Psychologists call these plans *implementation intention*, although you may know them as *if–then* plans (Gollwitzer and Sheeran 2006). These plans help make responses to setbacks automatic—things people just do rather than having to think about them first.

This is a popular technique among managers, since it is simple, practical, and effective. It involves only a few steps. First, ask the individual to think about what setbacks or problems they may encounter with the change in behavior they are seeking to achieve. Make a few suggestions of your own if they struggle to come up with a good list. Then, for each issue, ask them how they should respond, how they think about what the options and alternatives might be, and how effective each response would be. Again, feel free to make suggestions to help them. And that is it. It is that easy. Identify potential problems and then plan for them. It both reinforces people's self-confidence and helps them to cope with almost inevitable setbacks.

A good example of this was a senior engineer we worked with who had a tendency to talk over others in meetings and inadvertently close down debate by seeming too black-and-white and strong in voicing his views. The problem was that it was annoying his colleagues, preventing a good discussion of issues that needed discussing, and, as a result, it was irritating his manager. We worked with him to look at his underlying beliefs about wanting to make himself heard and we helped him identify ways of voicing his opinion in a less certain and aggressive manner. Yet although he was a willing individual, who wanted to stop annoying others, deep down he was not sure he could change.

Knowing that sometimes his old, historical behaviors would inevitably show through, we helped him prepare for this. We talked through what might happen and helped him develop a plan for how he should respond in each scenario—for example, apologizing to people after a meeting or approaching them and asking their opinion on the subject he had inadvertently closed down. Inevitably, he did sometimes fail in the behavior change and continued to talk over people and dominate meetings. But because he had a Plan B, he also had a constructive way to deal with these occasions. His setbacks became expected challenges with pre-prepared solutions, rather than confirmation that change was not possible.

Improving Resilience Key Facts

- Resilience is the ability to cope with setbacks.
- People's inner levels of resilience can be improved by promoting both a growth mindset (the idea that setbacks can stimulate growth) and self-compassion.
- Resilience can be "artificially" strengthened by helping people expect and plan for problems and setbacks.

From Inner Context to External Environment

Over the course of Chaps. 5 and 6, we have explored the third factor in our MAPS model for change—psychological capital. We have described how it is comprised of two key elements: self-belief and the inner strength to see things through. We have shown how they are vitally important parts of the context for change, capable of either significantly supporting or undermining people's attempts to change their behavior. And we have presented techniques for what you as a manager can do to improve or boost these aspects of their psychology.

The common element in the techniques we have presented so far in the M, A, and P of our model is that most of them involve you working fairly directly with people's psychology or capability, often through some form of conversation. Yet beyond the workplace, in fields as far apart as social policy, computer gaming, and education, professionals working to change people's behavior often work more indirectly. They make changes to the environment that

Video Fig. 7.1 Is willpower really limited? (▶ https://doi.org/10.1007/000-ak5)

people are working in, as a way to encourage or support certain behaviors and discourage others.

The idea is to provide some outside support for people's motivation, ability, and psychological capital in order to provide the "S" in our MAPS model for change: a supportive environment.

For brief reflections on the content of this chapter, new to the second edition, see Video Fig. 7.1.

Key Questions to Ask Yourself

1. How strongly would the individual rate their willpower? How strongly would you rate it?
2. In what situations might their willpower be reduced? What can be done to protect against this?
3. If their willpower is not as strong as it could be, which techniques could you use to boost it?
4. Is the individual capable of mindfulness? Can they remain focused on what they need to achieve and will they notice if they do not?
5. How would you and the individual rate their level of resilience? What types of situations do they most struggle to remain resilient with?
6. Does the individual anticipate potential obstacles and problems and plan for them? Are they adaptable in responding to problems?

Further Resources

- Angela Lee Duckworth's TED talk, *The key to success? Grit*, available on YouTube.
- Andy Puddicombe's TED talk, *All it takes is 10 mindful minutes*, available on YouTube.

References

Foster J. (2013) Will Smith isn't afraid to die…why should you be? *Wall Street Insanity*, February 18, 2013. From http://goo.gl/MYS0uc.

Duckworth, A.L., Peterson, C., Matthews, M.D., and Kelly, D.R. (2007). Grit: perseverance and passion for long-term goals. *Journal of Personality and Social Psychology*, 92(6), 1087.

Muraven, M., Collins, R.L., and Neinhaus, K. (2002). Self-control and alcohol restraint: an initial application of the self-control strength model. *Psychology of Addictive Behaviors*, 16(2), 113.

Baumeister, R.F., Bratslavsky, E., Muraven, M., and Tice, D.M. (1998). Ego depletion: is the active self a limited resource? *Journal of Personality and Social Psychology*, 74(5), 1252.

Muraven, M. and Baumeister, R.F. (2000). Self-regulation and depletion of limited resources: does self-control resemble a muscle? *Psychological Bulletin*, 126(2), 247.

Oaten, M. and Cheng, K. (2006a). Improved self-control: the benefits of a regular program of academic study. *Basic and Applied Social Psychology*, 28, 1–16.

Oaten, M., and Cheng, K. (2006b). Longitudinal gains in self-regulation from regular physical exercise. *British Journal of Health Psychology*, 11, 717–33.

Oaten, M. and Cheng, K. (2007). Improvements in self-control from financial monitoring. *Journal of Economic Psychology*, 28, 487–501.

Gailliot, M.T., Plant, E.A., Butz, D.A., and Baumeister, R.F. (2007). Increasing self-regulatory strength can reduce the depleting effect of suppressing stereotypes. *Personality and Social Psychology Bulletin*, 33, 281–94.

Muraven, M. (2010a). Building self-control strength: practicing self-control leads to improved self-control performance. *Journal of Experimental Social Psychology*, 46, 465–8.

Muraven, M. (2010b). Practicing self-control lowers the risk of smoking lapse. *Psychology of Addictive Behaviors*, 24, 446–52.

Muraven, M., Tice, D.M., and Baumeister, R.F. (1998). Self-control as a limited resource: Regulatory depletion patterns. *Journal of Personality and Social Psychology*, 74, 774–89.

Kirschenbaum, D.S. (1987). Self-regulatory failure: A review with clinical implications. *Clinical Psychology Review*, 7(1), 77–104.

Baumeister, R.F., Heatherton, T.F., and Tice, D.M. (1994). *Losing Control: How and Why People Fail at Self-Regulation*. San Diego: Academic Press.

Hatzigeorgiadis, A., Theodorakis, Y., and Zourbanos, N. (2004). Self-talk in the swimming pool: The effects of self-talk on thought content and performance on water-polo tasks. *Journal of Applied Sport Psychology*, 16(2), 138–50.

Miles, A. and Neil, R. (2013). The use of self-talk during elite cricket batting performance. *Psychology of Sport and Exercise*, 14(6), 874–81.

Hamilton, R.A., Scott, D., and MacDougall, M.P. (2007). Assessing the effectiveness of self-talk interventions on endurance performance. *Journal of Applied Sport Psychology*, 19(2), 226–39.

Landin, D. and Hebert, E.P. (1999). The influence of self-talk on the performance of skilled female tennis players. *Journal of Applied Sport Psychology*, 11(2), 263–82.

Theodorakis, Y., Weinberg, R., Natsis, P., Douma, I., and Kazakas, P. (2000). The effects of motivational versus instructional self-talk on improving motor performance. *Sport Psychologist*, 14(3), 253–71.

Landin, D. (1994). The role of verbal cues in skill learning. *Quest*, 46, 299–313.

Pace, T.W., Negi, L.T., Adame, D.D., Cole, S.P., Sivilli, T.I., Brown, T.D., and Raison, C.L. (2009). Effect of compassion meditation on neuroendocrine, innate immune and behavioral responses to psychosocial stress. *Psychoneuroendocrinology*, 34(1), 87–98.

Davidson, R.J., Kabat-Zinn, J., Schumacher, J., Rosenkranz, M., Muller, D., Santorelli, S.F., and Sheridan, J.F. (2003). Alterations in brain and immune function produced by mindfulness meditation. *Psychosomatic Medicine*, 65(4), 564–70.

Chiesa, A., Calati, R., and Serretti, A. (2011). Does mindfulness training improve cognitive abilities? A systematic review of neuropsychological findings. *Clinical Psychology Review*, 31(3), 449–64.

Irving, J.A., Dobkin, P.L., and Park, J. (2009). Cultivating mindfulness in health care professionals: a review of empirical studies of mindfulness-based stress reduction (MBSR). *Complementary Therapies in Clinical Practice*, 15(2), 61–6.

Roeser, R.W., Schonert-Reichl, K.A., Jha, A., Cullen, M., Wallace, L., Wilensky, R., and Harrison, J. (2013). Mindfulness training and reductions in teacher stress and burnout: results from two randomized, waitlist-control field trials. *Journal of Educational Psychology*, 105(3), 787.

Jha, A.P., Krompinger, J., and Baime, M.J. (2007). Mindfulness training modifies subsystems of attention. *Cognitive, Affective, & Behavioral Neuroscience* 7(2), 109–19.

Sedlmeier, P., Eberth, J., Schwarz, M., Zimmermann, D., Haarig, F., Jaeger, S., and Kunze, S. (2012). The psychological effects of meditation: a metaanalysis. *Psychological Bulletin*, 138(6), 1139.

Luthans, F. (2002). The need for and meaning of positive organizational behavior. *Journal of Organizational Behavior*, 23, 695–706.

Masten, A.S. (2001). Ordinary magic: resilience process in development. *American Psychologist*, 56, 227–39.

Luthans, F., Avolio, B., Walumbwa, F., and Li, W. (2005). The psychological capital of Chinese workers: exploring the relationship with performance. *Management and Organization Review*, 1, 247–69.

Luthans, F. and Youssef, C.M. (2007). Emerging positive organizational behavior. *Journal of Management*, 33, 321–49.

Youssef, C.M. and Luthans, F. (2007). Positive organizational behavior in the workplace the impact of hope, optimism, and resilience. *Journal of Management*, 33(5), 774–800.

Werner, E.E. (1993). Risk, resilience, and recovery: Perspectives from the Kauai longitudinal study. *Development and Psychopathology*, 5(04), 503–15.

Morehead, J. (2012, June). Stanford University's Carol Dweck on the growth mindset and education. *One Dublin*. Retrieved on August 12, 2014, from http://goo.gl/n2XTjw.

Dweck, C. (2006). *Mindset: The New Psychology of Success*. New York: Random House.

Witcher, L.A., Alexander, E.S., Onwuebuzie, A.J., Collins, K.M., and Witcher, A.E. (2007). The relationship between psychology students' levels of perfectionism and achievement in a graduate-level research methodology course. *Personality and Individual Differences, 43*, 1396–405.

Baker, L.R. and McNulty, J.K. (2011). Self-compassion and relationship maintenance: The moderating roles of conscientious-ness and gender. *Journal of Personality and Social Psychology,* 100, 853–73.

Breines, J.G. and Chen, S. (2012a). Self-compassion increases self-improvement motivation. *Personality and Social Psychology Bulletin*, 38(9), 1133–43.

Breines, J.G. and Chen, S. (2012b). Self-compassion increases self-improvement motivation.

Gollwitzer, P.M. and Sheeran, P. (2006). Implementation intentions and goal achievement: A meta-analysis of effects and processes. *Advances in Experimental Social Psychology*, 38, 69–119.

8

How to Build, Break, and Change Habits

The external environment in which people are trying to change behavior can include many things, all of which can impact their ability to change. Sometimes, the physical environment, such as office design, can play a role. Other times, factors such as team dynamics, organizational culture, and the support of key colleagues can be factors. Even work–life balance and the state of individuals' personal relationships outside of work can affect their ability to change behaviors in the workplace. The list of factors is long, because pretty much everything around individuals can affect them.

Rather than going through each and every possible external context factor, which would be a task worthy of a book in its own right, in Chaps. 9, 10, and 11 we are going to look at three *approaches* to creating a supportive environment for change. Each of these involves approaching the external environment in a different way, working with different factors. We will look at the use of incentives, tools for tracking progress, and the influence of social relationships. Two of the approaches we will look at—gamification and nudging—are fairly radical and relatively new. But we will begin by taking a fresh look at something that is not new: the science of how to build, break, and change habits.

Habits may not sound like part of the external environment, and over the course of this chapter we will look at aspects of people's internal context such as their psychology and even the physical structure of their brains. But in all of the techniques we then suggest, what we are trying to do is to create an external supporting structure within which people can make lasting changes in behavior.

A number of "pop-psychology" books have been written about habits recently, and you may already have read one. But do not skip this chapter yet, because although some of these books are great, they tend to oversimplify. For instance, some will tell you that it is not possible to get rid of habits, that it is only possible to change them. Yet as we will see, this is not true.

The Anatomy of Habits

A habit is a routine way of behaving that tends to occur automatically and unconsciously (Stern 2000). A great example is driving. Just turning a corner consists of a number of different behaviors, most of which we do not really think about as we do them. We check in the mirror to see what is behind us; look around to see what other cars are doing; then signal using the car's indicators to show which direction we are going in. And for the most part, these behaviors are routine acts that we do not have to be deliberate about or consciously decide to do. We just do them because we have learned to do them when we want to turn a corner. They are habits.

Half of all our behaviors are unconscious, automatic habits

There was a time, about 100 years ago, when habits were all that psychologists thought we had. As we described in Chap. 2, the early behaviorists saw all of our behaviors as more or less unconscious responses to external events. Times have changed, of course, and the cognitive psychologists who have dominated the profession since the 1950s have emphasized instead how we think about what we do and make conscious decisions about how to behave. Yet researchers still believe that around half of all our behaviors are unconscious, automatic habits (Quinn and Wood 2005).

That may sound like a lot, but think about your day so far: how many of your acts—the specific small behaviors you engaged in—were the result of conscious choice and deliberation? Sure, you may have decided to make a cup of coffee. But the individual behaviors involved in doing so—such as filling the kettle—probably did not take a lot of thought or decision-making. You just did them. Here are a few more examples of people we have encountered and their habits:

- The mid-level manager who had grown up in a large family with many siblings and who had, as a result, developed a habit of talking loudly and while other people were speaking. At his family dinner table, that was how conversations were held, but in team meetings the behavior went down less well.

- The engineer at a car manufacturing plant who had worked for a particularly perfectionist and stern boss in his early years and had taken on some of this behavior and developed the habit of *always* repeatedly checking his work to ensure there were no mistakes.
- The senior leader who—at some point in his past—had developed the habit of ending all his sentences with the word "the," as if he were about to start a new sentence. He hardly even noticed it, but it irritated his boss considerably.

The reason behavior change experts are so interested in habits is that once you have them, they can be tough to shake off. After all, how do you stop something that comes automatically to you and you do not really think about? Studies have repeatedly shown that once habits have become strong, they are more or less unaffected by current goals and objectives—by what you say you want to do (Neal et al. 2012). So you can decide to be more assertive all you want, but if you have a habit that means you speak quietly in group settings, it is not going to change immediately just because you decide you would like to do something different. This poses a problem for behavior change, but it also makes habits something of a holy grail because if you can turn a new behavior into a strong habit, then you will probably have it for life.

So if you want to help others change their behavior, you need to know about habits. You need to know how to change them or get rid of them when they are unhelpful, and how to form them so that new behaviors are more likely to stick. And to help understand how to do these things, we first have to explore what habits involve and are made of.

The Two Basic Components of Habits

Habits consist of two basic components: a behavior and a situation. The first of these—the behavior—is obvious. What is perhaps less obvious is that such behaviors tend to be very specific. For example, you may feel that someone has a general habit of always being on time for meetings. But the specific behavior involved may be the act of always setting a reminder alarm for five minutes before the meeting. Or you may have the impression that a manager has the habit of regularly walking the floor and getting out of his office and speaking to people. But the precise habitual behavior involved may be going to fetch a cup of coffee every morning and coincidentally walking past people and saying hello. Every habit involves at least one specific behavior and it may not be the obvious one.

The second component is a situation. Habits do not occur randomly, but in response to particular situations or events. For instance, the habitual acts people develop as they learn to drive round a corner only occur when they are in a car and about to turn. Similarly, the habitual acts involved in making a cup of coffee only occur when we are actually making coffee.

Pretty much anything qualifies as a situation. Psychologists call them *cues* because they act like triggers for the habitual behavior. In supermarkets and gas stations, the cue that can trigger you to buy a chocolate bar is the fact that the stores place them right by the checkouts. You see them, feel hungry, and so buy one. And if you pick up a bar enough times, then sooner or later you will start doing so automatically, whether or not you feel hungry.

Or take a finance director we worked with who was known among her team and peers for being edgy, firm, and direct. Yet she struggled to have a strong impact with her boss, who saw her as anxious and passive.

Working with her, we found that the cue that triggered this behavior was how she felt about authority, which dated back to when she was a young girl with strict parents. And now, all these years later, she immediately, automatically, and unconsciously started behaving in an anxious, more passive way every time she saw an authority figure such as her boss.

This case is also an example of how habits can spread from one cue to another through generalization. The original cue for the finance director's anxious behavior lay deep in her childhood, in her relationship with her firmly authoritarian parents. Over time, however, the cue had become generalized to other, similar authority figures, until eventually anyone in authority triggered the behavior in her, regardless of whether they were authoritarian in their style or not.

Habits can switch cues more radically, too. The most famous demonstration of this came from a Russian psychologist called Ivan Pavlov in the 1890s. Pavlov was studying how dogs salivated as they ate, when he noticed that his dogs would begin to salivate whenever he entered the room, even if he was not bringing them food. Curious, he experimented and started ringing a bell whenever he fed his dogs. And sure enough, they soon started salivating whenever the bell rang, regardless of whether there was food or not. The initial cue (the food) had become associated with a new and entirely different cue (a bell), as a result of which the behavioral habit of salivating had transferred from the food to the sound of the bell. Psychologists call the transfer process between very different cues *classical conditioning* (see Fig. 8.1).

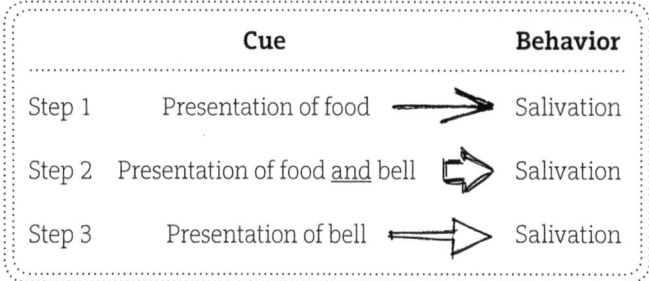

Fig. 8.1 Transferring cues through classical conditioning

A Third Component: Reinforcers

There is a third, slightly hidden and somewhat optional component of habits, too. We often need a reason to continue repeating a behavior enough times for it to become a habit. Psychologists refer to this reason as a *reinforcer*. It can be anything that makes it more likely that we will repeat a behavior—anything that reinforces it. With a chocolate bar, it is the enjoyment of eating it—the sugar rush! With the finance director, the reinforcer was her anxiety about what would happen if she displeased authority figures. And for one of your authors, a strong habit reinforcer for many years was caffeine.

Every morning on his way to work, he passed a coffee shop next door to his office. One day, feeling tired, he walked in and bought a cup of coffee to help him wake up. He liked it. So the next day, he went back in and bought another one. And before he knew it, he found himself buying a cup of coffee every morning. The coffee shop was a cue. Buying the coffee was the behavior. And enjoying the coffee and feeling more alert afterward was the reinforcer. What this reinforcer did was to encourage your author to carry on buying coffee enough times until it became a habit (see Fig. 8.2).

Even when reinforcers are necessary in order to establish a habit, they are sometimes only a temporary part of the equation. Indeed, part of the power of habits comes from the fact that they can continue long after the reinforcer has gone. Take the coffee example. Coffee is a drug, and if you drink it often enough, your body becomes used to it and adapts. As a result, you have to drink more of it to get the same "hit." This is why a double espresso will have less effect on a regular coffee drinker than on someone who does not normally drink it. And it is why your author's morning coffee eventually stopped working as a means to help him wake up. He kept going back to buy more because

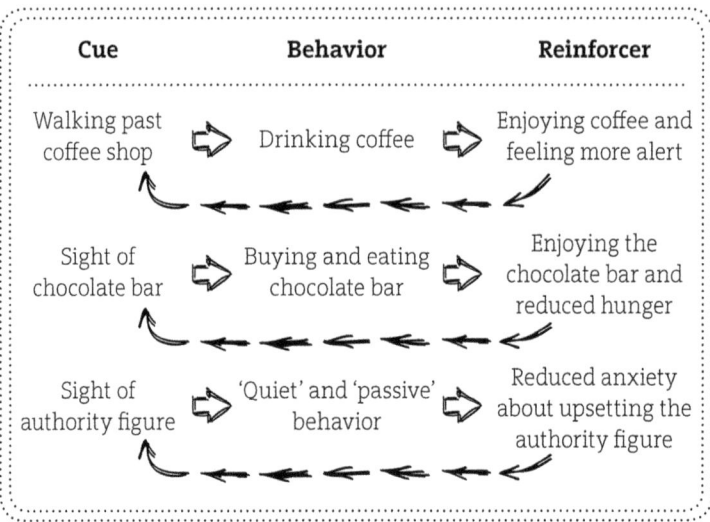

Fig. 8.2 The role of reinforcer

the behavior had become a habit. But it had become detached from the reinforcer and only the cue and the behavior remained.

These, then, are the two or three components of a habit: the situational cue, the behavior itself, and a reinforcer. It is a simple recipe. But understanding habits is one thing, using this understanding to help people change their behavior is quite another. So let's now consider three key questions about habits for people trying to help others change their behavior. How do you build habits? How do you break them? And how do you change them? As we will see, since habits involve automatic reactions and responses to the environment, most of the solutions to these questions require making changes to this external environment.

How to Build a Habit

The idea behind how habits develop is simple: If a specific behavior is performed in a specific situation enough times, then a habit forms (Lally et al. 2010; Triandis 1977; Wood and Neal 2009). People will then tend to automatically perform the behavior whenever they encounter that situation, without having to consciously think about it. That's the theory anyway. Anyone who has ever tried to develop a habit, though, will tell you that it is not always as easy as it sounds. This is backed up by research, too, since studies have shown that even when people are strongly motivated to create habits, approximately half of them do not perform behaviors consistently enough and long enough to turn them into habits (Lally et al. 2010).

This begs the question: How long is long enough? How long do we need to keep practicing a behavior before it becomes automatic? It may be longer than we think. For starters, there is no on-and-off switch with habits. It is not that we practice a behavior until suddenly, overnight, it becomes a habit. The change is more gradual. Behaviors slowly require less and less of a conscious decision to do them, until eventually they become automatic and require no conscious thought at all (Hull 1943, 1951).

There has been much debate over the precise point at which a behavior finally becomes completely automatic. Some self-help programs have claimed that it takes 21 days for this change to happen, but most researchers agree that it takes longer (Redish et al. 2008; Rothman et al. 2009). In fact, a recent study at University College London, which looked at how long it took to form a habit with a wide range of different behaviors, suggests that the average length of time it takes is 66 days (Lally et al. 2010). That's nine and a half weeks, or just over two months. This is an *average* number, though, and the length of time it took participants in the study to form habits ranged from 18 to 254 days.

Why the big difference in the time it took? Well, it depends on a range of factors, such as the person involved and the type of behavior they are trying to turn into a habit. Some people form habits more easily than others, and some behaviors are easier to convert into habits than others. Importantly, however, there are a few simple things you can do to ensure that you have as good a chance as possible of performing behaviors often enough to turn them into habits. In fact, you need to take four steps to build a habit: Identify a behavior, find a cue, think about a reinforcer, and promote repetition (see Fig. 8.3).

Step 1: Identify a Behavior

The starting point is usually the behavior. People typically use the identify/resolve approach we described in Chap. 1 to agree a behavior that someone needs to develop. And if the person gets stuck identifying the issues or finding solutions, you can use some of the questioning techniques we suggested in Chap. 3. There are three simple techniques to use when choosing a behavior to turn into a habit.

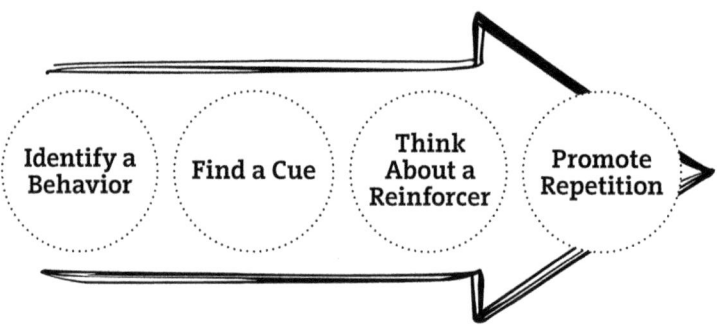

Fig. 8.3 How to build a habit

Behavior Technique #1: Be Specific

A critical technique here is that the behavior needs to be as simple and specific as possible. So, if you are helping someone identify a behavior they need to turn into habit, keep asking them, "Can we be more specific?"

Take, for example, the case of Noor—a manager who came to us saying that she wanted to "be more assertive in meetings." Seeing that this was rather vague as a goal, we worked with her to redefine her objective as "to voice an opinion at least once in every meeting, beginning with the phrase, 'My intuition on this is that…'."

Such specificity is important because it is easier to transform clearly defined and specific behavioral acts into habits than broad goals. This is why you are more likely to be successful trying to turn saying a particular phrase to customers into a habit than the more general behavior of being polite to customers. It is also why you will have more success with requests such as "Pick up the phone to six customers each week" than with "Be more proactive in calling customers."

Behavior Technique #2: Think Small

It is not only specificity that is important, but also *simplicity*. Or, put another way, size matters, because researchers have found that it is much easier to turn simple acts into habits than more complex ones (Verplanken 2006). This is why you may have heard some commentators repeating the phrases *small steps* or *tiny habits*. The idea is that so-called *proximal goals*—objectives that are more immediately achievable for the individual—are a good way to make change happen. These small steps may not be the whole change that someone wants to make, but it is generally accepted that it is better to achieve change through a series of small steps than to fail in a big one. For you, as a manager trying to help someone change, this means you have to think about how achievable the behavior is and whether there are some smaller steps they could take first. For example, being a better strategic thinker may well be the ultimate goal. But how about first trying to turn the behavior of reading one strategy-related article each week into a habit? It is far more achievable as a goal, the person is more likely to succeed and, in doing so, will build momentum for the ultimate change they wish to make.

Behavior Technique#3: As Few Behaviors as Possible

Building habits is hard enough without confusing things. So keep it simple. Rather than identifying a whole bunch of behaviors to change, choose only one, or at least as few as possible (Wood and Neal 2007). With our earlier example of Noor, who wanted to be more assertive in meetings, we could have identified a whole host of things for her to try doing in meetings. But we chose just one – voicing an opinion – so that she went into meetings with a clear and unambiguous idea about what she had to do. It was a small start, but we knew that once she had managed to do that, we could then focus on other behaviors.

Step 2: Find a Cue

Identifying the cue involved in a habit is usually fairly easy, too, although there are more factors to bear in mind than with behaviors. In fact, the best cues have four qualities—they are specific, salient, frequent, and consistent.

Just as with behaviors, the cue needs to be as *specific* as possible. Using the assertiveness in meetings example, rather than thinking of performing the behavior "in meetings" in general, think of specific regular meetings, or specific points in meetings, such as after the first three people have spoken in a debate.

Cues work better when they are *salient*, when they are very noticeable and it is hard to miss them (Lally et al. 2011). For instance, cues that occur at the beginning or end of a routine or process work better than those in the middle of something. That is why it is easier for people to form a habit of saying a particular phrase to customers at the beginning or end of their conversations with them rather than halfway through.

Cues work better when they are salient

Habits also form more quickly when they are *frequent* and people have the opportunity to practice them every day than if they can only practice them once a week (Norman and Cooper 2011). If the gap between cues is much longer than a week, you should probably think about a different cue.

Finally, cues need to be *consistent*, in that they need to look and feel the same. For example, they work better if they occur at the same time of day and in the same place (Danner et al. 2008). So, if you are helping someone to be more assertive in meetings and are trying to identify a specific meeting in which they can test the behavior and build up the habit, try *not* to pick a meeting that occurs in a different room or at a different time of day on every occasion.

Remember that you can use existing habits as a cue when you are identifying which cue to use. For instance, your coffee-drinking author decided one year that he wanted to eat more fruit as part of a drive to be healthier. So he simply used his preexisting habit of buying coffee as a cue to buy fruit and bought a small fruit bowl with every cup of coffee. By using the power of the existing habit, he made developing a new habit of buying fruit much easier.

Step 3: Think About a Reinforcer

Having a reinforcer is not absolutely necessary, but it *will* help and it will help a lot. Its role is to make sure that people carry on practicing a behavior long enough for it to become a habit. On days when someone is busy, stressed, or tired, it can be the reinforcer that ensures they still do the behavior. And let's face it there will be those days when good intentions are not enough. So, wherever possible, think about using a reinforcer.

We will look at what works best as a reinforcer in greater depth in Chap. 9, when we explore an approach to creating a supportive environment called *gamification*. For now, what is important is to remember three simple techniques.

Reinforcer Technique #1: Make Reinforcers Immediate

First the cue happens, which triggers the behavior, and finally the reinforcer acts to make the behavior more likely to happen again. It is like a prize or reward. One factor to bear in mind when choosing a reinforcer is that research shows that it works best when it follows as soon as possible after the behavior. Returning to the example of Noor again, who wanted to improve her assertiveness in meetings, we suggested that she take a small chocolate bar into the room, place it in front of her and only eat it after performing the behavior (speaking up and voicing an opinion).

Reinforcer Technique #2: Make Reinforcers Meaningful

What works as a reinforcer? Pretty much anything, but it needs to mean something to the person who is trying to form the habit. It needs to be something that they care about or enjoy, such as praise, a snack, or a cup of coffee. With Noor, the manager who took a chocolate bar into the room, we decided on that because she loved chocolate. And one commonly cited example in this context is the manager who wants to develop a habit of getting out of his office to speak with his team every day. The cue used is a specific time of day, say 10.30. The reinforcer is that after he has spoken to people—and only afterward—he gets himself a cup of coffee.

Reinforcer Technique #3: Remember the Premack Principle

One neat trick to bear in mind when choosing a reinforcer is what is known as the *Premack principle* after the psychologist David Premack, who first observed it. Essentially, he found that more enjoyable tasks could be used as reinforcers for less enjoyable tasks (Homme et al. 1963; Premack 1959, 1963). Consider the example of one of our colleagues, who—as part of his job—had to submit a report with some key data to senior leaders every week. He was ideally supposed to do it on Monday mornings, but somehow never got round to it. There were always other things to do. So we asked him to record what he did every Monday morning. When he showed us the list, we asked him to rate each activity according to how enjoyable he found it. Unsurprisingly, producing the report was right at the bottom of the list in terms of enjoyability, while catching up with colleagues, getting coffee, and even doing his e-mails were rated as more enjoyable. So, using the cue of first thing Monday morning and a reminder alarm, we created a reinforcer out of these other activities by getting him to agree that he would only do them *after* producing the report. In this way, the Premack principle is useful as it allows you to use existing activities as reinforcers.

Step 4: Promote Repetition

So far, we have shown a simple three-step approach to forming a habit: identify a behavior, find a cue, and think about a reinforcer. Yet we have also heard that about half of the people who start down the road of trying to build a habit ultimately fail. So what can you do to help people stack the odds in their favor?

Possibly the single most important thing you can do is to support individuals in repeating the behavior often enough for it to become a habit. Back in the early days of behavioral psychology, researchers thought that a behavior had to be repeated every single time a particular cue occurred in order for a habit to form (James 1890). Just one missed opportunity, they thought, and people would have to start all over again. These days we know it is not quite like that. For example, let's say there is a behavior someone wants to adopt in meetings. If they fail to do it in a particular meeting, it will probably mean that the habit forms more slowly, but it does not mean they have to start all over again (Lally et al. 2010). But consistency does matter, especially during the first days and weeks of behavior change, so anything you can do to ensure consistency will help the habit form (Armitage 2005). So with that in mind, below you will find six techniques to use to help promote repetition of behaviors (see Fig. 8.4). You can use some or all of them, and indeed combinations are likely to be most effective.

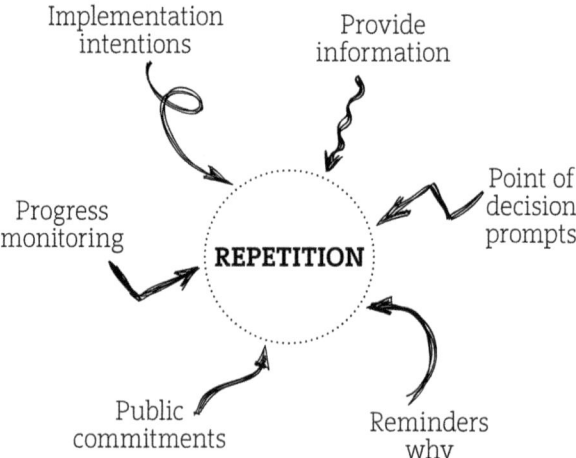

Fig. 8.4 Six techniques for promoting repetition

Repetition Technique #1: Provide Information About Habits

The simplest and easiest way to promote repetition of behaviors is to help people understand what habits are and how they work. Studies have found that by doing this and giving people information on how to form habits, they will be more likely to succeed in efforts to change their behavior (Lally et al. 2007).

Repetition Technique #2: Give Point of Prompts

Remembering is often a significant barrier to adopting a new habit. Cues can be overlooked or forgotten. So think about reminders and prompts, such as notes, signs, and alarms, to ensure people remember to act. For instance, the colleague we described earlier who used first thing Monday morning as a cue to act also left a large reminder note on his computer screen every Friday night, ready for him on Monday morning. Research shows that such reminders have a relatively short life expectancy—they soon lose their power to prompt us (Tobias 2009). But during the early days of trying to form a habit, they can be a useful tool. The key factor when designing prompts is to position them at the point of decision—the point where people either act out the desired behavior or do something else.

A great example of this technique is bitter nail polish—a product that is designed for use with children and other people who want to stop biting their fingernails. The polish tastes disgusting and so acts as a prompt or reminder to people not to bite their nails.

Repetition Technique #3: Remember Why

Reminding people *why* they are trying to change their behavior and why it is important can also lead to more successful outcomes. With this in mind, try sending the individual a couple of e-mails during the first few weeks of change pointing out why it is important.

Repetition Technique #4: Make Public Commitments

Research has shown that individuals are more likely to develop and sustain habits if they have made a verbal or written commitment to do so and then shared this with others (Schienker et al. 1994). Development plans do this to some extent, as do performance objectives. But it is the public sharing of these plans that really helps. This means someone sharing their plans with their boss, HR, coach, peers, or direct reports—a person who effectively acts as a witness and monitor. A neat example of this comes from Warren Buffett, who shared his goals in a unique way: by announcing to his family that he would write checks to his children if he failed to reach his weight-loss goals.

Repetition Technique #5: Monitor Progress

Backing up the previous point, putting in place a monitoring process to check progress can be extremely important. Sometimes this can be done by asking the individual to keep track themselves. Other times, you could use what are often referred to as pulse-checks. This involves sending a mini survey to maybe four or five people once a week or month to ask specific questions about whether the individual has been performing the behavior(s) in question. There are both paid and free online tools to help with this.

Using Technology to Build Habits

There is, we are told, an app for everything. So it should be no surprise to discover that there are apps available to help you build habits. They help in three main ways. First, they act as a form of commitment tool. Second, they serve as a prompt and reminder to act. And third, they help you track progress and can thus act as a reinforcer. Some of the best known examples of these apps at the time of writing were *Lift* and *irunurun*. Check them out. They are no substitute for proper planning and willpower, but they can help some people.

Repetition Technique #6: Create Implementation Intentions

We saved the big one for last. *Implementation intentions* are a type of planning that specifies what people will do in specific situations (Gollwitzer 1993, 1999). They are mini-scripts for how to act: "In situation X, I will do Y." Or, "If X happens, I will do Y." They are powerful because they can help people overcome the inevitable challenges they will face in building habits.

Let's say you are trying to help your sales team become more proactive in engaging customers. The goal you have set is for them each to call five customers a week, for a courtesy call. To turn this behavior into a habit, you need a cue and possibly a reinforcer. So you suggest that each person picks a specific time of day and rewards themselves afterward with a snack or drink. You provide some brief training to support these conversations. You have special prompt cards printed and attached to people's desk phones. And you even ask people to record their activity, so you can create a league table. So far, so good. But what about those pesky problems that can arise? That people will not be able to do it on some days because they have to attend certain meetings. That they will forget or they are too busy with other things. Or that maybe they cannot get hold of particular customers. What happens then? If they are unprepared for such obstacles, these sorts of seemingly minor issues can fundamentally undermine the focus on building a habit. Implementation intentions allow you to prepare people for moments like these. You can either provide them with a pre-prepared script for how to respond or, even better, get them to list potential problems and then ask them to think of the best responses. The goal is for people to have a simple script for each potentially problematic situation: "In this situation, I will do that." You are effectively automating their response.

Scripts like these have been shown to be highly effective in helping people successfully build habits across a wide range of behaviors (Gollwitzer and Brandstätter 1997; Bamberg 2002; Milne et al. 2002). Specifically, they have been shown to increase both the rate of performance of the planned behavior and the level of habit strength (Orbell and Verplanken 2010). Moreover, this seems to apply particularly in the early days of habit formation, when these scripts can effectively bolster willpower and help ensure that people's habit building is not derailed by events.

How to Break a Habit

So far, we have looked at how to build habits. We have stripped them down to identify what they are made of and then presented a simple four-step process for building them. But what about *stopping* them? We began the chapter by noting just how difficult to shift well-established habits can be. How on earth can we stop behaviors that are automatic, unconscious, and trigged by situational cues? This is particularly important, because to build new habits we often have to break old ones. Fortunately, you have three main options.

Option 1: Remove the Reinforcer

To be honest, this is not much of an option. But if a habit is weak—if it is newly formed or not always acted out—and if it is reinforced by a reward of some sort, you can remove the reinforcer. This only works for weak habits, but it is worth remembering as a first option. The one caution around using it is that it is not always easy to identify what is genuinely reinforcing a behavior.

Option 2: Avoid the Cue

A seeming lifetime ago, one of your authors quit smoking—a habit with a sting. If you stop it, your body starts experiencing withdrawal symptoms, unpleasant physical reactions to the withdrawal of the habitual behavior. It is about as strong a habit as someone can have. So how did your author quit smoking? He went on holiday.

That may sound like an odd way of stopping a habit. But it removed the major cues for the behavior. Your author typically smoked with friends, in coffee breaks at work. So he removed the friends and the coffee breaks from the equation. He still experienced withdrawal symptoms from the nicotine in the cigarettes, of course, but the change of situation helped him by enabling him to avoid the normal cues and triggers to smoke.

Habits, then, are so strongly rooted in the situations in which they occur that one way to break them is to change the situation (Wood et al. 2005; Verplanken et al. 2008). For instance, research looking at the exercising, newspaper reading, and TV watching habits of students transferring to a new university found that their old habits usually did not survive the transfer to the new situation (Wood et al. 2005). This is why the timing of efforts to break habits is so important and why people are most likely to succeed during times of change, such as changing jobs, moving desk, or starting work for a new boss.

So, when helping someone break habits, think about two key things. First, whether they can just avoid the cue involved in the habit they need to break. Taking a holiday to avoid the cue for smoking was a prime example of this. Another thing to bear in mind is that feeling tired or stressed is one of the biggest cues for triggering unwanted habits, so anything that can be done to reduce this during the period in which you try to break the habit is liable to help.

The second thing to think about here is whether there is a way to create or use periods of broader change to help people break their old habits. For example, consider the banking executive who wanted to improve levels of customer service in his relationship managers (sales people). He identified specific habits that he wanted people to build, but he was worried about the power of their existing behaviors and habits. So he announced a change program, restructured the department, and launched his initiative by having the office redecorated and rearranging people's desks. It wasn't that he did not like the old color of the walls or that he had a particular view on where people should sit. He just wanted to create a context of change and a sense of things shifting.

Of course, avoiding cues is often simply not possible. So what then?

Option 3: Ignore the Cue

Your next main option when it comes to breaking habits is to help people to ignore the cue—to consciously override it. The best way to do this is to help people move their habits from being unconscious, automatic responses to being things they are fully aware of. The challenge here is that it can take a high level of self-control to ignore cues, and when people get tired, stressed, or even hungry, their self-control can quickly disappear. Yet by adding some structure to what people are doing, you can help reinforce this self-control, using four techniques:

1. **Self-monitoring**. You can ask people to keep a record or diary of when and how often they perform an unwanted habitual behavior.
2. **Prompts**. If a behavior typically happens in a certain place or at a certain time of day, people can leave "Don't do it!" signs for themselves or create alarms to help remind them to consciously focus on not doing the behavior.
3. **Real-time feedback**. You can help people break a habit by ensuring that they get feedback that they are doing it. This could either mean telling them whenever you see them doing it or enrolling their peers or direct reports to do the same. This latter approach has the added benefit of effectively creating a public commitment by the individual to break the habit.
4. **Implementation intentions**. As we covered earlier, implementation intentions are a great way for people to pre-script how they will deal with the challenges involved in changing behavior. And you can use these scripts to help break habits as well as build them: "If I find myself doing X, I will do Y."

Sometimes, avoiding or ignoring the cue is not an option. Sometimes, the habit is just too strong and too ingrained to be broken. And when that happens, there is one final way forward: to *change* the habit.

How to Change a Habit

The practice of trying to stop unwanted behaviors by replacing them with alternative ones dates back centuries, but it was developed in detail by psychologists in the 1970s (Azrin and Nunn 1973). They sometimes referred to it as *competing response training* (CRT), and it was recently popularized by Charles Duhigg in his book *The Power of Habit*. As a method, it is often used to help people change some of the strongest unwanted habits it is possible to have, such as nervous tics, nail biting, and smoking. It is rarely used on its own and is usually paired with one of more of the other activities we have described in this chapter. It consists of three simple steps: understand the habit, select a substitute behavior, and make the substitution at every opportunity.

Possibly the most common example of this method in action is the use of nicotine gum and e-cigarettes (electronic cigarettes that are allegedly not as harmful to health) by people trying to give up smoking. Whenever they want a cigarette, the idea is that instead of lighting up, they chew some gum or vape an e-cigarette. One action is replaced by another. Now let's look at the three steps in turn.

Step 1: Understand the Habit

In order to make sure that someone understands their habit, you need to help them identify the behavior, cue, and reinforcer involved. But as Charles Duhigg has pointed out, it also means you discovering if there is some underlying need underpinning the habitual behavior. Smoking is again a good example here. Someone may have the habit of lighting up a cigarette after the cue of eating a meal, but the underlying need is a craving for nicotine. For most work-related habits, the underlying need is often to assuage anxiety—be it the social anxiety of being in a meeting, the professional anxiety of not wanting to let your boss down, or the performance anxiety of wanting to be seen as the best at what you do. You can find some examples of this in Fig. 8.5.

Not every habit has an underlying need. Some just build up over time. Or others may initially have satisfied some need that has long since gone. It is important, though, to help people understand whether such a need exists and, if it does, then to articulate what the need is. And the reason this is important is because your choice of substitute habit will ideally have to meet this underlying need. This brings us to the next step.

Need	Behavior	Cue	Reinforcer
Social anxiety	Nervous laughter	Whenever tension or heated debate occurs in large meetings	Temporary feeling of relief from reduced tension in the room
Desire to be thought well of	Saying 'yes' to extra requests without thinking through the implications	Boss asking someone to do extra tasks	Receipt of thanks and approval from boss
Drive to do well	Competitively talking over others in debates	Team situations	Feeling of having succeeded or won

Fig. 8.5 The role of underlying needs in habits

Step 2: Select a Substitute Behavior

This is sometimes easier said than done. We have already noted that a substitute habit needs to meet any underlying need that caused the original habit. But it also needs to follow a few other rules. As with building habits, behaviors involved in changing habits have more chance of sticking if they are simple, specific, and easy to do.

Note that all of the suggested substitute behaviors in Fig. 8.6 leave the original cue and reinforcer intact, and all seek to address the original underlying need that gave rise to the unwanted habit.

Step 3: Make the Substitution at Every Opportunity

The final step is to actually enact the new behavior. And here you can use pretty much all of the techniques suggested in the "Promote repetition" section, where we discussed how to build habits. So you can use prompts, progress reviews, and implementation intentions among other tools. The objective

Need	Cue	Original Behavior	Substitute Behavior	Reinforcer
Social anxiety	Whenever tension or heated debate occurs in large meetings	Nervous laughter	Using the phrase "There is some tension here", and then giving opinion on why	Temporary feeling of relief from reduced tension in the room
Desire to be thought well of	Boss asking someone to do extra tasks	Saying 'yes' to extra requests without thinking through the implications	Using the phrase "Let me go and check"	Receipt of thanks and approval from boss
Drive to do well	Team situations	Competitively talking over others in debates	Noting thoughts down before speaking them in a debate (creating a pause and opportunity to think)	Feeling of having succeeded or won

Fig. 8.6 Examples of substitute behaviors

is simply to help ensure that the new behavior is enacted enough times to turn it into a habit.

One factor to be aware of here is that people will sometimes need to practice the behavior. It may sound and feel odd to practice repeating a simple phrase or behavior, but research shows that it can help people to do it when they are faced with the cue for real.

Habits: A Structure for Change

In this chapter, we have looked at the anatomy of habits—what they are made of—and at how to build, break, and change them. Looking at change through the lens of habits is the first of our three approaches to building a supportive environment. And we have seen how, by thinking about behaviors as habits, and identifying cues, behaviors, and reinforcers, we can create a supportive structure for people's motivation, ability, and psychological capital for behavior change.

To some readers, it may feel slightly mechanistic: If this, then try that; pull on lever A to make B happen. And there is a degree to which they are correct. But habits, at their very core, are deeply mechanical in their structure, as might be expected from something that is essentially an unconscious, automatic process. So you need to approach them in a very tactical, planned way.

Moreover, this mechanistic approach is a common feature of most methods of building the supportive external context needed to help change happen. And we will see this even more with the next of our three approaches to building a supportive environment: the wonderful—if very misunderstood—world of gamification.

Key Questions to Ask Yourself

1. What are the behavior, cue, and reinforcer for the habit you are trying to help the individual create?
2. How can you promote repetition of the behavior, in particular in the early days of habit formation?
3. Have you given the individual information about the structure of habits and how they can be formed and broken?
4. Have they drawn up a list of implementation intentions to help them deal with situations and obstacles?
5. If you are trying to break a habit, how can you remove the cue or help the individual ignore it?
6. If you are trying to change a habit, has the individual selected a substitute behavior?

Further Resources

- Jeremy Dean (2013). *Making Habits, Breaking Habits*. London: Oneworld.
- Charles Duhigg (2013). *The Power of Habit: Why We Do What We Do, and How to Change*. London: Random House. Also available as a TEDx summary video on YouTube.

References

Stern, P.C. (2000). New environmental theories: toward a coherent theory of environmentally significant behavior. *Journal of Social Issues*, 56(3), 407–2.

Quinn, J.M. and Wood, W. (2005). Habits across the lifespan. Unpublished manuscript, Duke University, Durham, NC.

Neal, D.T., Wood, W., Labrecque, J.S., and Lally, P. (2012). How do habits guide behavior? Perceived and actual triggers of habits in daily life. *Journal of Experimental Social Psychology*, 48(2), 492–8.

Lally, P., Van Jaarsveld, C.H., Potts, H.W., and Wardle, J. (2010). How are habits formed: modelling habit formation in the real world. *European Journal of Social Psychology*, 40(6), 998–1009.

Triandis, H.C. (1977). *Interpersonal Behavior*. Monterey: Brooks/Cole.

Wood, W. and Neal, D.T. (2009). The habitual consumer. *Journal of Consumer Psychology*, 19(4), 579–92.

Hull, C.L. (1951). *Essentials of Behavior*. Westport, CT: Greenwood Press.

Hull, C.L. (1943). *Principles of Behavior: An Introduction to Behavior Theory*. New York: Appleton-Century-Crofts.

Redish, A.D., Jensen, S., and Johnson, A. (2008). A unified framework for addiction: vulnerabilities in the decision process. *Behavioral and Brain Sciences*, 31(04), 415–37.

Rothman, A.J., Sheeran, P., and Wood, W. (2009). Reflective and automatic processes in the initiation and maintenance of dietary change. *Annals of Behavioral Medicine*, 38(1), 4–17.

Verplanken, B. (2006). Beyond frequency: habit as mental construct. *British Journal of Social Psychology*, 45(3), 639–56.

Wood, W. and Neal, D.T. (2007). A new look at habits and the habit-goal interface. *Psychological review*, 114(4), 843.

Lally, P., Wardle, J., and Gardner, B. (2011). Experiences of habit formation: A qualitative study. *Psychology, Health & Medicine*, 16(4), 484–9.

Norman, P. and Cooper, Y. (2011). The theory of planned behaviour and breast self-examination: assessing the impact of past behaviour, context stability and habit strength. *Psychology & Health*, 26(9), 1156–72.

Danner, U.N., Aarts, H., and Vries, N.K. (2008). Habit vs. intention in the prediction of future behaviour: the role of frequency, context stability and mental accessibility of past behaviour. *British Journal of Social Psychology*, 47(2), 245–65.

Homme, L.E., DeBaca, P.C., Devine, J.V., Steinhorst, R., and Rickert, E.J. (1963). Use of the Premack principle in controlling the behavior of nursery school children. *Journal of the Experimental Analysis of Behavior*, 6(4), 544.

Premack, D. (1959). Toward empirical behavior laws: I. Positive reinforcement. *Psychological Review*, 66(4), 219.

Premack, D. (1963). Rate differential reinforcement in monkey manipulation. *Journal of the Experimental Analysis of Behavior*, 6(1), 81–9.

James, W. (1890). *The Principles of Psychology*. London: Macmillan.

Armitage, C.J. (2005). Can the theory of planned behavior predict the maintenance of physical activity? *Health Psychology*, 24(3), 235.

Lally, P., Chipperfield, A., and Wardle, J. (2007). Healthy habits: efficacy of simple advice on weight control based on a habit-formation model. *International Journal of Obesity*, 32(4), 700–7.

Tobias, R. (2009). Changing behavior by memory aids: a social psychological model of prospective memory and habit development tested with dynamic field data. *Psychological Review*, 116(2), 408.

Schlenker, B.R., Dlugolecki, D.W., and Doherty, K. (1994). The impact of self-presentations on self-appraisals and behavior: the power of public commitment. *Personality and Social Psychology Bulletin*, 20(1), 20–33.

Gollwitzer, P.M. (1993). Goal achievement: the role of intentions. In W. Stroebe and M. Hewstone (Eds.), *European Review of Social Psychology* (Vol. 4, pp. 141–85). Chichester: John Wiley & Sons.

Gollwitzer, P.M. (1999). Implementation intentions: strong effects of simple plans. *American Psychologist*, 54(7), 493.

Gollwitzer, P.M. and Brandstätter, V. (1997). Implementation intentions and effective goal pursuit. *Journal of Personality and social Psychology*, 73(1), 186

Bamberg, S. (2002). Effects of implementation intentions on the actual performance of new environmentally friendly behaviours—results of two field experiments. *Journal of Environmental Psychology*, 22(4), 399–411.

Milne, S., Orbell, S., and Sheeran, P. (2002). Combining motivational and volitional interventions to promote exercise participation: Protection motivation theory and implementation intentions. *British Journal of Health Psychology*, 7(2), 163–84.

Orbell, S. and Verplanken, B. (2010). The automatic component of habit in health behavior: habit as cue-contingent automaticity. *Health Psychology*, 29(4), 374.

Wood, W., Tam, L., and Witt, M.G. (2005). Changing circumstances, disrupting habits. *Journal of Personality and Social Psychology*, 88(6), 918.

Verplanken, B., Walker, I., Davis, A., and Jurasek, M. (2008). Context change and travel mode choice: combining the habit discontinuity and self-activation hypotheses. *Journal of Environmental Psychology*, 28(2), 121–7.

Azrin, N.H. and Nunn, R.G. (1973). Habit-reversal: a method of eliminating nervous habits and tics. *Behaviour Research and Therapy*, 11(4), 619–28.

9

Gamification

You may not know it, you may not have recognized it when it happened to you, but the chances are that you have already experienced gamification. If you have a loyalty card from a retailer, belong to a frequent flyer scheme with an airline, or are a member of LinkedIn, then you will have been on the receiving end of a gamified process.

Contrary to popular belief, gamification is *not* the use of games. In fact, it is not really about games at all. It is the use of a variety of methods and techniques to make activities as compelling and engaging as possible. The only reason it is called *gamification* is that the video gaming industry that emerged in the 1980s and 1990s was the first to master these techniques. Games generally have no other purpose than to keep people engaged and happy. So over the years, games designers developed a range of methods to ensure this engagement and keep people playing. What gamification does is simply take the best practices that games designers have mastered and apply them to other activities and behaviors that we want people to feel engaged with and to continue doing.

The most famous and common of these techniques include points systems, membership levels, and progress markers. So when you gain reward points on a retailer loyalty card for every item you buy, that's gamification.

Supplementary Information The online version contains supplementary material available at https://doi.org/10.1007/978-3-031-29340-5_9. The videos can be accessed individually by clicking the DOI link in the accompanying figure caption or by scanning this link with the SN More Media App.

When you get "leveled up" through increasing tiers of membership in an airline frequent flyer scheme (are you Platinum Elite yet?), that's gamification. And when you see a progress bar as you fill in your LinkedIn profile, that's also gamification. (Rumor has it that the progress bar took developers only two hours to code, but that it improved the proportion of users completing their profile by 55% (Chou 2013a).)

These techniques work because they help keep people engaged in a particular activity. For retailers, airlines, and LinkedIn, that means keeping you coming back to use their services and products. Seeing how well gamification techniques have worked with consumers, charities, governments, and organizations have all started looking at how they, too, can use these methods to encourage certain types of behavior. Gamification can now be found in schemes to increase the degree to which people recycle their trash, save energy, and take public transport. And organizations have started using it to engage employees around health initiatives and training programs.

One thing we want to acknowledge right from the start is that gamification is not for everyone. Just because of the name, if nothing else, some people are simply not interested in it. It is also true that many of its techniques are more suitable for middle and junior level staff than executives. And some people see it merely as points and awards. But there is much more to gamification than points and awards, and when it is done well, it can be a valuable tool. It provides a very different approach to creating a supportive environment that can boost people's motivation, ability, and psychological capital and thus their attempts to change behavior.

In this chapter, we are going to look at five types of gamification methods: progress tracking, achievement marking, challenge and competition, social connection, and narrative. We show how and when you can use them and give three basic rules you need to follow to make sure they work. Let's begin, though, by taking a brief look at gamification's rise to fame.

Why All the Headlines and Hype?

The term *gamification* was first used in 2002, as games developers started looking at how to apply what they had learned about engaging players in games to engaging people in other activities, such as buying particular products. In 2010, gamification went mainstream, as a number of influential conference speeches, a TED talk, and a book all coincided to make some serious noise. Organizations were quick to see the potential value, and headlines and hype about the power of gamification soon followed. Analysts and researchers started predicting gamification would be The Next Big Thing, and the years since have seen the emergence of a market for gamifying business processes that, according to estimates, will be worth over $37 billion by 2027.

Gamification is such a big hit because it offers a set of techniques that are affordable, relatively easy to implement, and that promise to significantly increase customer and employee engagement. It has also been accompanied by some high-profile early successes with big-name firms, including Nike and Ford.

Nike, for example, wants people to run, and keep on running. So it developed a way for users of its running shoes to gamify their experience of running. The techniques it used were simple: Give people feedback about their progress and create a sense of challenge and competition. To do this, it built accelerometers into the soles of shoes, which could send information about how far and how long people were running to a PC or smartphone. It then built a website and app where people could record their running performance, track their progress against goals, and mark achievements that they had set. The techniques obviously worked, because today the website boasts an impressive 28 million users.

Ford, meanwhile, was one of the first firms to use gamification to support employee learning. It needed to increase employees' engagement with an online training program, which relied on people proactively looking at the content and driving their own learning. The company's solution was to gamify the experience of using the learning resources. It created challenges for people around completing certain sections of the material, started tracking their usage, and began awarding badges when tasks were achieved. Through the use of leader boards, it also encouraged competition between individuals and teams, based on the extent to which people were participating. The program was a huge success, with employees' use of learning materials more than doubling.

One of the first examples of gamification being used to change employees' behavior, the Ford experience really turned heads. It started firms and consultants alike thinking about how they, too, could use these techniques. Gamification began to spread, and its use broadened, too. It is now used to support activities such as the adoption of new processes, collaboration and knowledge sharing, and innovation and process improvement. We have even seen it used to encourage people to use expense systems correctly.

Does It Work?

There is no doubt that some of the early headlines about gamification were overhyped, effectively positioning it as a solution to all problems. There is also no doubt that in the rush to use gamification, it has not always been accompanied by a strong understanding of how it works. But overhyping and poor implementation should not mask the fact that there is some pretty solid evidence that when gamification is done well it *can* be a highly useful and effective tool for behavior change.

Indeed, there is a strong bed of academic research that shows that gamification techniques can have a significant positive effect on people's level of engagement with particular activities (Hamari et al. 2014a). This should not really surprise us, since, although the gamification movement is relatively new, it is founded on century-old research and tried-and-tested methods that date back to the earliest behavioral psychology experiments (see Chap. 2).

There is also a growing collection of case studies demonstrating the real-life impact of gamification. Consider the global telecommunications firm T-Mobile. In 2013, it gamified a collaboration tool used by customer service staff to share knowledge and identify solutions to customer requests (T-Mobile's employee community collaborates to transform customer service n.d.). As a result, it saw a 96% increase in the use of the tool and a 583% increase in contributions, which in turn led to a 31% improvement in customer satisfaction scores. Or take the e-commerce company NextJump. In an attempt to support healthy behavior in employees, NextJump installed gyms in all its offices and then gamified them, creating competition by enabling employees to form teams and chart their team's progress on a leader board. As a result, 70% of NextJump's employees now regularly work out (Mulvey n.d.).

There is enough evidence, then, to show that gamification *can* work. To see how we can use gamification, though, we first need to understand *how* it works.

How Gamification Works

If we use the language of habits, then gamification works by creating reinforcers for behavior. It introduces elements into people's experience of doing something that make them more likely to do that thing again. And it achieves this in two main ways. These ways are not entirely distinct and often overlap, but the difference between them is important.

First, it creates and uses *extrinsic* motivators: rewards and sometimes punishments, too—the carrots and sticks that we discussed in Chap. 4. In gamification, these are often self-imposed. People will nominate a reward to receive when they achieve something, or indeed a punishment for themselves should they fail (such as a donation to charity). Sometimes, the rewards are created for them. The awarding of points is a type of reward, as is the giving of badges or promotion to different levels. The training for the Six Sigma approach to process improvement is a good example of this, in which "belt colors" reminiscent of martial arts are earned for increasing levels of training, up to the rank of "black belt." Reward can also come in the form of public recognition of success, which is why many gamification processes try to connect people and create an audience for progress and achievements.

The second way gamification works is by targeting the three sources of *intrinsic* motivation we described in Chap. 3: autonomy, mastery, and connection. Autonomy is reinforced by helping people track their progress and so see the impact of what they do: It gives them a sense of control (Coleman 1971). The desire for challenge and mastery is tapped into by setting goals, recognizing achievements, and creating a sense of competition. And connection is created by simply linking people to one another. For example, the online app Lift has focused on creating a community of people who can encourage and support one another. There is a good reason for this, too, because social factors such as coaching and public recognition have been found to be strong predictors of how well gamification processes are received and the degree to which users intend to continue using them (Hamari and Koivisto 2013).

The reason this difference between the two ways gamification works—using both intrinsic and extrinsic motivation—is important in that one of the reported weaknesses of gamification is that it may be subject to what researchers call *novelty effects*. In essence, the longer people use a gamified process, the less strongly they seem to enjoy it and benefit from it (Koivisto and Hamari 2014; Farzan et al. 2008; Hamari 2013; Hamari et al. 2014b). And this seems particularly true for gamification based purely on rewards and punishments. They only work for so long. This does not mean that this type of gamification is not useful, because frankly anything that can improve someone's chances of repeating a behavior in the early days of trying to build a habit is valuable. If the effect of gamification lasts only a few weeks that is fine, as long as it is enough for the habit to become established. But having said that, gamification that targets, builds, and reinforces intrinsic motivation is generally more sustainable (Simoes 2012).

Three Rules for Using Gamification

Taking the above into account, along with what we have already learned in previous chapters about extrinsic rewards and intrinsic motivation, we can lay out three basic rules for using gamification. Let's look at them now before we explore the tools and techniques you can use.

Rule 1: Only Use Gamification if People Want to

Research shows that gamification only works if people are open to using it. For example, a Wharton School of Business study looked at gamification's impact on employee attitudes and job performance at a technology startup (Mollick and Rothbard 2013). It found that people who consented to or embraced the gamification had good feelings about their job and improved their performance. Those employees who did not consent to it, however, ended up having negative feelings about their job and showed a slight decline in performance. So if you have an idea about how to gamify a change that someone is trying to make, always check with them first whether they are open to it and are willing to give it a go. Because if they are not, imposing it could do more harm than good.

Rule 2: Set Good Goals

Gamification provides support when people's intrinsic motivations, willpower, or resilience are not quite enough. In light of this, it tends to be used to help people change behaviors that they know they can and should change, but which they might otherwise put off doing or not persevere with long enough to change.

As a result, one of the most common scenarios in which it is used in business is to encourage people to read mandatory HR or compliance training materials: stuff that they know they should do, but are not really interested in or do not see how it is relevant to their day-to-day work. Typically, points and badges are awarded for completing the materials, which seems like an "easy win," since it promises to spur people to action and ensure the material is completed. Unfortunately, there is a problem. If people do not enjoy the material or see no purpose to it, gamification is not going to change that. Some people might be sufficiently motivated by the points and badges of the gamification, but many will not be. So completion rates may go up a bit, but gamification can only do so much if you do not have a good goal or activity.

This is especially so when trying to gamify a behavior change for specific individuals. If they have no motivation to change or do not feel able to achieve it, gamification is unlikely to work. So Rule 2 is simple: set a good goal, which people care about and feel is possible.

Rule 3: Gamify What Matters to People

One of the consequences of our first rule is that you need to know what matters to people, what motivates them. There has been some research into the kinds of things that motivate different types of people, but beyond the general finding that women tend to be motivated more by social activities, there are no hard and fast rules (Hamari et al. 2014c). So there is no shortcut: In order to find out what matters to people, you need to ask them.

One way of approaching this conversation is to use the model of intrinsic motivation we described in Chap. 3 (autonomy, mastery, and connection) to explore what types of activities and behavior motivate people most. Depending upon what you find, it can change which gamification techniques you use.

If it is *autonomy* that matters most to them, you can give them a sense of control over the change process by letting them design how to gamify it. For example, they can choose what their own rewards or punishments will be, set their own timelines, and choose other people to give them feedback on progress.

If it is challenge and *mastery* that matters most to people, you can use techniques such as tracking progress, marking achievements, and creating competition. (We will look at these in a minute.)

And if it is *connection* that matters most to people, you can use more social connection and narrative techniques. (Again, we will look at these later.)

Another way to approach this conversation is to think about what types of gamification will most motivate particular people. This is exactly what games designers do: They think about who will play the game and what types of games they enjoy most. One of the first people to recognize this was the British game designer and researcher Richard Bartle. Looking at what appealed to people who played video games, he described different types of players (Chou 2013b). For example, there are *Achievers*, who like to accumulate points, awards, and other concrete measurements of success, and there are *Killers*, who thrive on competition and enjoy interacting with other players and developing a reputation.

Bartle's categorization is not the only one and other people have come up with different lists of motivation types. Furthermore, Bartle's categorization

'Player' Type	What They Enjoy About Gamification	Main Type Of Motivation	Consequence For Gamification Design
Achievers - Consumers	Collecting rewards. Getting something tangible back for their efforts	Extrinsic: Rewards and punishments	Use rewards and punishments plus techniques that track progress and mark achievements
Free Spirits	The ability to choose, be in control, and design their own path forwards	Intrinsic: Autonomy	Involve them in gamification design. Offer them choices
Explorers	Progress and achievement	Intrinsic: Mastery	Use techniques that track progress and mark achievements
Socializers	Social connection	Intrinsic: Connection	Emphasize social connection techniques

Fig. 9.1 Gamification player types

was for video games, not gamification. But it serves to remind us that what motivates people varies. Taking his model as a starting point, we can apply it to gamification (see Fig. 9.1) (Chou 2013b). The results may be similar to using only the model of intrinsic motivation, but it provides a different way of approaching the conversation about what matters to people.

Which Methods to Use

These, then, are three simple rules that will help ensure that when you gamify a process it works. Now you need to know which methods to use.

Fig. 9.2 Five gamification methods

There is no room in a single chapter to describe all these methods in detail, so we are going to focus on five of the most relevant: tracking progress, marking achievements, competition, social connection, and narrative (see Fig. 9.2).

Tracking Progress

One of the most common gamification methods is tracking progress, enabling people to see how they are doing. It reinforces self-belief by showing people what they have accomplished so far. It appeals to their sense of mastery by showing how far they have to go. And it can reinforce willpower by reminding them of the need for progress. As we noted in Chap. 1, tracking progress is something that people should be doing anyway. That is why almost every gamification process includes some element of tracking. What gamification can do is to add a flourish to *how* you track progress and there are two techniques you can use here.

Tracking Technique #1: Points Systems

Most games use points of one sort or another to track progress. They create a way to see how far you have come and act as a kind of reward. Behavior change apps using gamification have largely followed suit, too. The Recyclebank app, for example, rewards people with points every time they recycle something. It has contributed to a 16% increase in recycling in the American city of Philadelphia, has over 100,000 fans on Facebook, and over 2 million members globally. Sometimes the points awarded—once you have enough of them—can be redeemed for prizes or rewards. But points do not always need prizes to work, since research shows that just seeing points accumulate can be enough to motivate some people (Cunningham 2012).

If you think that someone is an *Achiever/Consumer* or an *Explorer* and thus likely to be motivated by seeing points accumulate, you can easily create a simple system. For instance, consider the manager we worked with who was trying to ensure that he got out of his office more, walked the floors, and made himself available to his team. We suggested that he stick a simple piece of paper on his wall next to his computer monitor with a 10 by 10 grid on it. Every time he left his office and spontaneously spoke to his team he got to mark a cross in one of the 100 squares on the grid for each team member he spoke with. It was simple and low-tech, but for him it worked.

We have worked with accountants who prefer to track points on a spreadsheet, and IT people who have written their own small program to do so. No matter how you do it, though, using points of some sort or another is likely to be a key element in any gamification design as it provides a way to track how much or how often someone is actually doing the new behavior they wish to develop.

Tracking Technique #2: Progress Bars

The second and related technique here involves creating a way to visually show progress. In games, this is typically done with progress bars (see Fig. 9.3).

The use of these visual aids usually goes hand-in-hand with points systems. The idea is to create a visual reminder of how far people have come and how far they still need to go. The 10 by 10 grid we mentioned earlier is a simple example of how to do this. As with the points system, it does not need to be high-tech and you are likely to be surprised how much impact a simple visual aid like a progress bar can make.

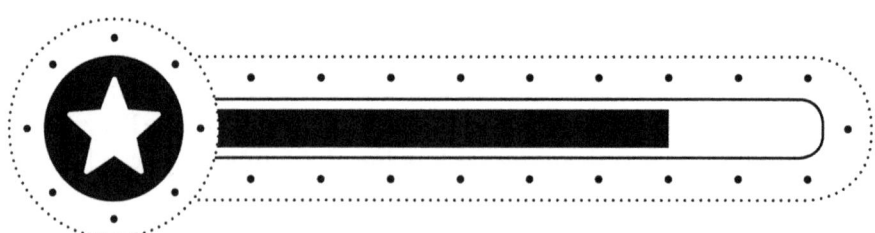

Fig. 9.3 A simple progress bar

Marking Achievements

Just as tracking progress is one of the basic building blocks of gamification, so is marking achievements. In video games, this is typically done by awarding badges or prizes. When you mark an achievement you are effectively rewarding someone for having done something, thus reinforcing their self-belief and making them feel good about their progress.

It may sound simple, but it works

It may sound simple, but it works. For example, a few years back Kaplan University decided to test whether gamification could have an effect on the motivation levels of students in higher education. It started giving badges to people as a visual marker of achievement and found that the students rewarded with these badges spent 155% more time actively engaged in classes than those who were not rewarded (Shane 2013). Obviously, employees might respond to different types of markers than students, but the principle is the same.

Before we look at some of the different ways you can mark achievements, we would like to highlight an important tip for using them. Make sure that what you are marking is genuinely an achievement. Imagine if you joined the army and immediately had a medal pinned on your chest that said, "Joining the Army Medal!" And the next day, you got another that said, "Completed My First Day Medal!" You would probably not feel that rewarded or accomplished, and the same holds true for recognizing accomplishments in behavior change. Make sure your markers genuinely mark something. With that in mind, let's look at the two main types of marker you can use.

Marking Technique #1: Tangible Markers

The most common type of marker used in behavior change processes with individuals is a tangible reward: something of real value to the person. This could be a cupcake or—as an extreme example—it could even be a car. A number of online gamified apps designed to support behavior change use this type of marker as one of their key techniques. They ask people to specify a goal, a reward they will give themselves if they achieve this goal, and a third party who can act as a referee and confirm whether the goal has genuinely been met or not.

It is not only tangible *rewards* that can be used, either. As strange as it may sound, punishments can also be used as markers. Consider the technician we worked with who wanted to try to read more in order to stay up-to-date with the latest developments in his field. We agreed a series of activities and goals with him, identified which of the more challenging ones we were going to mark, and then asked him to nominate a reward for each. These rewards were to be items that he would buy himself if he achieved these goals within a set timeframe. There was a twist to this agreement, though: We also asked him to agree that if for any reason he failed to achieve a particular goal, he would not buy himself the reward item and would instead pay half the value of the item to a charity that he disliked and did not support.

We talked a lot about how to use rewards and punishments in Chap. 4, and do not want to repeat it all here. Suffice to say, many gamification processes include tangible rewards that are given when targets are met and punishments that are applied if they are not. Asking individuals to nominate what they use as a reward or punishment is essential, since it helps reinforce their sense of choice and autonomy, vital for intrinsic motivation. This is particularly important for punishments, too, because imposed punishments tend only to breed a sense of unfairness.

Marking Technique #2: Symbolic Markers

In one sense, every marker of achievement is a reward. But some—like the badges given to students—are of no real, tangible value. They are more symbolic than anything else, more about recognition than reward.

The single best example of this is the gold star stickers given to children in kindergarten to recognize good behavior. They have no real prize-like value, but children can still become intently focused on how many stars they are getting.

In the workplace, one online app that tries to replicate this use of symbolic markers is Achievers. It provides a simple tool that allows managers to recognize the work of their people. Managers are provided with a pot of points from which they can distribute recognition points to their employees. This recognition can then be shared on social platforms like Facebook, Twitter, and LinkedIn.

Or consider Clarisse, a service center manager who was trying to improve the levels of customer service offered by the center's staff. New training was provided and key performance indicators put in place. Working with Clarisse, we developed a series of "levels"—particular titles—that people were awarded as they completed the training. Those who were only starting out were called *trainees*, those who had completed everything were called *champions*, and there were four other levels in between. Just as with the gold stars, these levels conferred no monetary value, but they did give people recognition and status. We actively reinforced this, too, by making it genuinely tough to make it all the way up to *champion* level. One year later, Clarisse told us that, thanks to all the measures put in place, customer service scores had improved significantly. And perhaps most interestingly, becoming a *champion* had come to be something that was aspired to by the service center staff.

Another way we have seen the same technique used is with companies such as IBM, which has used it to encourage senior technical staff to help train more junior people. They are given titles to recognize their contribution, and it has been so effective that having a title at IBM has become a status symbol. So, markers do not have to be tangible rewards.

Challenge and Competition

The third main type of gamification method directly targets the motivational drive of mastery by playing to people's desire for challenge and competition. Naturally, this is not a motivator for everyone, but for many—if not most—it will be. As a gamification method, creating challenge and competition is almost always combined with both tracking progress and marking achievements. Progress needs to be tracked to show how well someone is doing, and then once they have completed a challenge or competition, their progress is reinforced by marking the achievement.

Creating challenge and competition is fairly simple, and there are two key techniques you can use.

Challenge Technique #1: Targets and Tasks

A simple way to create challenge is through targets, tasks, and missions. Like all good goals, they need to be clear and specific if they are to work well. And, ideally, they should involve increasing levels of difficulty. For example, working with an ambitious young finance controller called Amr, who lacked confidence in presentations, we set up a series of challenges. First he had to do a presentation for his wife and seven-year-old son. (Including the son may sound strange, but we have found it a great teaching technique for presentation skills: After all, if you can keep a seven-year-old engaged, you can keep most other audiences engaged, too!) Then he had to present to us. Next, he presented to his team, then to his boss, and finally to a group of colleagues. In each presentation, his audience was asked to rate him as a presenter. If he scored under 8 out of 10, he had to repeat the presentation. Only after being rated 8 or above was he allowed to move on to the next step. With each step, the presentations became longer and more formal. And after he successfully completed each step, we marked the achievement with a small reward that he had chosen beforehand.

Challenge Technique #2: Comparison Points

The second way to create challenge and competition is by using a comparison point. You rate someone's performance at a particular activity compared with other people's. This is a favorite technique of online apps that seek to encourage environment-friendly behaviors. The app Opower, for instance, compares individual's consumption to that of their friends and neighbors. Benchmarks like this allow people to reevaluate how they are doing and can encourage a sense of competition.

For managers trying to help individuals change particular behaviors, there are two easy ways to use comparison points. First, you can simply refer to them. For example: "You know, when I think about how your peers do at this, I think they tend to do A and B better." You can also combine this with the rating scale questioning technique that we showed in Chap. 4: "When I think about how well you do this compared to your peers, I think you are performing at around 6 out of 10 and they at around 8. To step up to a 7, I think you need to do X and Y."

The second thing you can do is to use individuals as their own comparison point. For instance, consider Lěi, a director we worked with, who, like the technician we mentioned earlier, wanted to read more. Every month, *Harvard Business Review* and other magazines arrived on Lěi's desk, and every month they ended up getting filed without being read. Knowing that he was strongly competitive, we tried to create some competition for him. We did this by asking Lěi to record how many articles he read and to keep track of two metrics: the highest number of articles read in a single week and the average number. His task each week—and the competition—was not to read a particular number of articles, but just to increase the average. In fact, for Lěi, the average became his focus and the driver of his behavior, rather than the reading.

One final notable way of using comparison points is in leader boards. It does not really apply if you are working with a single individual to change a particular behavior, but when you are helping a whole team, leader boards can be useful. They are common to almost all video games. Both during and after a game, players are shown not only a points total for their performance but also how far up a league table their points total would be placed. One factor to be aware of is that there has been some criticism of leader boards, most notably that they can be demotivating if you are not at the top. So care needs to be taken with them, but in some circumstances and with the right group of people (competitive and resilient), they can be useful.

Social Connection

The fourth main gamification method you can use is to create social connection. It is a point we have made repeatedly in previous chapters, but trying to change in the dark—in isolation or when no one can see what you are trying to do—makes accomplishing the change more difficult. There are two reasons for this. First, knowing that other people are involved and can see us, helps us maintain our focus on what we are trying to achieve. It keeps us true to our objectives. Second, most people like to be connected—they prefer doing things with other people. This is why video games have become increasingly social. They encourage players to share their performance with their social networks and try to connect them to other people who are playing the game and have been struggling to overcome similar game challenges.

There are three techniques you can apply to gamify behavior change by using social connection.

Social Connection Technique #1: Publicly Share Achievements

When you publicly share achievements, praise, and other rewards, you make them more powerful. Some people can become embarrassed by public praise, but do not let this deter you. Making it public gives it more impact.

Social Connection Technique #2: Connect People for Support

Earlier, we described how you can connect people through comparison points to create competition. But people can also offer support. You can do this through "buddy systems," in which you ask someone to be a kind of coach or mentor for an individual trying to change a behavior. In one small business we worked with, the boss created a strong focus on behavior change by using a buddy system combined with a "leveling system" that marked people's achievements as buddies. Everyone trying to change a behavior was given a buddy to support them and whenever a buddy helped someone successfully change a behavior, the buddy was promoted to a higher level. Level one buddies were called *first buddies*, with level five ones being called *veteran buddies*. In effect, not only did the boss create a mechanism for providing social support to people trying to change behavior but he also encouraged people to take part by gamifying it with achievement markers.

Another common way of connecting people is to create groups and forums. In one business unit we worked in, where we were coaching several people to change various behaviors, we created a behavior change working group. Everyone who was working on a change was invited to a 30-minute meeting once every two weeks. This allowed people to share their objectives and progress and to discuss challenges.

Social Connection Technique #3: Group Quest

A final technique here is to use what video game designers call *group quests*. This involves binding the success of different individuals together. We know one leader, Jess, who every year asks her team to commit to one behavior change. Once objectives have been shared and agreed, she announces a prize that she will give to the whole team if—and only if—every single team member succeeds in the behavior change. This can be extremely powerful when working with groups, especially if it is combined with other approaches such as progress tracking and a buddy system. For instance, the same leader tracked people's progress in their various behavior change objectives and then publicly displayed this progress on a large sheet of paper on the office wall. This showed—in rough 10% increments—how close to achieving a behavior change each team member was. Once people reached 100%, they could still slide back down to zero if they stopped the new behavior, and in this way she created a focus not only on changing but also on staying changed.

Narrative

The fifth and final main gamification method we will look at is also perhaps the simplest. Most video games these days start with some sort of narrative or story that gives players some context about *why* they should play the game. Many of them seem to revolve around saving the world, solving a case, or even just helping a flock of very angry birds protect their eggs. Some of the stories can be extremely elaborate and game designers put a great deal of effort into developing them. Why? Because people like stories and—all things being equal—games with stories tend to be more engaging than those without.

Understanding this, the online gamified app SuperBetter uses narrative to help users boost their resilience and recover from setbacks. It achieves this through a rather unique story system. The app packages behavior change attempts into the elements of a super-hero story, with obstacles and challenges positioned as "bad guys" or "villains" that need to be defeated if a player is to win. It also seeks to bring people together as a means of social support. Users are encouraged to invite friends, colleagues, and other members of the SuperBetter community to become their "allies," who then assist in keeping them motivated with encouragement and by creating new targets or "quests" for them.

This kind of approach will obviously not suit everyone. But it can be very powerful to play to people's inner, intrinsic motivation for meaning and connection by placing their behavior change within a simple narrative. For instance, when discussing changes that people want to make, we always try to place them within a timeline story. We discuss how they have come to want to make this change now, at this point in their careers. We discuss how they have behaved in the past, and how they want to behave in the future. This is all very simple, and you may not even think of it as narrative, but it is using exactly the same technique as the fantasy story in the SuperBetter app. It is placing the behavior change within a bigger story.

Using Gamification

We have presented a number of different methods and techniques here, so where should you start? We would suggest simply going through the five main methods one by one. Check whether you can *track the progress* toward people's behavior change goals; look at whether you can *mark achievements*; think about how you can encourage a sense of *challenge and competition*; try to *connect* people; and create a broader *narrative* for the change. And, wherever possible, try to combine methods, as combinations tend to work better.

Gamification provides us with a very different approach to creating a supportive environment for change. And as you have read this chapter, hopefully many of the methods and techniques will have seemed familiar. In fact, unless this is the first chapter you are reading, they should do. This is because gamification pulls together many of the elements we have talked about in previous

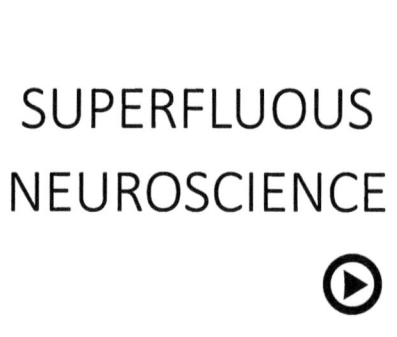

Video Fig. 9.1 Superfluous neuroscience (▶ https://doi.org/10.1007/000-ak6)

chapters. Most of the methods work by boosting people's motivation. Some support people's ability by making tasks easier, and others can act to reinforce people's self-belief, willpower, and resilience. And almost all of them act as reinforcers for creating habits. In this sense, gamification is like a supporting web that binds all these other factors and elements together.

Having explored habits and gamification, we will now look at one last approach to creating a supporting environment. It has recently generated even more noise and impact than gamification, and it has the potential to make managers completely rethink their role in helping people change behavior: It is called nudging.

For brief reflections on the content of this chapter, new to the second edition, see Video Fig. 9.1.

Key Questions to Ask Yourself

1. Is the individual open to gamification?
2. Are their goals truly intrinsically motivating?
3. Do you understand what drives the individual and which aspects of gamification, if any, are most likely to appeal to them?

Further Resources

- Jessie Schell's 2010 presentation *Design Outside the Box* is probably the single most cited and watched video about gamification and is available on YouTube.
- Karl Kapp (2014). *The Gamification of Learning and Instruction Fieldbook: Ideas into Practice*. Chichester: John Wiley & Sons.

References

Chou, Y. (2013a, June). The 8 core drives of gamification (#2): development and accomplishment. Retrieved August 15, 2014, from http://goo.gl/FwngCw.

Hamari, J., Koivisto, J., and Sarsa, H. (2014a, January). Does gamification work? A literature review of empirical studies on gamification. In *System Sciences (HICSS), 2014 47th Hawaii International Conference on* (pp. 3025–34). IEEE.

T-Mobile's employee community collaborates to transform customer service. (n.d.). Bunchball. Retrieved August 15, 2014, from http://goo.gl/k3jjQ7.

Mulvey, J. (n.d.). How gamification is changing health promotion campaigns. *Redbird*. Retrieved August 15, 2014, from http://goo.gl/CrUyD.

Coleman, J. S. (1971). Learning through games. In E. M. Avedon and B. Sutton-Smith (Eds.), *The Study of Games* (pp. 322–5). New York: John Wiley & Sons.

Hamari, J. and Koivisto, J. (2013). Social motivations to use gamification: an empirical study of gamifying exercise. In *Proceedings of the 21st European Conference on Information Systems*, Utrecht, Netherlands, June 5–8, 2013.

Koivisto, J. and Hamari, J. (2014). Demographic differences in perceived benefits from gamification. *Computers in Human Behavior*, 35, 179–88.

Farzan, R., DiMicco, J.M., Millen, D.R., Dugan, C., Geyer, W., and Brownholtz, E. A. (2008, April). Results from deploying a participation incentive mechanism within the enterprise. In *Proceedings of the SIGCHI Conference on Human Factors in Computing Systems* (pp. 563–72). ACM.

Hamari, J. (2013). Transforming homo economicus into homo ludens: a field experiment on gamification in a utilitarian peer-to-peer trading service. *Electronic Commerce Research and Applications*, 12(4), 236–45.

Hamari, J., Koivisto, J., and Sarsa, H. (2014b, January). Does gamification work? A literature review of empirical studies on gamification. In *System Sciences (HICSS), 2014 47th Hawaii International Conference on* (pp. 3025–34). IEEE.

Simoes, J. (2012, November). How gamification can drive behavioural change. *Gamifeye*. Retrieved August 15, 2014, from http://goo.gl/QAVLcA.

Mollick, E.R. and Rothbard, N. (2013). Mandatory fun: gamification and the impact of games at work. *The Wharton School Research Paper Series*.

Hamari, J., Koivisto, J., and Sarsa, H. (2014c, January). Does gamification work? A literature review of empirical studies on gamification. In *System Sciences (HICSS), 2014 47th Hawaii International Conference on* (pp. 3025–34). IEEE.

Chou, Y. (2013b, June). User and player types in gamified systems. Retrieved August 15, 2014, from http://goo.gl/NBGlX8.

Cunningham, T. (2012). How to make your brands playful to draw more customers. *Miami Herald Blog*. Retrieved August 15, 2014, from http://goo.gl/vJ9gwG.

Shane, K. (2013, July). Kaplan's gamification system shows 155% more student engagement. *Gamification Corp*. Retrieved August 15, 2014, from http://goo.gl/2tr1IS.

10

Nudging

Nudge (verb)
   to touch or push (someone or something) gently
   to push (someone) gently with your elbow in order to get that person's attention
   to encourage (someone) to do something
   Merriam-Webster Online English Dictionary

One of your authors works in a tall building. OK, so maybe it's not tall, but it has four floors, and first thing on a Monday morning or at the end of a long hot day, it can certainly *feel* like a tall building when you climb the stairs. Tiredness can make four floors seem like ten. Your author, though, does not get much exercise during the day, so he makes a conscious effort to walk up those stairs, every day, no matter how tired he feels. And he keeps doing this, despite the fact that every day he watches most of his colleagues making a different choice and taking the elevator instead. Or at least, they used to, because one day he decided to replicate a classic experiment in *nudging* (Burger and Shelton 2011).

In the first week, he simply recorded how many people took the stairs and how many the elevator. The next week, he placed a sign by the elevator that read "Taking the stairs is a good way to get some exercise," and checked to see

---

Supplementary Information The online version contains supplementary material available at https://doi.org/10.1007/978-3-031-29340-5_10. The videos can be accessed individually by clicking the DOI link in the accompanying figure caption or by scanning this link with the SN More Media App.

if more people would take the stairs. They did not. The sign seemed to make absolutely no difference to the number of people taking the stairs. So, in the third week, he placed a different sign saying "Most people use the stairs," and again he counted how many people walked up them. This time, nearly 50% more people took the stairs. He had not directly asked them to, there were no incentives or rewards for doing so—they had just been *nudged* to do so.

Climbing Stairs: An Alternative Nudge

To see an alternative, elegant, and downright fun way of nudging people to climb stairs, Google "Stockholm station stair nudge" and watch the two-minute video you find. It is well worth the watch.

What Is Nudging?

Nudging is a phrase commonly used to describe the techniques for changing behavior emerging from the field of behavioral economics. The word came from an influential 2008 book called *Nudge: Improving Decisions about Health, Wealth, and Happiness*, which looked at how indirect suggestions, incentives, and information could be used to influence people's decisions about how to behave (Sunstein and Thaler 2008). Building on research into how people make decisions and choices, the book was interested in how small and subtle changes to the environments in which people live could affect those choices and thus their behavior. Indeed, that's a good definition of what a *nudge* is: a feature of the environment that influences the choices people make without coercing them (Sunstein 2014).

For a good example of a nudge, just go into any shop. The way companies try to make product packaging attractive in order to encourage us to buy is a nudge. The way shops price items at $9.99 rather than $10, in order to make them sound cheaper and thereby influence our decision to buy, is a nudge. And the way they put chocolate in clear sight by the checkout, knowing that we are more likely to buy some if they do this, is also a nudge. Marketers are experts at nudging.

Research into nudging has primarily focused on how to nudge large groups of people—whole societies, in fact. And its techniques have been taken up by a number of governments, interested in how to help citizens eat healthier food, use energy more efficiently, and pay their taxes on time. But nudging is not just about large-scale behavior change. Its focus on people's decisions about how to behave means that nudging can provide us with techniques to help specific individuals change behavior, too, because *every* change in behavior involves a decision of some sort.

For someone to change a behavior, at some point—consciously or unconsciously—they have to *choose* to do so. It may not be a long thought-out decision; They may not even be aware of making it. But a decision is made: to take the lift or take the stairs; to wear a seatbelt or not; to have another piece of cake or just a coffee. And when they are trying to change a behavior, people usually have to make the decision more than once. In fact, they tend to have to make it time and time again, because before a new behavior becomes a habit, it usually requires conscious effort.

For example, consider Kaito, an experienced leader we were coaching on how to listen more to what others were saying before leaping to judgments. When he was first trying to change this behavior and turn it into a habit, he had to consciously remind himself and make a deliberate effort to listen more every day. This is where the science of nudging can come to our aid, by helping to make this decision making easier through something called *choice architecture*.

Choice Architecture

As organizations have come to realize the power of nudging, they have become interested in the techniques that can be used to achieve it. Efforts to increase healthy eating and safety behavior in employees using nudging are becoming increasingly common in organizations. Take Google and its work to encourage employees to eat more healthily (Kuang 2012):

- Research shows that the amount you eat is affected by the size of plate you use (Kallbekken and Sælen 2013), so Google put up a sign in some of its cafeterias informing people that they would eat less if they used smaller plates. As a result, the use of small plates rose by over 30%.
- Studies show that people tend to order or fill their plates with whatever they see first (Dayan and Bar-Hillel 2011; Thorndike et al. 2012). So Google makes sure the first thing they see is the salad.

- It made the sweets in its cafeterias less visible, partially hiding them in opaque containers, which resulted in a drop of nearly 10% in the amount of sweets bought.
- Bottled water is now stored at eyelevel in coolers, whereas soda has been moved to the bottom of the coolers, and this has increased water intake by nearly 50%.

Changing Shopping Habits

One of your authors once had a bad habit (or at least a habit that his wife viewed as bad). Whenever he went to his local supermarket to buy just one or two items, he almost always came back with bags full of shopping. Knowing that it irritated his wife, and aware of the research showing that using smaller plates leads to less food being eaten, he decided to try to nudge himself to change. He started using a basket at the supermarket, rather than a big trolley, and sure enough, the number of items he bought decreased. A simple change, perhaps, but it stopped his wife being irritated with him, and that was no small thing.

The term that behavioral economists use to describe these kinds of small changes to the environment in order to influence people is *choice architecture*. And there are three important factors you need to know about it.

First, context is unavoidable. Every decision about how to behave occurs in a context of some sort. Astronauts floating in space may seem to be operating in a complete vacuum, with nothing around them to influence their choices. But the voice of Houston Control on the radio, the capabilities of their spacesuit, and the fact that they are floating around in a gravity-less, air-less vacuum are all influences on how they behave. So every decision you make occurs within some sort of choice architecture.

Second, whether or not you notice it or realize it, context always influences you in some way. It may only affect you a bit, but there will be some kind of impact. For example, ask voters whether their choice of who they vote for is influenced by factors such as the order in which candidates are presented on the ballot sheet and they will almost all say no. Yet research shows that the order in which you encounter options invariably affects your choice. On a ballot sheet, you are more likely to select a candidate at the top of a voting list than one in the middle or at the bottom. In fact, candidates at the top of a list are likely to poll up to 5% more votes than if they are in the middle of a list—regardless of their policies (Gwynne 2010). The context in which you make choices always affects your decisions to some degree.

Finally, the key consequence of the previous two points is that whether you know it or not, and whether you like it or not, *you are* a *choice architect*. As someone's manager, peer, or even direct report, you have some degree of control over elements of the environment in which they are trying to change their behavior. You are able to make changes to the choice architecture. And that makes you a choice architect. The only questions are how deliberate you will be about it and how effective you will be in helping them change.

Five Types of Nudges

In the rest of this chapter, we are going to show you five key nudging methods that you can use to help people change behavior (see Fig. 10.1). Each of them involves making some kind of change to a person's environment with the aim of influencing their choices about how to behave.

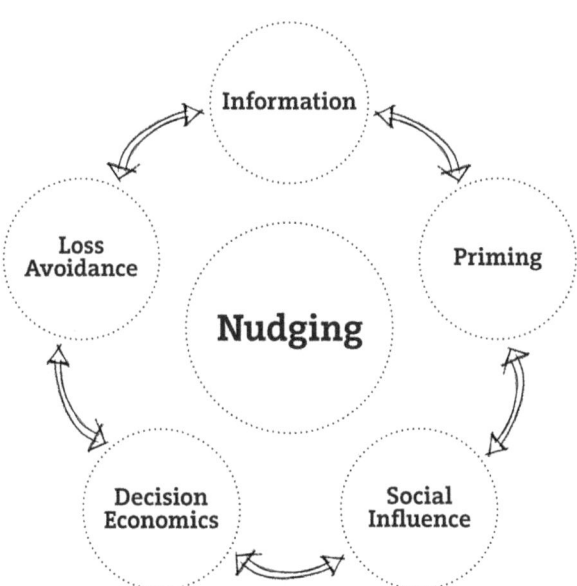

Fig. 10.1 Five types of nudges

Providing Information

Perhaps the simplest form of nudging is providing people with information. Indeed, you are probably already using the most common type of informational nudging—feedback. It provides people with information about their impact and how they are performing, which—in theory at least—leads to changes in their behavior and thereby improvements in their impact and performance.

We are not going to dwell on how to provide people with information because there is plenty written about that elsewhere. But we do want to briefly highlight two simple techniques that you can use to nudge people toward decisions about how to behave that will support any change they are trying to achieve.

Information Technique #1: Costs and Benefits

Possibly the most basic nudge is to remind people of the costs and benefits of different courses of action. Look at any pack of cigarettes in the United States or the United Kingdom and you will see precisely such a nudge, because on each and every packet there is a warning about the risks of smoking to your health. In a similar vein, researchers have found that using UV photographs that show individuals the existing (but not currently visible) damage to their skin from sun exposure can increase the degree to which people subsequently use protective sun cream (Mahler et al. 2008). Being reminded of the consequences of your actions focuses you on what you do.

Using this technique is easy. Returning to the example of Kaito we mentioned earlier, who was trying to develop the habit of listening more to those around him, we asked him to draw up a list of the costs and consequences of not listening. He then carried it around with him, and before each meeting, he made sure to read it. (Or, to put it in terms of the habits research in Chap. 8, the beginning of each meeting was his *cue* to read the list, which acted as a prompt to remind him of what he needed to do.)

One possibly counterintuitive thing to be aware of here is that reminding people of the costs of the behaviors they want to stop or replace seems to be more effective than reminding them of the benefits of the new behavior they are trying to adopt. We will return to this later. For now, it is enough to note that although we live in a world in which we are told that we should be positive, for most people, avoiding costs is a better motivator to action than gaining benefits.

Information Technique #2: Framing

The way you present information to people can have a significant impact on how they choose to act on it. The technical term for this is *framing*. In a classic experiment first conducted in 1982, researchers looked at the number of patients electing to have a particular operation after they had been given information about survival rates. They found that when patients are told that nine out of ten people who have the operation are alive after five years, they are more likely to have the operation themselves than when they are told that one out of ten dies within five years of the surgery (McNeil et al. 1982). Mathematically, the odds of them surviving are exactly the same whether 90% live or 10% die. But the way the information is presented has a big impact. And it is not only patients who are fooled by this. More recent research has found that even experts such as doctors are more likely to recommend the operation when they are told that 90% survive it than when informed that 10% do not (Tversky and Kahneman 1981).

So one aspect you need to think carefully about is how you are presenting information and the impact this may have. For example, to return to the example of Kaito, the leader who was trying to listen to others more, a key issue for him was confidence. Deep down, Kaito did not really think he could change. So we made sure to frame the changes he was trying to make as minor adjustments to his style rather than fundamental changes. And whenever we reviewed feedback on his progress with him, we always made sure to emphasize the positive. Working with another individual, who was extremely ambitious and a perfectionist, we did the opposite and focused more on the occasions when she was not doing things perfectly and how she could improve.

Priming

If providing information is the most basic type of nudging, priming is the most subtle. It involves placing cues in someone's environment that can subconsciously influence their behavior. The objective is to try to nudge people toward behaving in a certain way. This may sound a bit manipulative, but stick with us, because it need not be.

Consider sidewalks or pavements. They are designed to keep pedestrians safe. But recent studies have cast doubt on whether they really do help keep people safe. As strange as it may sound, researchers have found that when sidewalks are removed to create "shared spaces" for pedestrians and cars to use, the number of accidents decreases ("Riskier" streets reduce accidents 2012). The reason, it seems, is that removing the sidewalks creates a feeling of greater danger among drivers and pedestrians alike, which results in everyone being more alert and driving and walking more carefully. The design primes them to be careful. Examples of priming are plentiful:

- Placing a picture of an eye next to a bicycle rack reduces the theft of bicycles (Nettle et al. 2012).
- Playing German music in a supermarket increases the amount of German wine people buy (North et al. 1999).
- Showing people pictures of classrooms and school lockers increases the likelihood that they will subsequently support a school funding initiative (Kahneman 2011).
- Including a photo of a pretty girl on leaflets advertising loans increases the number of people applying for loans (Bertrand et al. 2009).
- Showing people lists of words that describe the elderly leads them to subsequently walk more slowly (Bargh et al. 1996).
- People report less pain after taking a painkiller when they are told that it cost $2 than when told it cost 20c (since they associate cost with quality) (Sunstein and Thaler 2008).
- People eat more when food portions are called "small" or "medium," and believe they have eaten less (Aydinoglu et al. 2009).
- Adding adjectives such as "succulent" or "homemade" to food packaging leads people who eat the food to report that it is both tastier and more filling (Wansink et al. 2005).
- And, to finish on a more business-related example, getting the CEO in a company to introduce a new initiative means that people are more likely to view it as important.

So, priming is a powerful tool. But how can we use it to help change people's behavior? Here are three examples of when we have used it that we hope will provide some inspiration.

Priming Technique #1: Priming Commitment

A recent, fascinating study has shown that people will respond more honestly when completing insurance claim forms if they are asked to sign the form at the beginning rather than at the end (Shu et al. 2012). There is something about writing your signature at the beginning of the form, confirming that the information in it is true, that primes you to respond more honestly.

So we built on this. When working with individuals who are trying to change their behavior in some way, we always encourage them to write out an action plan, which specifies what they are willing to commit to doing. We get them to sign it, their manager to sign it, and an HR representative to sign it. We have now started asking people undertaking a behavior change to sign the form at the beginning rather than the end (the witnesses—their manager and HR—still sign at the end). At the time of writing, we have not yet completed a full study into the impact this has on what people write in their action plans. But early indications are that they are more cautious in the number of actions they commit to, suggesting greater care being taken and potentially greater commitment to the actions they do include.

Priming Technique #2: Priming Openness

How much thought do you give to how meeting rooms are laid out when you walk into them? Just a table with some chairs, isn't it? Well, it may not be that simple. For example, researchers have shown that people given hard chairs to sit on take a tougher stance in negotiations than people given soft chairs (Sunstein and Thaler 2008). And any psychotherapist will tell you that if you want someone to be open with you, you should sit on chairs without a table between you.

Working with the leader who was trying to listen more to others, we explored with him how part of the problem had become that he had a reputation for not listening and so people tended to be less open with him. To try to counter this and prime people to be more open with him, he redesigned a meeting room to remove the table and include comfy chairs.

We also worked with a CEO who felt that his top team were too comfortable with one another and not challenging enough. So he replaced the soft leather-bound chairs in the boardroom with plainer, harder seats. And sure enough, feeling uncomfortable, people stopped acting comfortable and started questioning more.

Priming Technique #3: Priming Confidence

Researchers have shown that exposing students to lists of positive words can result in them working harder, longer, and with more motivation (Sunstein and Thaler 2008). This is why in some offices firms deliberately replace the pictures and other artwork with lists of positive words. Before you rush out to replicate this, however, we should note that the degree to which it works is heavily context dependent. For example, positivity—as a technique—tends to work far better in the United States than in Europe.

You can use this technique on a smaller scale, though, when working with individuals for whom confidence is a challenge. It is simple: Just pepper your conversations with positive words. It may sound contrived, but it works surprisingly well.

Social Influence

If providing information is the most basic type of nudging, and priming the most subtle, social influence is probably the most powerful. There are two main types: social norms and peer pressure.

Influence Technique #1: Using Social Norms

A social norm is a belief about how people should behave in particular situations. One of your authors is English, and for him it is a social norm to open doors for other people, in particular when he reaches the doorway first. But he also does a lot of work in Arab countries, where the social norm is to let people standing on the right walk through the doorway first. Both behaviors are examples of social norms, and although they may be subtle, they can be powerful influences on behavior.

There are two main types of social norms. Injunctive social norms tell us about how we *should* behave—about what is acceptable and unacceptable behavior. In most cultures and jobs, for example, it is not acceptable to turn up to work late. Descriptive social norms, by contrast, tell us how most people actually behave (Mahler et al. 2008). A good example is the sign outside the elevator described at the beginning of this chapter. The statement that "Most people use the stairs" set out a descriptive norm. It is worth noting here that it does not matter how many people in fact use the stairs. What matters is how many you *think* use them. Even if only a small number of people use the stairs in reality, if you think that most people use them, then that is the descriptive social norm for you.

Simply understanding what the social norms are around us and that influence us can be useful. For instance, consider Nastya, a manager who had repeatedly been given the feedback that she was "too confrontational," but who seemed unable to change her behavior. While exploring with her the reasons for her persistent style, we discovered that Nastya had inherited a family norm for how to discuss issues: loudly and with vigor! And once armed with this understanding of her behavior and how it clashed with the organizational norm for how to debate issues (which was far more reserved), Nastya was able to adopt a more open and objective approach to changing it.

As the elevator example shows, however, social norms can also be employed more actively to help modify behavior, because it seems that simply providing people with information about how others behave can exert a strong influence on their behavior. One of the most famous examples of this came in 1995 from the Minnesota Department of Revenue (Coleman 1996). Interested in finding a way to get more people to file their tax returns on time, it started including special messages on the tax return letters sent to individuals. One letter, which was sent to a random selection of 20,000 taxpayers, included a message that made a rational argument for paying taxes on time. It advised people of the services funded by taxes and the negative impact caused when they were not paid on time. Unfortunately, it made no difference to the number of people filing their tax returns on time. The second message, however, which was sent to a different group of 20,000 randomly selected taxpayers, included descriptive social norm information, along the lines of "Most taxpayers file their returns accurately and on time." And this message *did* have an impact, resulting in significantly more people filing their returns on time.

More recently, the UK government's Behavioral Insights Team took this nudge a step further by including special personally tailored messages in the letters sent to taxpayers reminding them to pay their taxes on time. This message told individuals the proportion of people in their local area that had already paid their taxes (usually a high figure). The information was accurate and genuine and drawn from real payment figures. Sure enough, rates of payment rose significantly. It seems that knowing that 90% of your neighbors have paid on time makes you more likely to do it, too (Hallsworth et al. 2014).

Other studies from around the world have shown that communicating descriptive social norms in this way can help modify all sorts of behaviors. Providing information that most people do not drink alcohol and drive can reduce drink-driving (Hellstrom 2014). Telling hotel guests that most other guests reuse their towels can make them more likely to reuse their towels, too (Schultz et al. 2008). And displaying signs advising that most people do not litter can cut littering in public settings (Cialdini et al. 1990). Moreover, studies show that not only are these descriptive social norms powerful but they are also more influential in changing behavior than most other types of information, such as feedback on performance or advice on the costs and benefits of particular behaviors. We are a social species and what other people think matters to us.

So how can you use social norms to help people change behavior? In exactly the same way: by simply asking or telling them what the descriptive social norms are. For instance, working with the leader who had received feedback that he was too confrontational, we would often either ask him what he thought most other people would do in particular situations or we would tell him, "What most other people do in similar situations is this…" This is a particularly helpful method if you are working with someone who wants to get better at something, but is unsure about how to do so.

Social norms can also be powerful when trying to change the behavior of everyone in a team. Consider the manager of a sales team who was tired of his team leaving the office kitchen in a mess. What particularly irritated him was that they left dirty coffee mugs sitting on the kitchen counter rather than putting them in the dishwasher. He had tried asking them again and again to stack the dishwasher, but with little impact. So at the next team meeting he lied, telling them how grateful he was that people were increasingly putting their coffee mugs in the dishwasher. At the same time, he took a lead from the priming research and put up a picture of two eyes in the kitchen. The week after, he put up a sign saying, "80 percent of people in this office put their used coffee mugs directly in the dishwasher." And sure enough, people started doing just that. There were always some people who did not clean up after themselves, but very soon 80% of people really did tidy up their dirty mugs.

A related technique here is to get a team to collectively agree to change their behavior—and thus create a new social norm. Studies show that this is more powerful than asking team members individually, especially when they are not convinced about the wisdom of a new practice (Raymond et al. 2013). With this in mind, the boss of Kaito—the leader who was trying to learn to listen more—decided to support him by gathering the whole team together and telling them that he wanted them all to become better at listening. He got the whole team to agree a set of standards or rules for listening—effectively new social norms. And in doing this, the boss was using not only social norms, but also the second major type of social influence: peer pressure.

Influence Technique #2: Peer Pressure

Most people care about how others view them. Their reputation matters to them. So one basic form of social influence that you can create around a behavior change intervention is peer pressure. To do so is simple. When Kaito's boss asked Kaito and his peers to all become better at listening, we reinforced this by asking both Kaito's peers and his direct reports to give him feedback every time they felt he was not listening. This not only gave him useful feedback but also created a kind of peer pressure for him to alter his behavior.

A second way of harnessing peer pressure is to create visibility about people's progress. We touched on this point in Chap. 9 when we talked about gamification, but it is worth repeating: Making performance levels and progress public can help drive change. In 1998, Los Angeles County introduced hygiene quality grade cards to be displayed in restaurant windows. As a result, restaurant health inspection scores improved, consumers' awareness of restaurant hygiene increased, and hospitalizations for food-borne illnesses decreased (Jin and Leslie 2003). Thus, while feedback and measuring performance can help, making them public makes them far more powerful. This is why you will often hear coaches asking people to share their development plans and behavior change goals with their team or other colleagues. It may not always be appropriate, but if it is, then you should encourage it because making things public creates pressure and thereby helps change happen.

Decision Economics

Behavioral economists may study behavior, but they are still economists at heart. This is particularly clear in our fourth type of nudge, which follows classic economic arguments. Economists see all choices and behavior as having both benefits and costs. Going to watch your son or daughter play soccer at the weekend costs you time and perhaps a bit of boredom, too, but with luck, it delivers the benefit of enjoying seeing your child play and the feeling of doing something together.

In order to encourage the adoption of a new behavior, it is important to make the economics of the behavior change work. People do not literally think about how to behave in terms of economics, of course. But when choosing how to behave, they *are* influenced—consciously or unconsciously—by the costs and benefits of the options. And when we say costs, we do not mean only monetary costs but also elements like time and effort.

For instance, studies have repeatedly shown that one way of getting people to eat more fruit and vegetables and to drink more water is to make them easily accessible (Cullen et al. 2003). For example, as the Google experiment mentioned earlier showed, displaying healthy foods conspicuously in a cafeteria increases their consumption, and putting water on the table, rather than 20 feet away, increases water consumption (Thorndike et al. 2012). In other words, if you want people to do something, you need to make it easy for them. Or at least, not difficult.

For behavior change to work, a new behavior needs to have more benefits or lower costs than the old behavior. And an added complication here is that people tend to focus on immediate, short-term costs and benefits, rather than on long-term ones. Take the leader who was trying to adopt more listening behaviors. The long-term benefit waiting for him was happier staff and possibly better decisions, but there was a short-term cost in his way—namely, the fact that listening took time and patience, neither of which he had much of.

With this in mind, there are three techniques you can employ to make the economics of behavior change work in a way that makes change more likely to happen.

Decision Technique #1: Make New, Desired Behaviors *Less* Costly

The first thing you can do is to carefully consider what the costs of a new, desired behavior might be and then try to reduce them. The costs may not always be obvious, but they are always there. Everything has a cost. Once you know what the costs are, though, reducing them is usually merely a matter of problem solving.

For an example of this, let's return to Kaito—the leader we described earlier who was trying to listen more. He was not a patient man and he was very busy. So we gave Kaito a script—a standard sentence—that he used in meetings both to encourage other people to speak on an issue and to limit the amount of time and patience required for him to listen to them. The sentence was, "I want to know what you think about this. We don't have much time, though, so I need you to tell me briefly. What are the headlines I need to know?" By placing a limit on their response in this way, it made it easier for Kaito to ask them and focus on what they were saying.

Decision Technique #2: Make Old, Undesired Behaviors *More* Costly

The flip side of making new, desired behaviors less costly is to make old, undesired behaviors *more* costly, which is usually much harder to do and also typically less effective. Yet one easy way of doing this is to ask people to comment, giving negative feedback, whenever someone acts out an old, undesired behavior. This is actually a type of punishment, so you need to be careful about using it, since punishments can often cause more resentment than anything else.

Decision Technique #3: Increase the Benefits of New, Desired Behaviors

The last aspect to consider is making a new behavior seem more beneficial and attractive by rewarding people for behaving in this way. We have already covered this in some detail in Chap. 4 where we discussed extrinsic motivation, so will not repeat it here. But we nonetheless wanted to list it here, as it is an important tool in decision economics. It also leads us into the last major type of nudge that we are going to look at: the curious case of loss avoidance.

Loss Avoidance

The fifth type of nudge we are going to consider is our rather strange approach to loss. In 2010, two groups of randomly selected Chicago school teachers were asked to participate in a pay-for-performance program. The first group was told that they would receive traditional bonuses at the end of the year, with the amount of the bonus being determined by student achievement. The second group was paid a lump sum in advance and was told that they would be asked to give back the money if their students did not meet certain performance targets. Which group do you think performed better?

It was the second group, the one that was paid upfront and told that they would lose the money if they did not perform well (Fryer Jr et al. 2012). The results of this experiment confirmed a classic, but perhaps surprising, finding from behavioral economics research: that avoiding losses can be a stronger motivator than receiving rewards.

Here's another example. In a wonderfully named 2008 study ("Put your money where your butt is"), smokers who were trying to stop smoking were asked each week to put the money they would have spent on buying cigarettes into a special savings account (Giné et al. 2010). They were told that after six months they would have to take a urine test to check whether they had smoked or not. If the drug test proved that they had succeeded in stopping smoking, they would get all the money back in a lump sum, but if it showed that they had smoked, they would lose all the money.

Just as with the pay-for-performance teachers, this loss-avoidance nudge helped motivate people, with smokers in the scheme more likely to succeed in quitting cigarettes than those who did not participate. Simply put, people hate losses. In fact, studies show that losing something makes people twice as miserable as gaining the same thing makes them happy (Sunstein and Thaler 2008).

People hate losses

As a manager trying to support people in modifying behavior, being aware of people's loss aversion gives you a powerful lever for change. So let's now look at some examples of how you can use this method.

Loss Avoidance Technique #1: Spot Bonuses

For one easy example of using loss avoidance, consider Maggie. She managed five direct reports and each year set aside $500 to support their development. When her people wrote their annual development plans, she agreed with each of them one particular behavior that they wanted to change. Maggie then gave them a $100 on-the-spot bonus and told them that if they succeeded in modifying that behavior, they could keep the money. If they failed, however, they would need to give it back at the end of the year.

In our experience, presented with this kind of deal, the majority of people work hard to avoid giving money back. You may have to adjust the amounts for different populations. Traders, for example, may need more than $100 to motivate them. But in general, you would be surprised how little the loss needs to be to motivate people.

Loss Avoidance Technique #2: Preemptive Praise

A closely related technique is to use nonfinancial losses. We once worked with a leader called Carlos, who did something very similar to Maggie, in that he agreed with each member of his team one particular behavior that they wished to change. But rather than paying them upfront, Carlos praised them upfront. He publicly announced what each individual had agreed to do in a team meeting, praised them for it, and got the whole team to applaud them for agreeing to change the behavior. Afterward, he made it clear to each individual that he would only comment on it again publicly if they failed to change the behavior.

Loss Avoidance Technique #3: Use Technology

One final tool you have at your disposal is to suggest to people that they use one of the online apps now available that seek to help people change behavior using loss avoidance as a lever. One such example is StickK.com. It is simple to use. You specify the behavior you wish to change, say how much money you wish to commit and then appoint someone to act as a referee. If the referee agrees you have changed the behavior, you get your money back. If not, the money goes either to the referee, a charity or what StickK.com calls an *anti-charity*—an organization you hate.

Pulling It All Together

Over the course of the last three chapters, we have explored how the external environment within which people are trying to change their behavior can affect how successful their efforts to change are. We have also seen just how much you—as someone's manager—can do to adjust this environment to give people a better chance of changing.

Whether it is creating a structure for people's attempts to make, break, or change a habit, applying gamification to make activities as engaging as possible, or nudging people to adopt certain behaviors, there is almost always something you can do to make change more likely to succeed. In fact, over the course of just the last three chapters we have looked at over 40 different techniques you can use.

Video Fig. 10.1 A quick thought on social norms (▶ https://doi.org/10.1007/000-ak7)

What the behavioral economics of nudging, in particular, encourages us to do is to think of ourselves as *architects* of this external environment, as people who have power to do things to it that can make behavior change easier. So in Chap. 11, we will look at how to pull together all the different elements of the MAPS model, and how to choose which of the many techniques in the book to start with. We will look at how to become an architect of change.

For brief reflections on the content of this chapter, new to the second edition, see Video Fig. 10.1.

Key Questions to Ask Yourself

1. What information could you provide the individual that might affect their decisions about how to behave?
2. Are there any situational cues that would prime the individual to behave in the desired way?
3. What are the social norms for the desired behavior? How are they different to how the individual is currently behaving?
4. What are the current costs and benefits of the desired behavior? How could adopting the desired behavior help the individual avoid losing something?

Further Resources

- Richard Thalerand Cass Sunstein (2008). *Nudge: Improving Decisions about Health, Wealth, and Happiness*. New Haven: Yale University Press. This is the book which launched behavioral economics into mainstream government policy.
- Steven Levitt and Stephen Dubner (2007). *Freakonomics: A Rogue Economist Explores the Hidden Side of Everything*. London: Penguin. See also Levitt's TED talk The freakonomics of crack dealing on TED. com with subtitles in different languages. And if you are interested in the behavioral economics approach and way of thinking, there is a regular *Freakonomics* podcast, too.

References

Burger, J.M. and Shelton, M. (2011). Changing everyday health behaviors through descriptive norm manipulations. *Social Influence*, 6(2), 69–77.

Sunstein, C.R. and Thaler, R. (2008). *Nudge: Improving Decisions about Health, Wealth, and Happiness*. New Haven: Yale University Press.

Sunstein, C.R. (2014). Nudges and public policy. *Behavioural Exchange*. Retrieved August 12, 2014, from http://bx2014.org/sites/bx/media/255.pdf.

Kuang, C. (2012, March). In the cafeteria, google gets healthy. *Fast Company*. Retrieved August 12, 2014, from http://goo.gl/KF9M7.

Kallbekken, S. And Sælen, H. (2013). "Nudging" hotel guests to reduce food waste as a win–win environmental measure. *Economics Letters*, 119(3), 325–7.

Dayan, E. and Bar-Hillel, M. (2011). Nudge to nobesity II: menu positions influence food orders. *Judgment and Decision Making*, 6(4), 333–42.

Thorndike, A.N., Sonnenberg, L., Riis, J., Barraclough, S., and Levy, D.E. (2012). A 2-phase labeling and choice architecture intervention to improve healthy food and beverage choices. *American Journal of Public Health*, 102(3), 527–33.

Gwynne, P. (2010) First among equals. *Kellogg Insights*. Retrieved August 12, 2014, from http://goo.gl/0O6OE3.

Mahler, H.I., Kulik, J. A., Butler, H.A., Gerrard, M., and Gibbons, F. X. (2008). Social norms information enhances the efficacy of an appearance-based sun protection intervention. *Social Science & Medicine*, 67(2), 321–9.

McNeil, B.J., Pauker, S.G., Sox Jr, H.C., and Tversky, A. (1982). On the elicitation of preferences for alternative therapies. *The New England Journal of Medicine*, 306(21), 1259–62.

Tversky, A. And Kahneman, D. (1981). The framing of decisions and the psychology of choice. *Science*, 211(4481), 453–8.

"Riskier" streets reduce accidents. (2012, April). *Open* Knowledge. Retrieved August 12, 2014, from http://goo.gl/6IWA5S.

Nettle, D., Nott, K., and Bateson, M. (2012). "Cycle thieves, we are watching you": impact of a simple signage intervention against bicycle theft. *PlOS one*, 7(12), e51738.

North, A.C., Hargreaves, D.J., and McKendrick, J. (1999). The influence of in-store music on wine selections. *Journal of Applied Psychology*, 84(2), 271.

Kahneman, D. (2011). *Thinking, Fast and Slow*. New York: Farrar, Straus and Giroux.

Bertrand, M., Karlan, D.S., Mullainathan, S., Shafir, E., and Zinman, J. (2009). What's advertising content worth? Evidence from a consumer credit marketing field experiment. Yale University Economic Growth Center Discussion Paper, (968).

Bargh, J.A., Chen, M., and Burrows, L. (1996). Automaticity of social behavior: direct effects of trait construct and stereotype activation on action. *Journal of Personality and Social Psychology*, 71(2), 230.

Aydinoglu N.Z., Krishna, A., and Wansink, B. (2009). Do size labels have a common meaning among consumers? In A. Krishna (Ed.), *Sensory Marketing: Research on the Sensuality of Products* (pp. 343–60). New York: Routledge.

Wansink, B., Van Ittersum, K., and Painter, J. E. (2005). How descriptive food names bias sensory perceptions in restaurants. *Food Quality and Preference*, 16(5), 393–400.

Shu, L.L., Mazar, N., Gino, F., Ariely, D., and Bazerman, M. H. (2012). Signing at the beginning makes ethics salient and decreases dishonest self-reports in comparison to signing at the end. *Proceedings of the National Academy of Sciences*, 109(38), 15197–200.

Coleman, S. (1996). The Minnesota income tax compliance experiment: State tax results. *Minnesota Department of Revenue*. Retrieved August 13, 2014, from http://mpra.ub.uni-muenchen.de/4827/.

Hallsworth, M., List, J.A., Metcalfe, R.D., and Vlaev, I. (2014). *The behavioralist as tax collector: Using natural field experiments to enhance tax compliance* (No. w20007). National Bureau of Economic Research.

Hellstrom, D. (2014). Reducing Risk: The Prevention Collaborative's Positive Social Norming Campaign. Conference presentation at the National Conference on the Social Norms Model, July 17, 2003, Boston, MA.

Schultz, P.W., Khazian, A.M., and Zaleski, A.C. (2008). Using normative social influence to promote conservation among hotel guests. *Social Influence*, 3, 4–23.

Cialdini, R.B., Reno, R.R., and Kallgren, C.A. (1990). A focus theory of normative conduct: recycling the concept of norms to reduce littering in public places. *Journal of Personality and Social Psychology*, 58, 1015–26.

Raymond, L., Weldon, L., Kelly, D., Arriaga, X. and Clark, A.M. (2013). Making change: norms and informal institutions as solutions to "intractable" global problems. Submitted to *Political Research Quarterly*, January 29.

Jin, G.Z. and Leslie, P. (2003). The effect of information on product quality: Evidence from restaurant hygiene grade cards. *The Quarterly Journal of Economics*, 118, 409–51.

Cullen, K.W., Baranowski, T., Owens, E., Marsh, T., Rittenberry, L., and de Moor, C. (2003). Availability, accessibility, and preferences for fruit, 100% fruit juice, and vegetables influence children's dietary behavior. *Health Education & Behavior*, 30(5), 615–26.

Fryer Jr, R.G., Levitt, S.D., List, J., and Sadoff, S. (2012). Enhancing the efficacy of teacher incentives through loss aversion: a field experiment. *National Bureau of Economic Research*, Working Paper, No. w18237.

Giné, X., Karlan, D., and Zinman, J. (2010). Put your money where your butt is: a commitment contract for smoking cessation. *American Economic Journal: Applied Economics*, 2(4), 213–35.

11

Becoming an Architect of Change

OK, so you have read most part of this book. Now what? There are over a 100 tools and techniques in it in total, so where do you start? How are you going to use them? What are you going to do differently because of them? What is actually going to change?

Rachel is the head of talent management for a big global pharmaceutical firm. Speaking with her the other day, we asked her how often she thought the company's talent development programs really worked, how often people really did accelerate their development. "Not often," came the reply, "and when it does work and people do develop, what makes it work is them. The individual. They find a way to drive their development."

This experience and perception seems to be a common one: When attempts to change and develop succeed, it is because the individual concerned somehow manages to make it work. They want it more, they try harder, or they are just more capable. This is why most development programs emphasize the role and responsibility of the individual in making change happen. And to be clear, we agree with this. A lot of the responsibility *does* lie with the individual: some people *are* more driven to learn than others, and some *are* more capable of changing and developing, too. So, yes, individuals matter and need to play their part.

Yet in many—if not most—companies, this emphasis on the individual has not been balanced by a similar focus on what organizations and managers need to do to help change happen. And they should be focusing on this, because the research shows—undeniably and unequivocally—that organizations and managers have a significant impact on whether change and development succeed.

The part they play—the responsibility they have—is to create a context in which change stands a decent chance of working. And to be fair, this has not been completely ignored. After all, most companies these days make sure that goal setting happens and that development plans are written. Of course these are both important and necessary, because poor goals and poor planning will kill change stone dead, but there is more to context than goals and plans. And in this book we have tried to show you what that something more is and what you—as a manager—can do about it.

In doing so, we are issuing a call to action, a plea for some measure of attention. We are advocating and arguing that you need to take charge of this broader context, start paying more attention to it and shape it. We want *you* to become an architect and builder of the context for change.

Using the MAPS Model

As a manager, as someone who is asking, encouraging, or supporting an employee to change, your first task is to help them explore the issue, identify objectives, and set goals. And when we say goals, we mean specific behavior changes. This is exactly what most coaching models are designed to help you do, and you are probably already doing it. But if you add our MAPS model to the mix, you can significantly improve the success rate of people's attempts to change behavior.

As we suggested in Chap. 1, the MAPS model fits in after goal setting, but before any action plan is written (see Fig. 11.1).

As we have seen, the MAPS model describes four key elements of the context for change: motivation, ability, psychological capital, and supporting environment. Each of the four is important, and if any one of them is missing or lacking, it can fundamentally undermine the chances of the desired behavior change succeeding. So, part of your task as a manager is to check how strongly each MAPS factor supports any change goals. Remember, too, that this should ideally be done *with* individuals and in conversation with them,

Fig. 11.1 Using MAPS

so that you obtain their perspective on each of the factors and also so that they feel they are driving the change.

One way to do this would be to ask individuals some general, exploratory questions. A complete list of questions to ask can be found in Appendix A, but prompts for the four basic questions are:

1. How motivated is the individual to achieve the goal? How do any rewards and punishments in place support their motivation?
2. How able are they to achieve the goal? Can you, as their manager, make it easier? Or at least seem easier?
3. How strong are their self-belief, willpower, and resilience in terms of achieving the goal?
4. To what degree does the environment around them incentivize, encourage, and nudge them to behave in this way and turn the new behavior into a habit?

A second approach—which we prefer—is to produce a *MAPS profile*, by plotting the level of support provided by each factor on a graph (see Fig. 11.2 for an example). Creating a profile is quick and easy, and it helps both you and the individual visualize what needs to be done. For instance, with the example in Fig. 11.2, you can immediately see that the individual has plenty of motivation and ability, but worryingly low levels of psychological capital and a work environment that does little to support the change.

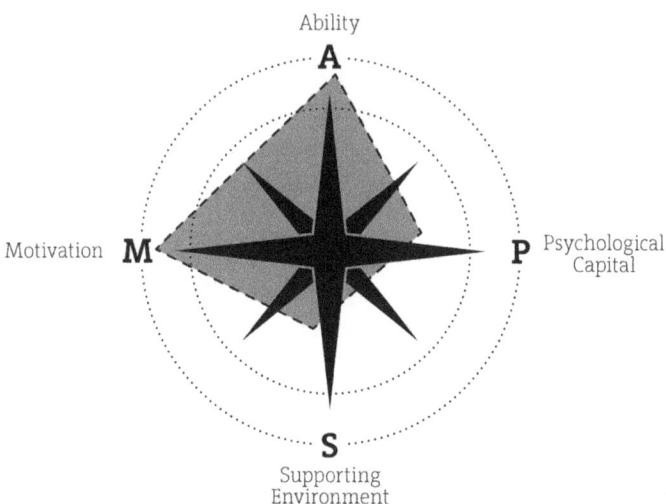

Fig. 11.2 Plotting MAPS

To help you produce MAPS profiles, in Appendix B you will find a brief profiler tool, a set of 16 ratings-based questions to ask about each of the four factors (e.g., "On a rating scale of 1 to 10, how much intrinsic motivation for this goal does the individual have?"). The tool shows you how to add up the answers to produce a score for each of the four MAPS factors, and you can then plot these scores on the blank MAPS profile graph in Appendix C. Alternatively, on the book's website—www.changingemployeesbehavior.com—you will find both an online version of this brief tool, which will produce a profile graph for you, plus a more comprehensive profiler tool.

You need to change the way you do action plans

Once this checking has been done—and only once it has been done—can action planning really begin. And this is where we get to probably the single most important thing you need to do in order to use the MAPS model and make sure someone's context supports change. *You need to change the way you do action plans.*

A typical action or development plan consists of four standard columns: what someone is trying to change, what specific actions they will take to change this, when they will take these actions, and how they will follow up and monitor progress. What needs to be added to this typical action plan is what *you*—as a manager—will do to support the behavior change through the four MAPS factors. There are a number of ways you could do this, but probably the easiest would be to add an extra column to the standard action plan (highlighted in Fig. 11.3).

This is probably as simple as it can get, and some may see it as too simple, or too little. For those who want something a little more comprehensive, there is a more detailed type of plan shown in Fig. 11.4. Free templates of both this and the simpler plan are available on our website. No matter how you do it, though, it is vital that the action plan *requires* people to think about the MAPS factors and account for them.

Is this extra work for you, as a manager? Yes, it is. We do not want to pretend otherwise. But it also means that change will be far more likely to happen. Few things are as dispiriting, cynicism-promoting, and timewasting as failed attempts to change behavior, so spending the extra time and effort getting it right is worth it.

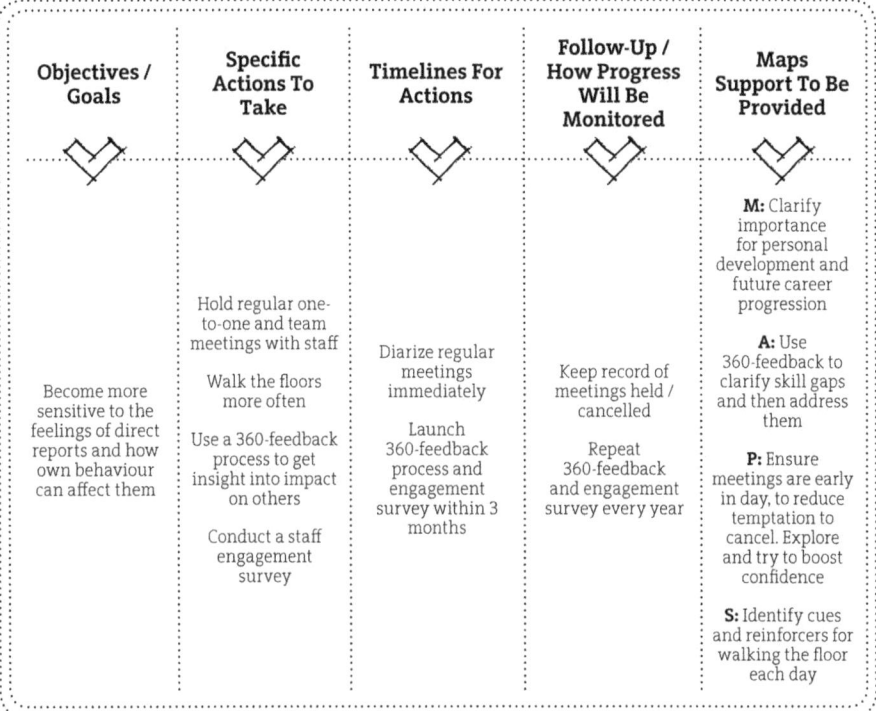

Fig. 11.3 Simple action plan with MAPS

What You Are Creating

The fact that bookshops are stuffed full of how-to-change books is evidence of just how much people want to change and feel they need help. The research showing that most training and development courses fail to translate into real, sustained behavior change only serves to reinforce this. And the persistently low satisfaction levels that business leaders are reported to have with the effectiveness of their learning and development functions is further proof—if proof were needed. Change is tough.

Yet change is also a core and critical part of your job as a manager, helping people to develop and improve at what they do. In fact, it is more than that—more than simply another task. It is a key part of your legacy as a leader. When you move on to your next role or next business, what will be remembered is the imprint you left behind you: the difference you made to people and the organization. And helping people to change and improve is a critical aspect of creating such an imprint or legacy.

Fig. 11.4 Comprehensive MAPS action plan

There are no easy answers, no instant results, of course. But by becoming an *architect of change* and actively and deliberately shaping the contexts in which people are trying to change, you can stack the odds in your and their favor and make change more likely. And by using the MAPS model, you are effectively giving yourself a bigger toolkit.

You are also making for a more collaborative type of behavior change, one that says, "Part of this is your responsibility, but part of it is ours, too. You do your bit, and we will do ours." This does not in any way reduce individuals' responsibility for driving their own development. It merely acknowledges that they—like everyone else—may need some help and support. In fact, in our experience, being clearer about what the challenges in changing behavior really are, and what everyone's roles in meeting them are, creates greater visibility on why change does or does not happen and thereby greater accountability for making the change work.

In this book, we have tried to provide you with practical tools and techniques that you can use to help change happen. We have also grounded them in brief overviews of four different approaches to change—behaviorism, cognitive psychology, systemic psychotherapy, and behavioral economics—so that you are better equipped to understand and shape the context for change. And we have provided a framework—the MAPS model—to help you navigate the tasks and challenges of being an architect of behavior change.

Throughout the book we have mainly looked at how to help individuals change, but the importance of context is just as true for helping teams, business units, and even whole organizations transform. Most of the techniques we have presented can be used at this level, and so the MAPS model provides a way to approach these larger-scale behavior changes, too.

Remember, too, that everything we have talked about in this book, all the techniques to help other people change, are just as applicable to you yourself. Changing employees' behavior begins with you—their manager—changing your own. Even if you are simply changing your approach to how you help them change, it begins with you and it is you who leads the way.

Make no mistake: what you—as a manager—do is critical

Make no mistake: what you—as a manager—do is critical and can make all the difference to whether individuals succeed in changing their behavior and in sustaining that change. Indeed, at the most fundamental level, above and beyond all the techniques and tools we have talked about, the key thing you can do and *have* to do is to *believe*. You need to believe that change is possible; believe in people's potential to change, develop, and improve; and believe in your ability to help them and make a difference to their efforts.

12

What We've Learnt

So, that was it. What you've read up to now was the original book. We left it as it was because there hasn't been any new research that has either contradicted what we wrote, or fundamentally changed our ideas about it. But the world *has* turned, time *has* marched on, and there *are* things we have learnt from both new research and our experience of applying the model, which have enabled us to build upon our original work.

This chapter and Chaps. 13 and 14 will explain what we've learnt. In this chapter, we're going to focus on new research into behavior change. In Chap. 13, we'll then explain how this research has led us to evolve what we focus on and do in organizations. And then, finally, there is a chapter that reveals our answers to some of the most common questions that we are asked by executives and managers about changing employee behavior and how best to apply the ideas in this book.

Before all this, though, we need first to briefly turn the clock back to 2020 and the COVID pandemic, because for many of us, it completely rewrote our expectations of change—about what is possible and what is needed to make it happen.

Lessons from the Pandemic

Perhaps the most obvious impact of the pandemic on our expectations of change was that for many observers—both academics and leaders—the speed with which change happened was shocking. We're not talking here about the imposed lockdowns so much, but about the responses that came after: the ways in which organizations and individuals had to rapidly transform what they did and how they did it.

There were the initial emergency issues of how to ensure continuity in the businesses that were still able to operate. Supply chains had to be reorganized, cash flows secured, and IT departments the world over had to perform miracles to enable a suddenly distributed workforce. And then, beyond all this, there were issues that emerged around how to adapt ways of working, run meetings, and keep people connected, all while avoiding *Zoom* overload and helping people manage the physical intrusion of work into their home lives. How, then, to support employees to remain effective, productive, and motivated while physically isolated in makeshift offices, sometimes in cramped conditions, and often with bored and frustrated children creating merry mayhem in the background.

Afterward, one thing we kept hearing was pride in leaders at just how fast they and their teams had been able to make some really quite radical changes. And the reverberation left by this is that many businesses and leaders now have higher expectations of just how much and how quickly change can be achieved.

There is something positive in this, in that for many firms changing how employees operate and behave is now more visibly on the table as an important strategic lever, in the same way that commercial strategy has always been. Balancing this, however, there were two other lessons from the pandemic that raised many leaders' awareness of just how difficult changing behavior can be.

The first of these lessons was the simple fact that people are different, their circumstances are different, and that to change their behavior often requires very different types of intervention and support. This was laid bare in the very first days of lockdown as the home environments of employees were suddenly made part of the workplace. Parents of young children, in particular, often struggled. We forget now just how many online meetings we had with leaders in which screaming children, barking dogs, and sometimes both, suddenly appeared in the background, seemingly intent on waging loud war with each other. For many parents, then, the change to homeworking was bigger and harder.

Then, as lockdowns lengthened, personality tended to come more into play, most visibly in the differences between how introverts and extroverts managed the change. Introverts tended to find working at home relatively easy, enjoying it even, but often found themselves exhausted by the social demands of seemingly endless online meetings. Many extroverts, meanwhile, found their motivation—and in some cases their mental health and happiness—strained by the physical isolation of lockdown.

In this way, the pandemic made clear one of the key challenges of changing people's behavior: that people and their contexts are different, and that although the overarching solution—such as homeworking—may be the same for all, the implementation needs to vary according to individual needs. This is something we stressed in the original book, but the pandemic suddenly and significantly raised awareness of it as an issue. As a result, many businesses have since turned to us to ask what this means for large-scale behavior change initiatives, such as culture shift programs. The challenge they now see in particular is how to implement widescale change programs in a way that supports individual needs. We'll explain how we have helped firms navigate this in Chap. 13.

The second, related, lesson from the pandemic about the challenges of change was just how important one particular type of individual difference is: psychological capital. Just as those early *Zoom* meetings laid bare people's home circumstances, the stress of the challenges of change also left many people's inner, psychological worlds on display for colleagues to see. Individual's optimism and resilience, in particular, came to the fore, affecting their ability to adapt and remain agile in the face of rapidly shifting work demands. Indeed, we saw the most reserved, private, and traditional leaders openly talking about their feelings, stress, and the importance of social connection in a way we had just not witnessed before. And as a result, many—if not most—firms started paying more attention to the emotional well-being of their people, and the importance of this for helping employees remain productive.

So, the heightened expectations of change that the pandemic brought were balanced by the suddenly more visible challenges of individual differences and psychological capital. In the best of worlds, the impact of this would have been an increased desire to support behavior change, coupled with a greater understanding of the challenges involved, which together would have produced more sophisticated change initiatives. And in some businesses, that has undoubtedly been one of the positive legacies of the pandemic.

However, not all organizations seem to have learned all the lessons of the pandemic equally. For we have noticed that some firms seem to have retained their greater expectations of change while having seemingly forgotten what COVID taught us about the challenges involved. This is dangerous, because the risk here is that more ambitious or stretching change programs are launched, but without the focus on MAPS required to ensure the programs are successful or that any change produced is sustained. In the wake of the pandemic, we have thus seen big one-size-fits-all performance and culture change programs launched, which take little account of the challenges and context involved, and that have therefore inevitably not had the impact desired. And, as is often the case, it is usually not the initiators of the program who take the blame, but those left trying to implement it—senior leaders, middle-managers, and employees themselves, who are accused of "just not getting it," or something similar. The result is not just a failed change initiative, but reduced motivation, impacted performance levels, and often increased cynicism and turnover, too.

Three New Findings

We will come back to how we believe businesses can best navigate these tensions between higher expectations of change and the challenges of actually doing it later, when we describe how our focus and work with businesses has evolved. But before we do so, we want to describe three key new research findings related to the MAPS model, which we believe reinforce the lessons from COVID and provide ideas for how to apply the MAPS model to the post-pandemic new normal now facing firms.

Finding #1: Motivation Is Even More Situational Than We Previously Thought

Motivation continues to be one of the most studied factors in behavior change. Some of our favorite research of the past few years has been the studies looking at the neurological basis of motivation—which parts of the brain are involved and how. But it is still early days in this research and so for the moment it has little in the way of practical implications for most of us.

There has also been some fascinating research showing that one of the reasons that intrinsic motivation tends to be more powerful than extrinsic reward is that people expect the outcome of an activity to be better when they are motivated by inner desire. As a result, they are more likely to then repeat these behaviors (Meng and Qingguo 2015). This is helpful because it suggests that reminding people of the positive impact of changing their behavior can be a powerful lever.

Yet these interesting nuggets aside, the real advance in motivation research has been the flurry of new studies showing just how much the effectiveness of intrinsic and extrinsic motivation depends upon the situation, the behavior being targeted, and the people involved. The constant refrain of this book has been that *context matters*, and what these studies continue to show us is just how much.

First, in the original book we explained how the use of external interventions such as targets and incentives can end up inadvertently decreasing people's intrinsic motivation for things. The implication was that only offering rewards for changing behavior, without also trying to evoke or appeal to someone's inner desire to change, could in the long run undermine their motivation for that change. New research, however, suggests that this isn't always true.

For example, there is evidence that when first trying a new behavior or activity, immediate rewards can actually boost people's enjoyment of it and thereby their intrinsic motivation to do it again (Wenzel et al. 2019). So, continued rewards may not help, but initially, on first trying something, a little reward can help.

There is also growing evidence that the nature of the task or activity involved can affect how successful different extrinsic motivators are. In complex tasks, for instance, financial rewards can be very effective and have little (or at least, far less) negative impact on intrinsic motivation. In simple activities, however, they are far more likely to damage intrinsic motivation. For praise and recognition, on the other hand, it is the other way around, in that they are most effective when used to reinforce simple activities than complex ones (Malek et al. 2020).

Similarly, the effectiveness of rewards can also be affected by the broader organizational culture. If a business is viewed as generally fair, for instance, then rewards tend to work better as extrinsic motivators of change, than in businesses that are thought to be less fair (Mikkelsen et al. 2017).

Finally, new research is also shedding further light on how extrinsic motivators can work better with some people than others. Specifically, there is evidence that one of the best indicators of how well someone is likely to respond to extrinsic motivators is how much they need to feel a sense of autonomy (Farzan et al. 2013). Studies show that people who have a high need for autonomy usually don't respond as well to extrinsic motivation as those with a low need for it. So, a quick way of working out how effective external motivators will be with any one person is to gauge their need for autonomy.

What each of these studies show, then, is that the effectiveness of any intrinsic or extrinsic motivator in helping someone change behavior is even more situational—and therefore more complex—than we originally thought. And the consequence of this for us is that there is just no getting round the fact that how you help motivate people to change their behavior needs to vary with every person in every situation. We all love rules of thumb—guidelines we can follow in most situations. But the evidence keeps mounting that when it comes to motivation at least, the more we rely on general rules, the more we're likely to get it wrong and not have the motivational impact we wanted.

Finding #2: Using Gamification Is Also More Complicated Than Previously Thought

In Chap. 9, we introduced a relatively modern approach to change called *gamification*. As it built upon many of the other ideas in this book—boosting people's motivation, reinforcing self-belief and resilience, and reinforcing habits—we suggested that it could be thought of as a kind of framework or structure that binds all these other factors together. And while acknowledging that it may not work for everyone, we suggested that managers could extrapolate five key techniques from gamification, which could be used to create a stronger supporting environment for change.

In the years that followed, research into gamification has moved at quite a pace, providing more detail in particular on three things: when it works, how it works, and when it doesn't.

First, there has been a steady stream of success stories, showcasing the benefits of gamification. Gamified apps such as step counters on phones have been used to motivate less physically active people to be more so. And gamification techniques have been used to successfully motivate a range of consumer behaviors, such as completing surveys and accessing new websites (Mollick and Rothbard 2014).

There has also been a raft of research shedding more light on how these techniques work. For example, just as with the new research into motivation, there is evidence that gamification—which mainly involves applying extrinsic motivators such as points, levels, and leaderboards—often works by increasing *intrinsic* motivation. For example, many gamification elements work by increasing feelings of achievement and competence, adding to the enjoyment of an activity and thereby increasing intrinsic motivation for it. So, these techniques may involve extrinsic motivators, but they often get their power from boosting how we feel inside about things. And it is this aspect of gamification—how people personally experience the elements of it—that has received the most attention from researchers.

In this vein, there have been studies showing that gamification techniques often work best with people who are competitive (Keller et al. 2021). Similarly, people who are more confident also tend to respond more positively to gamification (Lauren et al. 2016). Moreover, it isn't just that some people respond more positively, but that when applied in the wrong way or to the wrong people, gamification can actually lead to a decrease in motivation and performance. For example, one study showed that when people give their consent for gamification to be used, it can increase their enjoyment of tasks and thus their intrinsic motivation for them. However, when people do not want gamification to be used on them, but it is anyway, it can lead to a decrease in their enjoyment of tasks and thus a drop in their engagement and performance (Lauren et al. 2016).

What this all points to is two things. First, that when thinking about whether to use gamification techniques, taking individual differences into account is even more important than we thought. While it can undoubtedly be powerful, it isn't for everyone. Second, while gamification tries to create a supportive context for change to occur within, it is also affected by the context in which it occurs, too. So, just as with any technique, how it is introduced, talked about, and set up can be critical. Likewise, the broader business context is important as well. Just as with motivation, if people believe the broader business is not fair in how it treats people, then any gamification efforts are likely to be viewed with suspicion, and thus less likely to work (Perryer and Scott-Ladd 2016).

We have talked in the book about how the context in which change occurs is critical for whether change is successful or not. Well, in the same way, the context in which we use techniques to support change is also important for whether these techniques actually work, and this appears to be particularly true for gamification.

Finding #3: People Are Talking More About Change Maintenance

The third main body of research has involved a shift in focus away from how to change behavior toward how to maintain change. It is as if researchers have decided that changing behavior is the easy bit that anyone can do; and that it is maintaining a change where the real challenge lays.

For example, one recent study reviewed 117 theories about behavior change and from these pulled out five themes that academics have identified as critical levers for maintaining change. The first is obvious—making sure that people stay motivated. The second is resources—both psychological and physical. Next comes maintaining self-regulation or discipline. Then there is the formation of habits; and finally, there is social support (Kok et al. 2015). Keen-eyed readers will have already noticed that these themes bear a strong resemblance to our MAPS model. What is most interesting to us though is not so much that other researchers are coming to the same conclusion as we did, but that the language of 'change maintenance' is becoming mainstream.

We see this is our clients. Increasingly, we are being approached by both individuals and firms who have already made a change and being asked by them how they can best sustain it. For us, this feels like a hugely positive step forward. And it reminds us just how important it is to plan—right from the beginning—not just how to make a change, but how to keep it, too.

With this in mind, we have also seen useful new research focusing on which of the MAPS elements are most important for maintaining change. The most accurate answer to this question is of course that it depends upon the person and situation. But in trying to answer the question *in general*, academics have come to one of two conclusions. On the one hand, there has been a group of researchers who have pointed to the evidence showing how important motivation is, and concluded from this that the best thing that can be done to support change is to try to keep people's motivation for it high.

The second group, however, suggest a more cautious approach. Noting that individuals tend to start an attempt to change their behavior when their motivation for it is very high, the researchers suggest that it is therefore inevitable that over time, motivation will fall a bit—maybe not to zero, but certainly closer to the average for motivation. They thus argue that the problem with supporting motivation as a solution is that you could become trapped in forever having to do this. That it is only natural for motivation to rise and fall over time, and that any attempt to stop this is destined to be hardwork and ultimately to fail. The solution they suggest instead, therefore, is to focus on psychological capital—and willpower and confidence, in particular. For it is willpower, they have found, that keeps people going when their motivation dips; and it is confidence that seems to most determine whether a newly adopted behavior grows within the person, becoming applied in new and different situations.

For us, there is utility in both these approaches. Motivation for change can be extremely important in the early days, and regular top-ups—reminders of the importance and benefits can undoubtedly help. But in the long run, discipline, willpower, and resilience are what tend to keep people going.

A Common Thread

The central theme running through all this research has—to us, at least—been a reinforcement of our core argument: that individuals' internal and external contexts need to be supportive of a change in behavior for that change to succeed and be sustained. What events and research since we wrote the first edition of this book have mainly taught us is that however complex we thought this context was, it is even more so. Because year after year, new research has been published showing some new way in which people differ, and in which techniques that help some people, can hinder change in others.

The immediate impact of these events and research was to reinforce in our minds how managers need to adjust their approach with every single person: how the optimal context depends upon the situation, the person involved, and the change being attempted. Yes, this can feel complex and tiring, but the evidence just keeps stacking up. If you want behavior change to work, then the approach you take to supporting it *needs* to vary between individuals. And there is just no short-cut, no getting around this.

Beyond this though, the new events and research also led us to look more broadly. For the element of context that we increasingly found ourselves focusing on was the supporting environment. And not just the supporting environment created by the techniques we use to support change. But the supporting context beyond this. The context of the broader relationship between an employee and their boss, and the context of the wider business culture. Because—again—the evidence here just kept stacking up.

We described earlier how the level of fairness perceived in the broader business culture can change the effectiveness of external motivators and gamification techniques. But there are other things, too. The degree to which people generally enjoy their jobs and say they like working for their employer can also affect the techniques described in this book and how likely change is to succeed. This is because content employees tend to have higher levels of motivation and psychological capital, whereas unhappy employees tend to have lower levels and so expend less effort on trying to change.

Similarly, the level of cynicism or trust in an organization's culture can affect more or less every technique we have mentioned. If employees do not trust the business—or if they do not trust you, their manager—then any attempt you make to help them change is less likely to succeed. In fact, any attempt to do anything with them is less likely to succeed.

When we originally wrote this book, we focused on the aspects of employees' context that most directly affect whether attempts to change and develop succeed, and that you—as a manager—could quickly and easily do something about. And the four aspect of culture that we focused on—MAPS—are indeed critical for creating a supportive context for change.

But as time has passed, we have increasingly been drawn to the relationships between employees and their organizations, and between employees and you, the managers they work for. Because these relationships are the wider context within which everything we wrote about within this book happens.

And if the wider context isn't right, if it isn't positive, then everything you do to support change will be harder, and, ultimately, less likely to work.

So, it is this broader relationship and its effect on employees, more than anything else, that has been the focus of our attention in the years since we first published this book. And our research into this relationship, and our work with businesses across the world, has left us firm in the belief that it holds the key to solving almost all the challenges involved in changing employee behavior, whether that be to develop skills, improve performance, or change the whole culture of a team or business.

References

Meng, L. and Qingguo, M. (2015). Live as we choose: The role of autonomy support in facilitating intrinsic motivation, *International Journal of Psychophysiology*, 98(3), 441–447.

Wenzel, A.K., Krause, T. A., and Vogel, D. (2019). Making Performance Pay Work: The Impact of Transparency, Participation, and Fairness on Controlling Perception and Intrinsic Motivation. *Review of Public Personnel Administration*, 39(2), 232–255.

Malek, S.L., Shikar, S., and Haon, C. (2020). Extrinsic Rewards, Intrinsic Motivation, and New Product Development Performance. *Journal of Product Innovation Management*, 37(6), 528–551.

Mikkelsen, M.F., Jacobsen, C.B. and Andersen, L.B. (2017). Managing Employee Motivation: Exploring the Connections Between Managers' Enforcement Actions, Employee Perceptions, and Employee Intrinsic Motivation. *International Public Management Journal*, 20(2), 183–205.

Farzan, R., DiMicco, J. M., Millen, D. R., Brownholtz, B., Geyer, W., and Dugan, C. (2013). When the experiment is over: Deploying an incentive system to all users. *Proceedings of the 2008 ACM conference on Computer supported cooperative work*, 711–720.

Mollick, E.R. and Rothbard, N. (2014). Mandatory Fun: Consent, Gamification and the Impact of Games at Work. *The Wharton School Research Paper Series*.

Keller, J., Kwasnicka, D., Klaiber, P., Sichert, L., Lally, P., and Fleig, L. (2021). Habit formation following routine-based versus time-based cue planning: A randomized controlled trial. *British Journal of Health Psychology*, 26(3), 807–824.

Lauren, N., Fielding, K.S., Smith, L. and Louis, W.R. (2016). You did, so you can and you will: Self-efficacy as a mediator of spillover from easy to more difficult pro-environmental behaviour. *Journal of Environmental Psychology*, 48, 191–199.

Perryer, C. and Scott-Ladd, B. (2016). Enhancing Workplace Motivation Through Gamification: Transferrable Lessons from Pedagogy. *The International Journal of Management Education*, 14, 327–335.

Kok, G., Gottlieb, N.H., Peters, G.-J.Y., Mullen, P.D., Parcel, G.S., Ruiter, R.A.C., Fernández, M.E., Markham, C., and Bartholomew, L.K. (2015). A Taxonomy of Behavior Change Methods; An Intervention Mapping Approach. *Health Psychology Review*, 10(3), 297–312.

13

What We Do Differently

When we started writing the first edition of this book, back in 2014, we thought it was about helping you, as a manager, to help other people change and develop. And it was. But as we talked about it more and more, we realized we had also written about something else: How to help *you*—the managers and leaders of people—to change your own behavior. Because for every factor we discussed that could affect one of your direct reports' efforts to change, we looked at how *you* could help them by adjusting and adapting how *you* behave. In this light, *Changing Employee Behavior* has—it seems—actually all been about changing you, and what you can do to change and optimize the impact you have on your team and organization.

Two Pathways; Same Destination

We are jumping ahead a bit though, so let's step back. We finished Chap. 12 by noting that research and events since we published the first edition of this book had led us to increasingly focus on broader elements of context (such as the relationship between employees and the organization) and how they could affect both individuals' attempts to change, and your attempts to support them.

Supplementary Information The online version contains supplementary material available at https://doi.org/10.1007/978-3-031-29340-5_13. The videos can be accessed individually by clicking the DOI link in the accompanying figure caption or by scanning this link with the SN More Media App.

One of the key drivers of this expanding focus was our consulting work with organizations, and two very different types of requests we received. On the one hand, we had organizations asking us how they could use the MAPS model to change the behavior of everyone in their business in the same way—or in other words, how to change the culture of their firm. On the other hand, we had companies asking us if their managers could use the MAPS techniques to not just support change but also to drive the highest levels of performance.

On the face of it, these were two very different requests. But where they inexorably led us was to the same end point: you, and your relationship with your people.

Changing Behavior to Change Culture

All culture change is about changing behavior. It is just about changing the behavior of a group of people in the same way, so as to shift expectations and norms for how people usually behave in that group, be it a team, a business unit, or a whole organization.

The traditional, standard approach to doing this is well established. Processes differ, of course, but they typically involve a number of common components. There is often some kind of analysis of the existing culture. There is a process to identify or define the new, desired culture and the behaviors it requires. There is a focus on the role of a business' most senior leaders to role model and support the desired behaviors and culture. And then there is some kind of a large-scale program to develop people's understanding of how they need to behave and equip them with any new skills or techniques they may need.

There are variations, but that's usually the core of it. And we want to be clear, it's not a bad approach. It's ok. Done well, it can work, especially if it involves a great communication plan and some kind of measuring of progress and follow up. But it does, we feel, still suffer from five key flaws.

Too Many Fronts Assuming this isn't the first bit of the book you've read, you'll know that one of the most consistent findings in the research is that change is more likely to succeed when you try to change just one, simple thing. Increase the number of goals you have, or the complexity of them, and you automatically decrease your chances of succeeding on all of them. It's just math: Multiply the probability of successfully changing behavior by the number of goals, and the end result—your chances of success—will always get smaller the more goals you have. And yet we've lost count of the number of times we have seen firms identify not just one aspect of culture they want to change, but four, five, six, or even more things they want to improve. We understand and applaud the desire to change. But too many culture change programs try to move forward on too many fronts at once. So, if you want culture change to work, pick a fight—one thing you want to change—and then stick to it. Too Much Uniformity Again, if you've read the rest of this book—and Chap. 12, in particular—you'll have seen us repeat the mantra that change is more likely to work when it is tailored to the specific goals, needs, and motivations of individuals. This is just as true when it comes to large-scale culture change in organizations. Initiatives need to be tailored to each of the various departments, units, and teams within them. This could mean having one overarching cultural goal for the whole company—such as greater levels of proactive collaboration, or a greater focus on customer service—but then having separate plans for how to drive this in each business unit. Alternatively, it could mean having different change goals in each business unit, since what is most important to help drive growth in one business unit may be different in another. For example, back-office functions may need to create quicker, leaner processes, while for customer-facing business units more proactive service and selling may be the most important goals. Whatever the specifics, assuming that one goal or one program is right for every part of your business is a really big assumption, and in our experience, often a wrong one. Too Short a Span Just as with individual change, culture change does not come overnight, and if anything, takes longer. Most organizations seem to be aware of this, but seem to underestimate just how long it can take. We have seen multiple studies showing that it usually takes at least three years before any attempt you make to change culture can be said to have successfully taken hold, and to be lasting. Before that, it needs constant reinforcement. But how many firms have you seen introduce a three-year culture change program, with different activities in each year all focused on a singular change? Not too many, in our experience. Too Much Focus on the Most Senior Leaders One long-held belief has been that if a business' most senior leaders do not support and role model a culture change objective, then it cannot succeed. There is certainly no doubt in our minds that such support is critical and helpful and there is no shortage of examples showing how senior executives can radically alter the culture of their business should they choose to do so (think Elon Musk in Twitter). But is senior executive support the make or break of culture change? No. We've witnessed countless examples where a firm's senior executives behave one way, but the leader of a specific business unit decides to instill a different way of behaving, and succeeds within their area of creating a kind of cultural oasis. In fact, there is increasing evidence that all the focus on senior executives has become counterproductive, and for two reasons. First, because it can inadvertently disempower leaders and managers below the executive level. Too often we've heard managers say that they can't do anything to change culture because it is set by the executive team. The tragedy of this lies in the second reason that focusing on executives can be counterproductive. Because however important executives are, the fact remains that the day-to-day culture of a business—the everyday experience of employees—is not usually set or driven by them. It is instead created by the managers of teams. By you. The people above you—your boss, for instance—will certainly have some impact on your team. But the higher up leaders go, the further removed they become from people, and so the less direct impact they have. For example, in his book, *Who Says Elephants Can't Dance*, on the most successful transformation in IBM's history, Lou Gerstner, IBM's CEO at the time and the person who was recognized as the one who made it happen, argued that it was not about him but about the thousands of managers across the organization who drove the necessary behavioral changes. It is you—as a manager or leader—that leads and is the main driver of the local culture of your team. Yes, it is influenced by the broader business culture, but it is individual managers who lead it. And that is why culture change programs are increasingly focusing less on senior executives, and more on the leadership levels below them, and what everyday managers need to do to create the culture businesses need to succeed.

Too Much Focus on Behavior The final flaw is that all too often, culture change initiatives tend to focus too much on how people need to behave, and then on motivating and teaching people to do this. There is no doubt that defining the specific behaviors required and providing skills training on these can be useful. But, as you hopefully know by now, the key to any successful behavior change is making sure that the day-to-day context that people work in supports this change. So, to be successful, instead of just focusing on teaching behaviors, culture change initiatives need to also focus on creating a context in which these behaviors are supported. Which again, brings us back to you, as a manager or leader of people who directly creates this day-to-day context for employees. Since publishing the first edition of this book, we have taken the MAPS model and applied it to culture change in organizations across the world, using it to address these five flaws. In Video Fig. 13.1, you will find an example of how we have done this. In brief, our approach involves taking the traditional approach and building on it.

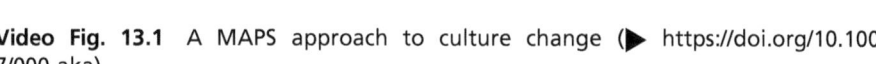

Video Fig. 13.1 A MAPS approach to culture change (▶ https://doi.org/10.1007/000-aka)

- We still think a brief analysis of existing culture is useful, though we place an emphasis on doing so quickly and efficiently.
- We still emphasize the importance of identifying clear goals and specific behaviors. However, we push businesses to prioritize just one or two goals, and to consider whether different goals for different areas would both have a greater chance of succeeding and have a stronger impact on business performance. (The compromise often made here is to have one goal for the overall organization and then offer each business unit or function the option of adding a second local goal just for them).
- For each goal and behavior, we make sure to also identify the context required to enable, encourage, and reinforce it. For example, we might ask "in what ways would the day-to-day working environment of your people need to be different, in order for the behavior you want to see to occur spontaneously, without you having to do anything else to make it happen?"
- We always ensure there is a three-year plan. Sometimes we use the principles of simple goals (described earlier in the book) to have easy steps in year one, and slowly build up to the full change required by year two or three. Other times, we drive for the full change in year one and then have reinforcement plans for years two and three. This always involves the measurement of progress and building feedback loops. Whatever the specifics, we ensure the plan does not stop after the initial intervention and that it was clearly laid out before any activity began.

- We create different communication and intervention plans for different layers of the organization. In a medium to large-sized firm, for example, we might have one plan for the board (providing governance for the change), another for the executive team, a third plan for the two to three layers below the executive team, a plan for the managers below this, and then finally a plan for non-supervisory staff. Each, tailored to the specific needs of the population at that level, their different roles in driving and supporting the change, and the different challenges they face.
- Most important of all, every plan focuses not just on changing people's behavior but also on changing people's context so that it enables, encourages, and supports this change. And using MAPS, this means creating a context that ensures people have the motivation and ability to behave in the desired way, the psychological capital needed to make the change, and a supporting environment that helps them initiate and sustain this change.

This focus on using context to drive culture change, rather than just relying on teaching behaviors or skills, is the key difference in a MAPS approach to culture change (see Video Fig. 13.2). And it unerringly brings us to what tends to become the core focus for us in every culture change initiative: You. What you and every other team leader, at all levels in the organization, need to do to drive and support a certain shift in behavior. Because when you, and enough of your colleagues, all create the right kind of context to support a

Video Fig. 13.2 One key difference in a MAPS approach to culture change (▶ https://doi.org/10.1007/000-ak9)

specific change, then over time, behaving that way will become the norm across the company. It will become the culture.

Yet in focusing on what you can do to drive and support change, we also found ourselves looking at something else: why your efforts to help people change can seem easier or harder in some situations than others. Or in other words, what are the things that can affect how effective your attempts to support people are.

In trying to answer this, we started researching the role of broader contextual factors. For example, we looked at the behavior of more senior stakeholders, different commercial scenarios, industry type, national culture, and even the broader political environment and the impact of social trends. Yet as we investigated how factors like these could affect both people's attempts to change and your attempts to support them, the evidence kept piling up: the biggest factor affecting these things is the quality of your broader relationship with people.

It is the general environment that you—as their manager—create in the team. Whether your team feels cared for; whether they feel a strong sense of ownership for what they do; and whether they enjoy their work. And it is your personal relationship with each of your direct reports. Whether they respect you; whether they trust you; and whether they feel confident around you. Because if people don't feel cared for, if people don't enjoy working with you, or if people don't trust you, then no matter what you do to try to support them, it is far less likely to work.

Just as the more important determinant of whether employees manage to change behavior is the everyday context they work in, the most important determinant of whether your attempts to support them are successful is the context that this occurs in. And this means the team culture you create and the personal relationships you have with people. If these aren't right, everything becomes harder.

We often think of culture as an abstract thing. And culture change initiatives have traditionally tended to feel a bit like huge machines, with big programs rolled out across organizations with an emphasis on following the lead of senior executives. But making culture change work requires something far more personal. Because, ultimately, it's really all about individual teams, the people within them, and their working relationships.

Changing Behavior to Drive Performance

The second type of request we received from organizations was whether managers could use the techniques in this book not for supporting change in individuals, but for driving high performance in their teams.

On the one hand, we could see a clear rationale for why the MAPS techniques could be used for this. Leaders drive performance in two ways. They can do so directly; for example, through pushing sales or deciding something that directly affects results. Or, they can do so indirectly, through supporting other people to do things. And it is this second way that tends to become the main lever that leaders use to drive performance as they rise into more senior roles. They do it by affecting things like what their team focuses on, how motivated people are, how decisions get made, levels of accountability, and the degree to which people support each other. In other words, they create a working context or environment for their people that directs, drives, and supports them to deliver. So, as the MAPS techniques are all about how to adjust and adapt this context that people work within, they certainly seem like good candidates for methods leaders could use.

However, the four MAPS factors were what research showed were the most important contextual factors for supporting change. What we were now being asked, was whether they were also the most important factors for driving performance. To answer this, we did what we always do, which is to dive into the research. We reviewed over 1000 academic studies (see Video Fig. 13.3 for more details), and then conducted research of our own, involving over 2500 leaders and managers from different industries across the globe.

What we discovered was that three contextual factors in particular stand out as critical for individuals' performance. These are elements of both overall team culture and leaders' one-to-one relationships with direct reports that our research showed *need* to be in place in order for a leader to drive sustained high performance. And importantly, they are slightly different from the MAPS factors important for change. They are trust, clarity, and momentum.

Trust

Trust stands out as the single most important element of context for performance. It is a vital driver of both individual and team performance and of organizational indicators such as sales figures and net profits. And it is more important in driving these things than how motivated employees feel, how empowered they are or how much they enjoy their job. Trust is crucial because

```
┌─────────────────────────┐
│                         │
│   RESEARCH INTO         │
│   LEADER -              │
│   EMPLOYEE              │
│   RELATIONSHIPS         │
│            ▶            │
└─────────────────────────┘
```

Video Fig. 13.3 The research into leader-employee relationships (▶ https://doi.org/1 0.1007/000-ak8)

of the types of performance it drives. Followers who trust their leaders show higher levels of discretionary effort—the extra mile people will go to ensure success. They also show higher levels of employee voice—the tendency to speak up and challenge thinking. This is essential for innovation, good decision-making and risk management.

Clarity

The second key contextual element is clarity. It is the understanding that exists about the strategy of the business, who is accountable for what, why certain things are important, and how things should be done. Clarity is important because with it comes the essential alignment, unity and community that are critical for strategy implementation and business success. And through these things, clarity also drives both better teamwork and higher levels of employee commitment.

Momentum

The final element of context critical for performance is momentum—the energy and drive for sustained activity. This includes motivation, confidence, and empowerment, as well as the sense of connection, togetherness and team that people feel. Just as with trust and clarity, the importance of momentum

> HIGH-PERFORMER VS. HIGH-PERFORMING LEADER ▶

Video Fig. 13.4 Being a high performer vs. being a high-performing leader (▶ https://doi.org/10.1007/000-akb)

lies in the behavior it tends to drive. People who have higher levels of momentum are more likely to take the initiative, drive creativity and innovation, and show higher levels of entrepreneurialism. They have been shown to work harder and persist longer when they encounter difficulties. And they are more likely to show loyalty to the organization and demonstrate commitment to it.

Our research showed that the leaders of high-performing teams create significantly higher levels of these three factors than the leaders of lower-performing teams. Which of these is most important can vary between situations. How leaders can best go about creating them depends upon the individuals concerned and the broader national and organizational culture. But no matter where in the world leaders work, what industry they are in, or the specific commercial challenges they are faced with, high-performing leaders produce higher levels of trust, clarity, and momentum (see Video Fig. 13.4).

Changing People's Context

Our research into these three contextual factors and what leaders could do to create them eventually culminated in what became the follow-on to this book: *Leadership OS: The Operating System Leaders Need to Succeed*. The factors we focused on—trust, clarity, and momentum—were different from the factors needed to support change that we have described in this book. But what they had in common was that they were all about the context you create for others. So, just as with how to drive culture change, exploring how to drive performance led us to you, and your impact on others through the relationships you have as a leader, manager, and colleague.

There is a movie quote (which has been in a surprisingly large number of films), that seems to capture where we have arrived in our work and research: *It's you; it's always been about you.* The key to leadership—be it supporting people to develop, driving culture change, or enabling the highest levels of performance—is what *you* do, the impact *you* have, and the context *you* create.

That is why we said this book is actually all about how to change you. And why, in retrospect, we probably should have called it *Changing People's Context*.

14

Frequently Asked Questions

One of the things we love about writing books is that we get to present the findings to you—the managers and leaders of organizations. Whether it is through the IMD business school open programs, customized development interventions for organizations, or our online offerings, the thing we love most about doing this is the questions you ask us and the conversations we get into with you. Because when that happens—when you say, "what about *this*" or "what about *that*"—it helps push the boundaries of what we know and understand about behavior change forward. So, to finish up, we wanted to give back to you some of the nudges you have kindly given us, in the form of our answers to some of the questions we are most frequently asked about changing employee behavior.

How Can We Help People to Identify What They Need to Change and Develop?

It's not always easy to know what you need to develop. And sometimes, even when people do know, they don't want to say. So, to help open up this conversation, we often use a simple mnemonic: RISC-E. These letters stand for the five critical factors that decision-makers usually think about when considering whether someone can do a role or are ready to be promoted.

Supplementary Information The online version contains supplementary material available at https://doi.org/10.1007/978-3-031-29340-5_14. The videos can be accessed individually by clicking the DOI link in the accompanying figure caption or by scanning this link with the SN More Media App.

© The Author(s), under exclusive license to Springer Nature Switzerland AG 2023
N. Kinley, S. Ben-Hur, *Changing Employee Behavior*,
https://doi.org/10.1007/978-3-031-29340-5_14

- The **R** stands for results and execution. It's a basic and fundamental question: Do they deliver the numbers? Can they get things done?
- The **I** stands for interpersonal skills, or in other words, are they liked, can they get on with people, and can they manage the politics of the business.
- The **S** stands for strategy, or put another way, are they a strong thinker? The precise emphasis here will depend upon the role, but the question asked here is usually can they create a strategic plan, do they have good judgment, and will they drive innovation?
- The **C** stands for the culture or climate that a leader creates within his area. Whether people want to work for him and whether he develops and improves his team.
- And finally, the **E** stands for experience and expertise: whether the individual has the previous experiences and technical expertise required by the role.

In terms of importance, the five factors should probably read E-RISC; but RISC-E just sounds more memorable.

Once we've presented the five factors to people, we then ask them to rank order the factors according to how strong or weak decision-makers may think they are in each of them. So first they identify the factor that they think stakeholders will view them as being strongest in; and then we work through the factors down to the one they think people will have the most doubts about them with. We then focus the development plan on the factors that they identified as weaker.

By positioning this rank ordering as not being about what they are strong and weak at, but about their reputation and what other people think about them, it depersonalizes development needs and seems to make them easier for people to talk about.

What's the Best Way to Open People Up to the Idea of Change?

This is a perennial challenge, but one recent piece of research has suggested that asking people what is important to them makes them more likely to take on advice and change their behavior. The finding comes from a study that scanned people's brains as they were given some typical advice about the need to exercise more.

Before receiving the advice, some of the participants were led through a simple exercise that involved thinking about what was important to them—family, work, religion, or anything that had meaning for them. The rest of the participants were just given the advice as normal, without being asked this.

All the participants were then tracked to see whether they took the advice on and did more exercise. And sure enough, the participants who have been asked to reflect on what was important to them went on to heed the advice and exercised more than the group who were not asked the question.

The reason for this link was not looked at in the study, but it is likely that by asking people what is important for them, we are reminding them of it, and thereby enabling them to more easily connect the advice to what is important to them. In terms of the MAPS model, what we are doing is increasing people's intrinsic motivation, using a technique we describe in Chap. 10 called priming. It's simple, but seems to work.

So, the next time you are going to give someone some advice, make sure you start with what's important to them.

Are There Any Other Models of Behavior Change That You Like and Have Used?

This is a nice little mnemonic to emerge from work conducted by behavioral economists from Cornell University for the Department of Health in New York State. They were looking at how to get children to eat more healthily at school. In thinking about how to influence children's decisions about what to eat, they came up with what they called the *CAN* approach. It stands for *convenient, attractive,* and *normative*.

Convenient means just that—making it *easy* to do something. Making sure that people know exactly what is required of them and that the action is made as easy for them as possible. That may involve breaking the goal down into a series of smaller steps. Or it may involve providing resources or tools of some sort. Either way, it is about making sure that performing the desired behavior is as effortless as possible.

Attractive means making sure the desired behavior is more attractive relative to whatever alternatives exist. You don't have to make the behavior *amazingly* attractive; just more attractive than other potential behaviors in the situation. This is where intrinsic motivation and incentives come into play.

Finally, normative means ensuring that performing the desired behavioral is seen as expected, usual, and the normal thing to do. What everyone should and does do. This means leaders role-modeling, publicly recognizing people who do it well, and advertising the fact that most people do the desired behavior.

It is, then, a very simple model. It picks up on aspects of the M, A, and S of our model—missing out on Psychological Capital. As such, for us it is incomplete. But it is nonetheless a neat little mnemonic that you can use to help others understand some of the basics required to help people change behavior.

Do People Need Be Aware of the Need to Change Before They Can Start Changing?

Generally speaking, people do need to be aware of the need to change before they can start trying to change. In fact, many of the classic psychological models of behavior change have self-awareness as a critical first step in the process. Take, for example, what is probably the most frequently used model of behavior change in Psychology, called the Transtheoretical Model, or TTM for short.

It was developed in the late 1970s by a group of US psychologists led by James Prochaska and it suggests that when changing people go through a number of stages:

- Pre-contemplation (Not Ready): People are not intending to take action and may be unaware that their behavior needs to change.
- Contemplation (Getting Ready): People are beginning to recognize that their behavior needs to change, and are starting to look at the pros and cons of their behavior.
- Preparation (Ready): People are intending to take action in the immediate future, and may begin taking small steps.
- Action: People have made specific attempts to modify their behavior.
- Maintenance: People have been able to sustain the new behavior for six months.
- Termination: Individuals are sure they will not return to their old behavior.

This, then, is the classical psychological model, and it describes becoming aware of the need to change is a key step in the process. As models go, it feel fairly logical, and using it can help you figure out where people are in their change journey and the type of support they may need at any particular point in time.

But is awareness absolutely always necessary? Well on that we're not convinced. The reason for this is that sometimes people change their behavior without actually being aware that they are doing so. They might, for example, change their attitude and behavior toward a key stakeholder—and not deliberately or thoughtfully, but just in the moment and in response to a particular situation or something the stakeholder says or does. In these situations, because the change is not deliberate or conscious, it is not driven by self-awareness. The awareness can often come after the change has happened.

So—strictly speaking—no, we do not think that self-awareness is always *needed* for people to change. But is it useful? Yes. Usually. For the most part behavior change seems to work best and last longer when people are aware of the need to change and make a deliberate, conscious attempt to do so. Which brings us to the next question.

What Can Be Done to Improve People's Level of Self-Awareness?

There are three main ways in which self-awareness can be improved:

1. Specific feedback – or in other words, give the individual specific information relating to them and their behavior;
2. General information – give the individual general information either about the situation involved or people and how they tend to behave, and hope that it provokes the individual to ask questions or draws conclusions about themselves (this is effectively what self-help books do);
3. Questioning – ask the individuals questions about themselves and their behavior.

The more you can help an individual engage in one or more of these three processes, the more self-aware they are likely to become.

Something to remember though is that self-awareness is not just something that you have, but something that you do. It is about being continually curious about your own behavior and impact on others. Indeed, being self-aware of the need to change a particular behavior may be what is required in specific situations, but in general, it is being self-questioning that is perhaps the more valuable and critical capability.

Do You Have Any Suggestions for How to Make Development Plans More Useful?

The problem with development plans is that all too often they just do not work. Or at least not work very well. The issues with them are well documented and we described most of them earlier in this book. Plans may not be taken seriously. They may contain too many goals or insufficiently specific ones. Or they may not be behavioral enough and overrely on training programs or coaching as solutions. However, there are two growing trends that may hold some hope of making development plans more reliably effective.

Support Writing Plans

The first is a move toward coaches and managers becoming more involved in the writing of development plans. Traditionally, the opposite has been true. There was a pervasive belief that people needed to 'own' their plans, and should not feel that development actions had been imposed upon them. There was much sense in this, too, because if people feel that they have no choice in development actions then they are far less likely to complete them. Unfortunately, this often resulted in individuals being left to write their development plans on their own, or at least to put the first draft together. And all too often the result of this was that the development plans were not good quality, and that individuals' managers—excluded from the process—were less motivated and able to support the plan.

So, recently, there has been a move to try and rectify both these issues by involving managers and coaches more in the actual writing of development plans. For example, we have recently led a change program in which coaches played a far more active part in writing development plans. Our team of coaches sat with leaders and their managers over a laptop and wrote the plan with them. And not with the coaches constantly saying 'what do you think?' to the leader; but with the coaches playing a very active role in making suggestions about potential development actions the individual could try. In addition, afterward, the coaches had a brief one-to-one conversation with individuals' managers to brainstorm ideas for how they could create a supportive context for the development. The result was far better-quality development plans, greater involvement and support from managers, and a significantly higher rate of plan completion.

In another program we recently ran, we didn't use coaches, but just taught leaders a simple process they could use to write development plans with their direct reports. The outcome here was similar to using coaches. Development plans were better quality than when individuals wrote them on their own, there was greater manager involvement, and again, higher plan completion rate. Program evaluation showed that neither plan quality nor completion rates were quite as high as when coaches were involved, too, but they were nonetheless better than the traditional approach of just leaving individuals to write their own development plans.

Shorter Timeframes

The second trend is a move toward shorter timeframes for development plans. The standard at present is for annual plans, with perhaps quarterly or half-yearly reviews of progress. But if a leader has not acted on their plan in the first three months, they usually aren't going to. So why not focus plans on things that people can do more or less immediately and give them a timeframe of 3–6 months? There may be some actions (such as attending certain courses) that cannot be completed in that time, but these can just be carried over to the next plan. And that is the real bonus of shorter timeframes for development plans–that they put a greater emphasis on continual development.

So, if you think most development plans in your business end up being put in a drawer and never looked at again, try more active involvement from managers and coaches in writing them, and shorter timeframes.

How Can People Improve Strategic Thinking?

This is one of the most common questions we get asked. The first hurdle here is that strategic thinking can mean different things to different people. Generally speaking, though, it refers to one of three abilities:

- The ability to think and plan ahead;
- The ability to see the bigger picture and broader context—to look beyond an individual deal or issue;
- And finally, the ability to join the dots—to see the connections between issues and events, and identify patterns in the data.

To help leaders improve these thinking skills there is a range of executive education courses. The ones we like best are the ones that focus on strategy in relation to a very specific issue, or the ones that involve bringing people from a range of different industries from all over the world together to discuss and debate case examples. Both types can be highly effective. What about outside these courses, though? Well, there are typically five basic things people can do.

1. You can write a two-year strategic plan or discussion document for how you would develop your area. This doesn't need to be a 38-page masterpiece: a one-pager or SWOT analysis will do. And once done you can then present it and discuss it with your boss. This both gives you practice in writing a plan and forward-thinking and showcases to your boss what you can do.
2. You can read. Then read, read, and read some more. Ideally it should be something business-related; but frankly anything that stretches your thinking and gets you looking at things from different perspectives would work. The challenge here is that finding time to read regularly can be tough, but there are two solutions that can help. Ideally you should use both. First, you can try to turn your reading into a habit. Make it something that you do every day at a particular time, say just before bed or after dinner. And keep it bite-sized, say just ten minutes, to make it manageable. Second, you can skip the reading and try watching videos or listening to podcasts instead. With the huge number of TED Talks videos available and podcasts on almost every topic you can imagine, accessing information has never been easier. And for many people watching a video or listening to a podcast feels easier than reading. So, choose a media that works best for you.
3. One simple build on the idea of reading is to try presenting on one article or video to your team once a month. The act of articulating the ideas and your thinking about them will help cement the learning. And of course, it becomes a learning opportunity for your team, too. Alternatively, as another way to accomplish the same thing, you could agree with your team to all read a particular article or watch a video and then discuss it as a group. This adds an element of debate, which can then help you see things from different angles.
4. Find a strategy buddy. What we mean by this is find someone with whom you can discuss issues and with whom you can have a good debate—preferably someone who tends to see things differently to you. You could both arrange to read the same article or watch the same video and then meet over coffee to discuss it. And it's the discussion that's key to learning here: the fact that you are articulating your thinking and debating things.
5. Finally, a more frivolous but potentially still useful suggestion. Try playing brain games. Soduko. Crossword puzzles. Whatever takes your fancy—there are certainly enough to choose from these days. But something that

```
   IMPROVE
   CREATIVE
   THINKING &
   INNOVATION
        ▶
```

Video Fig. 14.1 How to help people improve creative thinking and innovation (▶ https://doi.org/10.1007/000-akc)

gets you thinking and literally exercises your brain. Because just like physical muscles, your brain can benefit from a good workout, too.

For our suggestions on how to help people improve another thinking skill—creative thinking and innovation—please see Video Fig. 14.1.

How Can We Help People Who Have Low Willpower?

We made some suggestions for this in this book, but since publishing it, two new research papers have come to our attention that each describes a way to help or support people's willpower when trying to change behavior.

The first is called *temptation bundling*. It involves combining something we really like—such as watching a favorite TV show, or listening to a particular audio-book—with something we are more ambivalent about—like going to the gym. This is essentially a variation on something that we cover in the book called a commitment device. These are mini-contracts that we make to try and incentivize ourselves or other people to behave in certain ways. These contracts say, 'do this, and you'll get that reward'; or they may say, 'fail to do this, and you need pay that forfeit'. For example, we might reward ourselves for reading a book by eating a chocolate bar. Or we may penalize ourselves for failing to read it by paying an amount to charity. What is different about temptation bundling is that we are outing the two things together—at the same time—rather than making one of them the consequence of the other.

The second willpower hack is called the fresh start effect. It shows that people are more likely to tackle their goals following particular temporal landmarks—such as the start of a new week, month or year, or a birthday or holiday. The researchers suggest that these landmarks may work by signaling the start of a kind of new mental accounting period, which "induce people to take a big-picture view of their lives, and thus motivate aspirational behaviors."

So, if you feel someone's willpower needs a little support (and hey, whose doesn't?), try giving these a go.

How Can You Tell if Someone's Resilience Isn't Strong Enough to See Through a Change?

In our experience, asking just two questions can help identify someone's resilience for a task—their ability to persevere and find ways around challenges.

As we have noted in this book, resilience is a critical capability for success. It is the ability to find ways around potential challenges and develop new or alternative ways of doing things. It is the capacity to cope with adversity and sometimes even grow stronger from it. Now a seemingly unrelated new piece of research may hold a clue for something simple that all managers can do to help people improve the resilience of their people for tasks.

The research in question involved experienced pilots completing a flight simulator exercise. The pilots were told beforehand that the exercise would involve an engine failure that would occur shortly after take-off (one of the most difficult situations a pilot can face). And they were then asked two simple questions: "How demanding do you expect the task to be?" And, "How able are you to cope with the demands of the task?"

What the researchers found was that the pilots' responses to these questions accurately predicted how well they subsequently coped with the engine failure. Pilots who saw themselves as less able to cope were indeed less able to do so. Moreover, their answers to these two questions predicted their ability to land the plane safely more than any other relevant factor such as their age and years of experience.

So, when you next set one of your direct reports a task or a project, try asking them these two questions. They may not be totally open with their concerns, but it will help you understand how they feel about the task and as the study with the pilots shows, what people feel is important.

Does Resilience Training Work?

With research showing that the pressures of work are steadily increasing, and that managers and leaders are feeling more stressed than ever, it is little wonder that workshops aimed at helping people improve their resilience have become one of the fastest growing trends in leadership development. Indeed, training in resilience is all the rage at the moment, with both big-name vendors and businesses reporting significant gains from running resilience-building development interventions. The question is do they really work?

Two recent studies have shed new light on this issue. The first of these was the first major review to be conducted into all the research that has been published about the effectiveness of resilience training. It started with 155 English language studies into the effectiveness of resilience training published in peer-reviewed academic journals since 2003. After applying careful criteria, it concluded that only 14 of the studies were robust enough to draw solid conclusions from.

The resilience programs covered in these 14 studies varied massively in what they involved. They included everything from single 90-minute individual coaching sessions to workshops run over 12 weeks. They included both online programs and 2½ day retreats. And they included approaches based on Cognitive Behavioral Therapy, positive psychology, mindfulness, Acceptance and Commitment Therapy, and the stress-reduction-focused Attention and Interpretation Therapy. One program even used high-tech biofeedback machines.

The conclusions drawn by the study were that resilience training can indeed improve levels of resilience and have a positive impact on employee's subjective well-being, self-confidence, and performance. However, it also pointed out that the evidence on effectiveness was thin (14 decent studies in ten years is not a lot), and that due to the limited evidence and wide variety of different approaches to developing resilience it was not possible to draw any firm conclusions about which approach or methodology was the best. It did, though, make two tentative suggestions. First, the study suggested that most successful interventions included an element of one-to-one training and support that addressed individual needs. Then, noting that what organizations mean when they say resilience can vary considerably, the study suggested that firms need to begin by clearly defining what specifically they mean by resilience. Firms are then probably better off designing an intervention around this definition rather than buying a ready-made off-the-shelf intervention.

The second and more recent piece of research looked at 37 other studies into the effectiveness of resilience training. It concluded that overall the effectiveness of resilience-building programs was small and that benefits of these programs often fade fairly quickly. However, it went on to add that development programs aimed at those most needing help were far more effective. It therefore concluded that identifying those most in need of developing their resilience levels and focusing interventions on these individuals was important for ensuring the effectiveness of development programs. In other words, if you put everyone through a program, don't be surprised if not all of them benefit from it. Instead, you should just focus on those most in need.

So, before you build or buy a resilience-building program, it's worth bearing in mind the key findings of these two pieces of research:

- Resilience-building interventions can work, if carefully targeted at those who need them.
- Begin by clearly defining what you mean by resilience—what behaviors typify it in your organization—and then choose or design an intervention that specifically addresses these behaviors.
- Include an element of one-to-one coaching and/or mentoring.

You Talk a Lot About the Power of Praise, but Isn't There a Risk in Over-Praising?

Yes, absolutely. We recently came across an interesting study coming out of Utrecht University, looking at the impact praise can have on people. Specifically, it looked at the tendency in adults to give inflated praise to children with low self-esteem.

Apparently, about 25% of adults tend to do this when faced with child lacking self-esteem. This is not just something that people do with kids, either. Most people, if faced with someone who is clearly not feeling good about themselves, will tend to change how they speak—the words they use—to try and help the other person feel better about themselves. And quite right, too, you may think. Except, there's a kicker here.

The researchers found that inflated praise—such as simply saying "that's incredibly beautiful," rather than just "that's beautiful," seemed to discourage children with low self-esteem from subsequently taking on challenges. (With children with high self-esteem it has the opposite effect—it seems to encourage them.)

Why it has this negative effect on children with low self-esteem isn't clear. The researchers suggest that it may be because inflated praise inadvertently sets a high bar for children that they don't believe they can achieve again going forward, and so they avoid future challenges. But the researchers acknowledge that this is essentially just a guess. So, for the moment we don't know the why of it.

What is useful about this research, though, is not the why but the what. It is the reminder that it is an almost natural impulse to adapt our language to soften our words and inflate our praise when we are with people who are clearly not feeling good about themselves. And it is the fascinating finding that inflating praise in this way can have a completely unintended consequence that is the exact opposite of what we were hoping for. Yes, this research was on kids, but we'd bet the findings with adults would be very similar, if not identical.

So, be nice. Give praise. After all, it's cheap and probably the single most effective motivator available in the managerial toolkit. But don't go over the top and beware of inflated praise.

What's the One Thing That You Think Every HR Department Should Do to Support Behavior Change in Their Organization?

A few years ago, a group of Dutch researchers published some pretty depressing findings. They had conducted a systematic review of the quality of other studies looking at what works in behavior, culture, and organizational change. Their conclusions were simple, that despite the growing volume of articles looking at what techniques work best, the quality of these studies is generally low and getting lower every year. In other words, the evidence for what works is dodgy, and getting dodgier.

There are three main reasons for this. The first is that much of the research is driven by vendors and so open to—well, let's call it bias. They have a product to sell, and they do their best to sell it.

The second is that even when both vendors and academics have a genuine interest in objectively investigating what works in successfully driving and supporting change, they can struggle to get hold of the data they need. Things like feedback and performance ratings. Some firms just don't want to share it, and while others may be willing to in principle, getting formal approval can be difficult.

The final reason is that most firms are actually not that interested in looking at what works for themselves. They expect outside experts and vendors to bring that. And they tend instead to be focused on just single change initiatives and making sure that they work. For the individual senior or mid-level leader running a particular change project, there is little to be gained from figuring out learning for future initiatives. They just need to make sure this one works. Or at least that it doesn't go horribly wrong, anyway.

If the success rates of change initiatives are to improve, though, we need more and better information about what works and what doesn't. And the only way that this can start happening is if firms start doing one of two things. Either they need to start actively partnering with academics and properly sharing their data, so that the vendors or academics can do the research. Or, firms need to stop looking at this problem with such a short-term, single-initiative focus, and start building up a reliable body of knowledge about what works for themselves. In other words, they need to stop relying on vendors being the experts in change and start becoming the experts themselves.

For us, the solution probably needs to be a mix of both: some partnering with academics, and some investment in their own expertise. And the reason we think this is so important is that—if you'll forgive us saying it one last time—context matters; and as the context for change is different in every business, what is needed to drive and support change will also be slightly different in every organization. So, our one piece of advice—not just to HR, but to all managers and leaders—is become experts in your own context. Share knowledge and learnings. Build up your own body of evidence about what works for your people in your organization. Because through becoming experts in your context, you lay the foundations for also becoming masters of it. And if you can master your context, anything is possible.

Appendix A

Key Questions to Ask Yourself

For convenience, we have gathered here all of the "Key questions to ask yourself" presented in each chapter. You can use the list as a prompt to help you think about the various aspects of the MAPS model.

Motivation

Motivation consists of *intrinsic* and *extrinsic* motivation. Intrinsic motivation is fueled by internal feelings. Extrinsic motivation comes from external motivators such as rewards and punishments.

Intrinsic motivation

- On a rating scale of 1 to 10, how strongly does the behavior change appeal overall to the individual's intrinsic motivation?
- What would the rating be for how strongly the change appeals to each of the three elements of intrinsic motivation: autonomy, mastery, and connection?
- Does the individual have a sense of autonomy, choice, and involvement in the change process?
- What can you do to highlight competence, progress, and challenge? Does the individual know how to go on—what to do next—and understand the relevance and importance of the change for them?

- How might the individual's culture, age, role, and gender affect their intrinsic motivation for this change?
- How might the individual's career concept and personality affect their intrinsic motivation for this change?

Extrinsic motivation

- How do the extrinsic motivators you are using support and play to what intrinsically motivates the individual?
- Might the individual's culture, experience level, and personality impact the effectiveness of the extrinsic motivators you are using?
- How many different nonmonetary rewards are you using?
- Are you getting the timing and frequency of rewards and punishments right?
- Will employees feel that the distribution and handling of rewards and punishments are fair and consistent?

Ability

- Does the person have sufficient opportunity to perform and practice the desired behavior?
- Are there any physical resources lacking that could limit the progress of the behavior change?
- What skills and knowledge might the individual need to succeed in this behavior change? Do they have these already, or will they need to learn them?
- Have you agreed a set of proximal goals that will act as a successful pipeline to the ultimate desired behavior?
- Are there any competing commitments or psychological blockers that could impede the change process?

Psychological Capital

Psychological capital consists of four key components: self-belief, optimism, willpower, and resilience.
Self-belief and optimism

- On a rating scale of 1 to 10, how self-confident is the individual in general?
- On the same scale, how confident are they that they can change behavior?

- Is there anything concerning the behavior change that they are worried about?
- Are they usually optimistic, or less so? How could this affect how they feel about the behavior change?

Willpower and resilience

- How strongly would the individual rate their willpower? How strongly would you rate it?
- In what situations might their willpower be reduced? What can be done to protect against this?
- If their willpower is not as strong as it could be, which techniques could you use to boost it?
- Is the individual capable of mindfulness? Can they remain focused on what they need to achieve and will they notice if they do not?
- How would you and the individual rate their level of resilience? What types of situations do they most struggle to remain resilient with?
- Does the individual anticipate potential obstacles and problems and plan for them? Are they adaptable in responding to problems?

Supporting Environment

We highlighted three key approaches to shaping a supportive environment: habits, gamification, and nudging.
Habits

- What are the behavior, cue, and reinforcer for the habit you are trying to help the individual create?
- How can you promote repetition of the behavior, in particular in the early days of habit formation?
- Have you given the individual information about the structure of habits and how they can be formed and broken?
- Have they drawn up a list of implementation intentions to help them deal with situations and obstacles?
- If you are trying to break a habit, how can you remove the cue or help the individual ignore it?
- If you are trying to change a habit, has the individual selected a substitute behavior?

Gamification

- Is the individual open to gamification?
- Are their goals truly intrinsically motivating?
- Do you understand what drives the individual and which aspects of gamification, if any, are most likely to appeal to them?

Nudging

- What information could you provide the individual that might affect their decisions about how to behave?
- Are there any situational cues that would prime the individual to behave in the desired way?
- What are the social norms for the desired behavior? How are they different to how the individual is currently behaving?
- What are the current costs and benefits of the desired behavior?
- How could adopting the desired behavior help the individual avoid losing something?

Appendix B

MAPS Profiler Tool

This simple profiler tool is designed to help you determine which areas of the MAPS model you need to focus on most or first. It is best to answer the questions after speaking with the employee you are trying to help, or to work through the questionnaire with them.

For each area of the MAPS model there are five questions. Answer them using the rating scale provided, and then plot the scores on the graph provided in Appendix C.

An online version of this tool is also available on the book's website, at www.changingemployeesbehavior.com (Figs. AB.1, AB.2, AB.3 and AB.4).

Motivation

On a scale of 1-5, where one is low, not very often, or not very much; 3 is medium or average; and 5 is high, very often, or very much

How strong is the individual's sense of autonomy in relation to the proposed behavior change? (Do they feel they have choice and are involved?)	1	2	3	4	5
How strong is the individual's sense of mastery in relation to the proposed behavior change? (Do they feel competent and/or challenged?)	1	2	3	4	5
How strong is the individual's sense of connection to the proposed behavior change? (Do they see the change as important for them and do they know how to go on?)	1	2	3	4	5
To what extent are there extrinsic motivators in place to support the desired behavior change?	1	2	3	4	5
To what extent are extrinsic motivators aligned to the individual's intrinsic motivation	1	2	3	4	5
Total					

Fig. AB.1 Motivation

« Ability »

On a scale of 1-5, where one is low, not very often, or not very much; 3 is medium or average; and 5 is high, very often, or very much

Question	1	2	3	4	5
How much opportunity does the individual have to perform and practice the new, desired behavior?	1	2	3	4	5
To what extent does the individual have all the resources they need to achieve the behavior change?	1	2	3	4	5
To what extent does the individual have the skills and knowledge the need to achieve the behavior change?	1	2	3	4	5
To what extent are proximal goals in place to help build up to the desired behavior?	1	2	3	4	5
To what extent is the individual free of competing commitments or other potential psychological blockers to change?	1	2	3	4	5

Total ➔

Fig. AB.2 Ability

⟪ Psychological Capital ⟫

On a scale of 1-5, where one is low, not very often, or not very much; 3 is medium or average; and 5 is high, very often, or very much

How strong is the individual's self-confidence in their ability to achieve the desired change?	1	2	3	4	5
How optimistic is the individual in general?	1	2	3	4	5
How strong is the individual's willpower and personal discipline?	1	2	3	4	5
How able is the individual to maintain good levels of energy and protect themselves from tiredness?	1	2	3	4	5
How strong is the individual's ability to cope with a set-back in the behavior change process?	1	2	3	4	5
Total ⟹					

Fig. AB.3 Psychological capital

≪ Supporting Environment ≫

On a scale of 1-5, where one is low, not very often, or not very much; 3 is medium or average; and 5 is high, very often, or very much

To what extent are processes in place to support the repetition of the new, desired behavior?	1	2	3	4	5
To what extent does the individual have implementation intentions and other support tools and processes in place to help them deal with potential challenges and obstacles?	1	2	3	4	5
To what extent are there processes in place to track progress and highlight competition and challenge?	1	2	3	4	5
To what extent do the benefits of adopting the new, desired behavior to the individual outweigh the costs of adopting it for them?	1	2	3	4	5
To what extent do social norms support the new, desired behavior?	1	2	3	4	5

Total ⟶

Fig. AB.4 Supporting environment

Appendix C

MAPS Profiler Graph

You can plot the scores obtained on the profiler tool in Appendix B on this graph. It allows you to more easily see which areas of the MAPS model need most attention. A high score on a dimension means that that element of the model is already being addressed. A low score means that you need to take action on that element to support the individual trying to change.

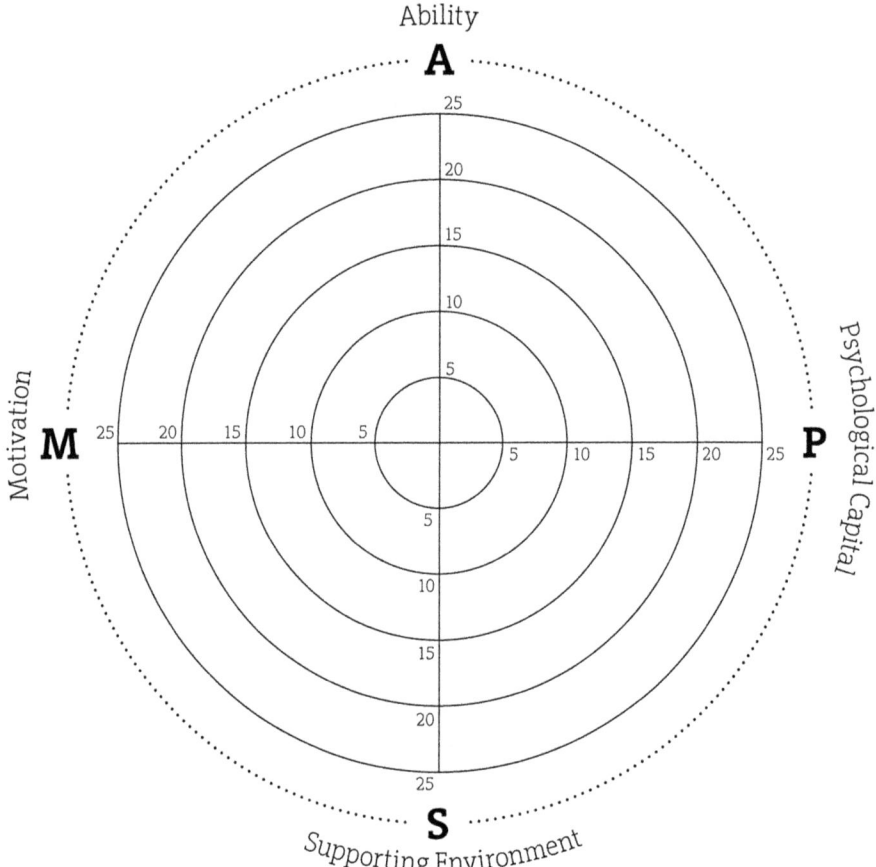

Index

A

Ability, 1, 3, 8–10, 12, 13, 28, 31, 38, 43, 44, 47, 51, 52, 85–94, 100, 101, 103–108, 111, 118, 119, 122–130, 135, 155, 160, 171, 176, 182, 202, 203, 207, 211, 218, 220, 222, 224, 232, 235, 237, 239, 240, 246, 251
Absenteeism, 99
Achievers, 165, 168, 170
   See also Apps
Adversity, *see* Resilience
All-or-nothing thinking, *see* Cognitive distortions
Anti-charity, 195
Anxiety, 19, 20, 65, 87, 106–108, 123, 139, 152
Applied behavior analysis, *see* Organizational behavior management
Apps
   Achievers, 165, 168, 170
   irunurun, 148
   Lift, 148, 163
   Nike, 161
   Opower, 172
   Recyclebank, 167
   SuperBetter, 175
Ariely, Dan, 36, 45, 46, 61, 62, 78
Association of stimuli, 20
Attentional control, 123, 124
Attitudes, viii, 3, 21–28, 164, 235
Autonomy, 22, 28–31, 38–42, 45, 47–52, 55, 63, 66, 74, 76, 77, 102, 119, 122–124, 127, 136, 152, 163, 165, 170, 179, 180, 182, 183, 191, 213, 236, 245
Availability heuristic, 29

B

Baby steps, *see* Proximal goals
Badges, *see* Marking achievements
Banking crisis, *see* Financial crisis
Bartle, Richard, 165
Bateson, Gregory, 25, 26
Behavioral economics, 28–31, 41, 180, 193, 196, 197, 207

Behavioral engineering, 21
Behavior change
    managers' beliefs about behavior change, 11, 111, 129
    most common behaviors, vii, 169
Behaviorism, 19–24, 26, 27, 31, 32, 207
Behavior modification, *see* Behavioral engineering
Being assertive with stakeholders, 111
Biases, *see* Heuristics and biases
Bicycle theft, 186
Blockers, 90, 92–94, 111, 246
Body language, 107
Bonuses
    pay inequality, 63
    spot, 68, 194
Brainwashing, 7
Buddy systems, 173, 174

C

Capability, *see* Ability
Career concept model, 51–53, 77
Caring, ix, 119
Case studies
    aggressive communication style and dealing with setbacks, 126
    autonomy, 39–42, 66
    being assertive with stakeholders, 111
    career concept model, 51–52
    communicating with large audiences, 87
    confidence in giving presentations, 76
    culture change, 211, 220–225
    customer service behavior, 21
    directiveness, 27, 72
    habits, 20, 135–155, 182, 247
    improving customer service through gamification, 162, 170, 171
    listening, 39, 41, 54, 190, 192, 239
    making an impact in team meetings, 122
    messy office kitchens, 190
    motivation, 9, 10, 24, 28, 31, 54, 78, 130, 155, 160, 165, 176, 187, 202, 203, 210, 212–214, 216, 224, 227, 245–246, 250
    persuasion to increase self-confidence, 104–106
    preemptive praise, 195
    pride, 45
    promotion and prevention focus, 53, 54, 72, 75, 77
    reading more, 1, 103
Cecchin, Gianfranco, 13
Challenge, *see* Mastery
Change architect, 196, 201–207
Choice, *see* Autonomy
Choice architecture, 29, 31, 181–183
Choices and options, 30, 77
Circle technique, 106
Classical conditioning, 138, 139
Coaching, 1–3, 5, 7, 8, 12, 13, 23, 102, 163, 174, 181, 236, 241, 242
Coaching models, 5, 6, 9–11, 202
Cognition, *see* Cognitive psychology
Cognitive distortions, 109–111
Cognitive psychology, 22–27, 29, 31, 38, 53, 207
Collectivist cultures, *see* Culture
Commitment, *see* Intrinsic motivation
Communicating with large audiences, 87
Communication and tone, 40
Comparison points, 172–173
Competence, *see* Mastery
Competing commitments, *see* Blockers
Competing response training (CRT), 152
Competition, 45, 118, 160–163, 165, 167, 171–173, 175
Conditioning, 138, 139

Confidence, 2, 8–12, 22, 23, 25, 43, 44, 64, 68, 69, 74, 76, 87, 88, 97–108, 111, 121, 122, 128, 129, 167, 169, 171, 176, 185, 187–188, 203, 214, 216, 227, 241, 246–247

Connection, 20, 38, 45–48, 50, 55, 65, 66, 101, 108, 110, 159, 160, 163–165, 167, 173–175, 211, 227, 233, 237, 245

Consistency, *see* Habits, repetition

Context, vii–ix, 6–11, 13, 18, 21, 24–28, 31, 32, 35, 40, 41, 43, 53, 64–66, 73, 75–78, 87, 88, 90, 91, 94, 97, 99, 101–103, 106, 110, 129–130, 135, 137, 138, 140, 144, 145, 148–151, 154, 155, 160, 174–176, 180, 182, 183, 185, 188, 190, 195, 196, 202–204, 207, 210–219, 222–228, 233, 235–237, 240, 244, 247–248, 253

Control, *see* Autonomy

Coping, *see* Resilience

Costs and benefits, 28, 184, 190–192, 196, 248

Criticism, 20, 21, 44, 59–66, 68, 71, 72, 128, 173
  experts and novices, 72

Crowding out, 63

Cues, 10, 11, 138–141, 143–155, 184, 185, 196, 247, 248
  See also Habits

Culture
  collectivist, 49, 69, 71
  extrinsic motivation, 70
  face-saving, 71
  hierarchical, 71
  individualist, 49, 71
  intrinsic motivation, 49, 246

Culture change, ix, 17, 211, 220–225, 228, 229

Customer satisfaction, 162

Customer service behavior, 21

Cybernetics, 25

D

Decision economics, 191–193

Decision-making, 28, 29, 136, 181, 227

Deep breathing, 107
  See also Mindfulness

Default options, 30

Deliberate practice, 93–94

Depression, 7, 8, 25

Development plans, 24, 35, 91, 107, 108, 147, 191, 194, 202, 204, 232, 236–237

Dietary behaviors
  coffee, 137, 139
  healthy eating, 181
  shopping, 41, 182
  See also Losing weight

Directiveness, 27, 72

Drink-driving, 189

Drugs, *see* Quitting drugs

Duckworth, Angela Lee, 117

Duhigg, Charles, 152, 155

Dweck, Carol, 73, 126

E

Engagement, 22, 159, 161, 162, 215

Environment, *see* Context

Ericsson, Anders, 93

Exercise, 36, 65, 162, 239
  elevators *vs.* stairs, 179
  exercising and going to the gym, 65, 239

Experts and novices, *see* Criticism; Mastery; Praise

External environment, 129–130, 135, 140, 195, 196

Extrinsic motivation, 36, 59–78, 163, 193, 212, 213, 245, 246

F

Family therapy, *see* Systemic psychotherapy
Fear, *see* Anxiety
Feedback, 1–3, 5, 18, 39, 44, 47, 52, 64, 68, 71, 72, 77, 79, 87, 88, 92, 94, 102, 105, 151, 161, 165, 184, 185, 189–191, 193, 223, 235, 243
Feedback loops, 26–28, 31, 223
Financial crisis, 36, 64
Financial incentives
  effectiveness, 63
  effect on intrinsic motivation, 63, 213
  ethics, 63
  organizational productivity, 61
  See also Rewards
Fixed mindset, 126
Ford, 161
Ford, Henry, 100
Framing, 185
Free templates, 204
Frequent flyer scheme, 159, 160

G

Galatea effect, 100
Game design, 165, 174, 175
Gamification
  hype, 160, 161
  market, 161
Gender differences and effects
  confidence, 104
  motivation, 55, 246
Gladwell, Malcolm, 93
Goals, 1, 4, 5, 8–11, 21, 24, 35, 39, 40, 43–49, 61–64, 68, 69, 72, 74, 75, 91, 92, 94, 100–102, 104–106, 108, 117, 119, 120, 122, 123, 126, 127, 135, 137, 142, 143, 145, 148, 149, 161, 163–165, 169–172, 175, 176, 191, 202–205, 207, 213, 215, 220, 221, 223, 233, 236, 240, 248
  See also Stretch goals
Golem effect, 105
Golf, 93, 104
Google, 180, 181, 192
Governmental behavior change departments, 28
Grit, 117–129
Group quest, 174
GROW model, 5
Growth mindset, 126–127, 129
Gym, *see* Exercise

H

Habits, 53, 150
  breaking habits, 151, 155
  changing habits, 13, 150, 153, 182
  effect of new situations, 150
  forming a habit, 146
  giving people information about habits, 147
  habit components, 137–140
  repetition, 141, 146, 147, 155, 247
  routine, 65, 78, 136
  substitute behaviors, 152, 153, 155, 247
Heuristics and biases, 29, 31, 243
Hormones, 107
Hygiene, viii, 191

I

IBM, 171, 222
If–then plans, *see* Implementation intentions
Implementation ideas, 39
Implementation intentions, 128, 148–149, 151, 153, 155, 192, 247
Incentives, 8, 10, 11, 21, 22, 29, 31, 54, 62, 66, 135, 180, 213, 233

Information nudging, 184, 188, 248
Inner commitment, *see* Intrinsic motivation
Inner steel, 118, 125
Intelligence tests, 100
Intentions, ix, 2, 22, 36, 40, 144, 148–149
Intrinsic motivation, 35–55, 62–69, 74, 76–78, 92, 93, 101, 119, 147–148, 151, 163–166, 170, 175, 186–187, 204, 212–215, 227, 228, 233, 239, 245–246
Introspection, 20
Irunurun, 148
　See also Apps

K

Kahneman, Daniel, 29, 185, 186
Kaplan University, 169
Knowledge sharing, 161

L

Law of effect, 59
Leader boards, 161, 162, 172, 173
Leadership behaviors, 24
Learning and development
　common themes, 215, 216
　effect of self-confidence on training, 101
　gamifying mandatory training materials, 161, 165
　online and gamified training programs, 169, 175, 241
　success of training, 2
　training market, 2
Levels, 8, 11, 25, 30, 37, 39, 61–64, 72, 93, 94, 99, 101, 104, 105, 107, 109, 117, 119, 120, 127, 129, 149–151, 159, 160, 162, 163, 169–171, 174, 191, 203, 205, 207, 212, 214, 217, 220–222, 224, 226–229, 235, 241, 242, 246, 247
Lift, 148, 163, 181
　See also Apps
LinkedIn, 159, 160, 170
Listening, 39, 41, 54, 184, 187, 190–192, 238, 239
Littering, 190
Little Albert experiment, 19
Locus of control (LOC), 102–103, 108
Losing weight, 8, 39, 65, 101
　food diary, 120
　money, 65
Loss avoidance, 31, 193–195
Low-tech solutions, 168
Loyalty card, 159

M

Making an impact in team meetings, 122
Managers
　beliefs about behavior change, 128
　role in behavior change, 9, 110, 176
Managing low performance, 243
　See also Case studies
MAPS action plan, 206
MAPS model, 9–11, 13, 18, 22, 24, 28, 31, 32, 78, 85, 94, 98, 129, 130, 196, 202–204, 207, 212, 215, 220, 222, 233, 245, 249, 255
MAPS Profiler Graph, 255
MAPS profiler tool, 204, 249–253, 255
Marking achievements, 161, 163–165, 167, 169–171
Mastery
　becoming an expert, 93, 244
　guided mastery, 101–103
Meaning, *see* Connection
Mental illness
　depression, 7, 8, 25
　schizophrenia, 25

Merritte, Douglas, 19, 21
Messy office kitchens, 190
Military, 46
Mindfulness, 25, 107, 120, 123–125, 241
Minnesota Department of Revenue, 189
Modeling, 101, 103–104, 108, 220, 221
Money, *see* Financial incentives
Motivation
   behavior change, 2, 36, 119, 155, 175, 212
   extrinsic motivation, 36, 54, 59–78, 163, 193, 212, 213, 245, 246
   intrinsic motivation, 35–55, 62–69, 74, 76–78, 119, 163–166, 170, 175, 204, 212–215, 233, 245–246
   money, 61–62
   motivators, 36, 37, 45, 51–55, 59–70, 72–78, 103, 163, 171, 184, 193, 213, 214, 217, 243, 245
   performance, 36, 37, 55, 61, 64, 122, 212, 215
   positive and negative extrinsic, 59–61
Muraven, Mark, 118–120

N

Navy, 105
Negative extrinsic motivators, *see* Positive and negative extrinsic motivators
New situations, *see* Habits
New year's resolutions, 1, 2, 39
NextJump, 162
   See also Apps
Nicklaus, Jack, 104
Nike, 161
   See also Apps

Novelty effects, 163
Nudge, 30, 32, 179, 180, 182–195, 203, 231
   See also Nudging
Nudge: Improving Decisions about Health, Wealth, and Happiness, 180, 197
Nudging, 13, 30, 31, 41, 135, 176, 179–196, 247, 248

O

Obstacles, 5, 8, 149, 155, 175, 247
   See also Setbacks
Opower, 172
   See also Apps
Opportunity, 47, 53, 68, 69, 86, 102, 103, 126, 144, 146, 152–154, 238, 246
Optimism, 11, 12, 97–100, 108–112, 211, 246–247
Organizational behavior management, 21
Organizational citizenship behaviors, 99
Overgeneralization, *see* Cognitive distortions
Ownership, 39, 72, 74, 225

P

Pavlov, Ivan, 138
Pay-for-performance, 61, 62, 193, 194
Pay inequality, *see* Bonuses
Paying taxes, 189
Pedestrian sidewalks, 185
Peer pressure, 188, 190, 191
Pension schemes, 30
Perfectionism, 127
Performance, ix, 1–2, 36, 37, 46, 55, 61–64, 71, 72, 93, 94, 99, 105, 107, 111, 119, 121, 122, 127, 148, 149, 152, 161,

164, 170, 172, 173, 184, 190, 191, 193, 211, 212, 215, 218, 220, 223, 226–229, 241, 243
Perseverance, *see* Grit; Psychological capital; Resilience
Personalization, *see* Cognitive distortions
Persuasion, 101
Pessimists, 109
   See also Optimism
Physiological states, 101, 106–108
Pink, Daniel, 63
Point of decision prompts, 147
Points, 13, 20, 30, 62, 76, 88, 89, 92, 94, 100, 110, 119, 137, 141, 143, 147, 148, 159, 160, 163–168, 170, 172–173, 175, 181, 183, 191, 214, 215, 220, 234
Positive and negative extrinsic motivators, 60, 61
Positive psychology, 98, 121, 241
Practice, 50, 86, 90, 91, 93–94, 101–104, 107, 120, 124, 125, 141, 144, 154, 159, 190, 238, 246
Praise
   experts and novices, 64, 72
   preemptive praise, 195
Premack, David, 145
Premack principle, 145
Presentation skills, 86, 87, 104, 171
Pret a Manger, 64, 68
Prevention focus, *see* Promotion and prevention focus
Pricing, 180
Pride, 45, 210
Priming, 185–188, 190, 233
Prison
   fairness of rewards, 75
   prisoner of war camps, 7
   prison therapy, 42

Prizes, 59, 69, 73, 144, 167–169, 174
   See also Rewards
Problems, 7, 13, 17, 27, 35, 59, 74, 104, 108, 120, 121, 123, 126, 128–129, 137, 149, 162, 164, 187, 192, 216, 236, 244, 247
Productivity, 21, 37, 61
Professionalism, 21, 24
Progress
   framing progress feedback, 185
   monitoring and tracking, 148
   progress bars, 160, 168
   See also Mastery
Promotion and prevention focus, 53, 54, 72, 75, 77
Prompts, 27, 68, 147–149, 151, 153, 184, 203, 245
Pro-social rewards, 63
Proximal goals, 91, 142, 246
Psychological capital, 10–12, 24, 28, 31, 97–111, 117, 119, 125, 129, 130, 155, 160, 202, 203, 211, 216, 217, 224, 234, 246–247, 252
Psychology, the history of, 19
Public commitments, 147–148, 151
Public policy, 30
Public recognition, 69, 74, 163, 173
Punishment, 12, 20–22, 26, 36, 37, 54, 59–78, 163, 165, 170, 193, 203, 245, 246
Purpose, *see* Connection
Pygmalion effect, 105

Q

Questions
   key MAPS model questions to ask yourself, 245–255
   miracle question, 89–90
   rating scale question, 40, 44, 88–89, 102
   See also MAPS Profiler Tool

Quitting drugs, 7, 8, 101, 118, 139, 194
Quitting smoking, 2, 8, 39, 62, 65, 101, 120, 150, 152, 184, 194

R

Reading, 1, 91, 103, 143, 150, 172, 175, 238, 239
Recognition, 59, 73, 170, 171, 213
  public, 69, 74, 163
Recyclebank, 167
  See also Apps
Reinforcers, 139–141, 144–146, 148–150, 152, 153, 155, 162, 176, 247
Relatedness, *see* Connection
Reoffending rates, 6
Resilience, 8, 10–12, 97–99, 106, 107, 109, 117–130, 164, 175, 176, 203, 211, 214, 216, 240–242, 246, 247
Resistance, 40, 41
Resources, 2, 10, 11, 68, 69, 86, 97, 161, 215, 233, 246
Rewards
  culture, 70–71, 213
  experience, 72
  fairness, 75–76
  intrinsic motivation, 62–63, 66–68
  promotion and prevention focused personalities, 72
  promotion and prevention focus situations, 72
  pro-social rewards, 63
  public *vs.* private, 69
  timing, 68
  what to motivate people with, 73–76
Role, effect on motivation of, 55, 246
Role models, *see* Modeling
Ronaldo, Cristiano, 104

S

Safety behaviors, 21, 181
Satisfaction, 43, 68, 69, 99, 162, 205
Schizophrenia, 25
Scripts, *see* Implementation intentions
Self-belief, *see* Confidence
Self-compassion, 126–129
Self-concept reinforcement, 110–111
Self-confidence and proactivity, 108
Self-confidence, *see* Confidence
Self-control, *see* Willpower
Self-criticalness, *see* Self-criticism
Self-criticism, 127
Self-determination theory, 38, 45
  See also Intrinsic motivation
Self-efficacy, 101
  See also Confidence
Self-monitoring, 151
  See also Progress
Self-reflexivity, *see* Mindfulness
Self-talk, 122
Seligman, Martin, 98, 109
Setbacks, 99, 109–111, 125, 126, 128, 129, 175
  See also Resilience
Shared spaces, 186
Sharing achievements, *see* Public recognition
Sharing goals and development plans, 147
Shopping habits, 182
Signatures, 187
Signs, 30, 46, 121, 147, 151, 179–181, 186–188, 190
Simple habits, *see* Proximal goals
Situation, *see* Context
Six Sigma, 163
Skills, *see* Ability
Smith, Will, 117
Smoking, *see* Quitting smoking
Social connection narrative, 160, 165, 167

Social influence, 188–191
    See also Social norms; Social support and networks
Social norms, 10, 22, 30, 31, 188–190, 196, 248
Social support and networks, 11, 65, 173–175, 215
Social systems, *see* Systemic psychotherapy
Sport, *see* Exercise
    See also Football; Golf
Spot bonuses, 68, 194
Stanford University, 126
StickK.com, 195
Strategic thinking, 91, 237–239
Strengths, 43, 77, 88, 92, 97, 99, 105, 106, 108, 109, 111, 117, 122, 129, 149
Stress, 99, 106, 119, 123, 211
Stretch goals, 21
    See also Goals
Sun cream, 184
SuperBetter, 175
    See also Apps
Supporting environment, 10, 11, 22, 28, 31, 176, 202, 214, 217, 224, 247–248, 253
Symbolic markers, *see* Marking achievements
Systemic psychotherapy, 7, 23–28, 31, 42, 88, 207

T

Tangible markers, *see* Marking achievements
Targets, 1, 4, 17, 24, 26, 30, 43–45, 49, 61–64, 68, 69, 74, 75, 91, 94, 100–102, 104, 105, 108, 119, 120, 122, 123, 127, 135, 145, 161, 163, 170–172, 175, 176, 193, 202, 205, 207, 213, 215, 240
    See also Goals
Tasks, *see* Goals; Targets
Technology
    accepting new technology/IT, 37, 168, 210
    apps and tools, 148, 195
    See also Gamification
TED talks, 10, 36, 160, 238
10,000 hour rule, 93
Therapy, *see* Systemic psychotherapy
    See under Prison
T-Mobile, 162
Towel use, 190
Training, *see* Learning and development
Triggers, *see* Cues
Turnover, 63, 212
Tversky, Amos, 29, 185
Two-step method of behavior change, 5

U

Underlying needs, 152, 153
University College London, 141
University of Colorado, 93
University of Missouri, 110

V

Visualization, 104
Voting, 182

W

Watson, John Broadus, 19–21
Wharton School of Business, 164
Willpower, 8, 10–12, 97–99, 117–130, 148, 149, 151, 164, 167, 176, 203, 216, 239–240, 246, 247
Wittgenstein, Ludwig, 47
Work satisfaction, *see* Satisfaction

Ingram Content Group UK Ltd.
Milton Keynes UK
UKHW022320240723
425703UK00006B/236